CONVERGENCE
THE GLOBALIZATION OF MIND

BY THEO HORESH

For Alia
My Best Friend and Love of My Life

Library of Congress Cataloging-in-Publication Data

Horesh, Theo

Convergence: The Globalization of Mind

p.cm

1. Consciousness. 2. Globalization. 3. Psychology

ISBN 13: 978-1-936955-14-5

Bäuu Press
Golden Colorado
www.bauuinstitute.com

CONTENTS

It's a strange world. It seems around fifteen billion years ago there was, precisely, absolute nothingness, and then within less than a nanosecond the material universe blew into existence.

Stranger still, the material universe so produced was not merely a random and chaotic mess, but seemed to organize itself into ever more complex and intricate forms. So complex were these forms that, many billions of years later, some of them found ways to reproduce themselves, and thus out of matter arose life.

Even stranger, these life forms were apparently not content to merely reproduce themselves, but instead began a long evolution that would eventually allow them to represent themselves, to produce signs and symbols and concepts, and thus out of life arose mind.

Whatever this process of evolution was, it seems to have been incredibly driven - from matter to life to mind.

But stranger still, a mere few hundred years ago, on a small and indifferent planet around an insignificant star, evolution became conscious of itself.

And at precisely the same time, the very mechanisms that allowed evolution to become conscious of itself were simultaneously working to bring about its own extinction.

And that was the strangest of all.

KEN WILBER, SPIRITUAL PHILOSOPHER

INTRODUCTION

Seek knowledge as far as China.
THE PROPHET MUHAMMAD

So far as we know, humans are the only animals that think globally. We are the only animals that band together in global associations. And we are the only animals who possess the power to instantly destroy the planet. It took thousands of years of human civilization before we began to build comprehensive global institutions. While those institutions are but a century or so old, they are now commonplace. In fact, it has become difficult to conceive of a lasting human civilization without the support of global institutions. But to run those institutions we must possess global consciousness.

Global consciousness is the capacity to experience the world as an integral whole. The ability to think globally is now quite common. Turn on any major news channel and you will be barraged by global events. To comprehend those events, you must be able to situate them in global causal chains. Most people in the developed world today more or less possess this capacity. But global consciousness is not just about how we see the world. Like nationalism and team spirit, it is a form of group identification. The globally conscious self identifies with the world and its multitude of beings, human and otherwise. The sense of identification need not be strong. Marketers talk about saving the planet because somehow the idea appeals even to the otherwise indifferent. But global consciousness can seep into the deepest reaches of one's being: stirring feelings for peoples unmet, places unseen, species yet undiscovered. And the image of the planet has for many bypassed the flag as a symbol of allegiance.

The story of how we became conscious of the world as an integral whole, how our lives were knit together into a planetary civilization, and how some of us began to identify with all of humanity, and with the fate of the earth, is the story of global consciousness. It is an incomplete epic about the emergence of global civilization and its fragile fate; few took an interest in the fate of the planet before it became possible to destroy it in an instant. But the story begins with mundane developments: more accurate maps and more frequent exchanges; more rapid communication and increasing travel; wars, migrations, and standardized measurements. Micro-developments at the margin, strand by strand, knit us together into one integrated world. Now we have reached a tipping point: to live well in the world, we must possess a comprehensive awareness of planetary civilization.

The concept of global consciousness can be explored through a range of disciplines. Strictly speaking, the category of global consciousness is psychological. Global consciousness is a mental framework, a lens through which events are viewed. Each local event – a vote, a purchase, a spoken word– has global reverberations. And the globally conscious self takes these wider ripples seriously. Maintaining the broad scope of global consciousness is psychologically demanding. There is more information to keep up with: more people, more issues, more nations, more history. And this is not just a linear increase in the volume of polling results or trade statistics calling for interpretation. Whole new areas of concern appear with the emergence of global consciousness: loose nukes, melting glaciers, barriers to trade, and border disputes; space junk, species loss, water wars, genocide, climate change, the balance of power, and international exchange rates. The result is an exponential increase in information that matters. Globally conscious individuals must somehow make sense of a vast and variegated world of concerns and distribute their attention accordingly. This raises questions about how the brain organizes information, how much of it we can process, and how we forge our identities.

The globally conscious self is a world citizen, a cosmopolitan thinker, simply a human being, one amongst seven billion, but never just an American, a Muslim, a Hindu, or a Han. Multiple mechanisms socialize the average Russian or Japanese to his or her nation of birth. Universal primary schooling, shared cultural norms, and a common public sphere channel attention and focus drives. The same goes for any culture. Members are taught conventions, and over time, the conventions become a part of themselves, integral to their expressions and relations and the values they hold dear. But it is different for the cosmopolitan. As she frees herself from the norms into which she was socialized, others become possible. Freed from one set of commitments, the next becomes more a matter of choice.[2,3,4] The shift can be disorienting, for it throws all values and meanings into question. Suddenly the world we were preparing to enter in our youths grows in size by several orders of magnitude and we are plunged into a life for which we have not yet been prepared. Few of us are prepared for global citizenship; meanwhile, more and more of us are making the leap to global consciousness.[5]

Multiple historical forces draw us together in one integrated world. War and trade, the development of science and the evolution of religion: each contributes to the emergence of global consciousness, because each grows over time to a global scope. Their growth is fueled by historical trends stretching back hundreds of years, if not millennia. World trade has grown in staggered spurts for thousands of years along with the pace of transport and the ease of communication.[6,7] As air travel became increasingly practical, world leaders began to meet at regular intervals. As drug trafficking and terror networks went global, inter-state cooperation increased. Each increase in the distance and accuracy of bombs brings about a corresponding growth in communications amongst states. Each new global challenge increases global consciousness.

These are historical forces for which any survey of global consciousness must account. This makes the study of global consciousness, amongst other things, an historical investigation. But the history of global consciousness is a revolution in the making, and we have hit a watershed. At the heart of this upheaval lays a vast transformation in the way we communicate. The information revolution is far from complete.[8,9,10,11] There is an immense backlog of innovations slowly coming online and little reason to believe the ideas of today will not continue to become the innovations of tomorrow. The revolution in telecommunications allows us to distill the world into bits and to re-arrange those bits into new patterns, thereby making the world anew. In so doing, we level hierarchies and realign social classes, shatter conventions and widen vistas.[12] Information technologies speed up the spread of knowledge and thus fuel the growth of global consciousness. Facebook, Twitter, Blogs, and the Internet each alter the nexus of personal concerns and transform the sources of human identity, and in contributing to a vast sphere of interconnected technologies, they inadvertently stimulate global consciousness.

Transformations in the ease and pace of transportation have a similar affect. We are increasingly likely to live and work in foreign lands, increasingly likely to immigrate and marry foreigners. The changes in residence broaden social, political, and religious affiliations. And they widen the circle of ethical commitments. Humanity is being brought closer together, literally. Global associations of regulators and professionals, judges and legislators, activists and aid groups, can now organize on the Internet and meet with ease from across the planet.[13] The networks encompass the globe in a growing web of awareness that would be impossible to imagine without recent developments in telecommunications and transportation.[14] To understand global consciousness, we must understand technological development. But the connection is a human one: information technologies transform the very sense of who believe ourselves to be.

Global consciousness is largely about who and what we identify with. These questions thrust us into a thicket of ethical conundrums. While ethical systems are almost always expressed in universal terms, seldom do their adherents value all people equally.[15,16] Few Americans value the life of an Iraqi civilian so much as that of an American. And few parents give as much thought to the billion malnourished people living in the world today as they do to each of their own children. Something is morally amiss. Our ethical commitments increasingly appear perverted. Global consciousness raises questions about how and why we should concern ourselves with people living in remote and distant places. As we grow in global consciousness, we open our eyes to the suffering of people and animals that otherwise would not count. Global consciousness challenges us to redistribute our attention, our care, and often our resources. But while it raises questions, it offers few answers. Somehow we must balance local and global priorities, and each of us will do this in our own ways. Such concerns are central to the field of ethics. And ethical debates have a way of bleeding into broader philosophical questions concerning the nature of the good life and structure of the ideal state.

We are now all members of a global civilization whether we know it or not, like it or not. Wired to global media; swept up in the international labor market; nodes in a virtual world of interconnected circuits; parties to the destruction of rain forests and oceanic fisheries; producers and consumers in a global economy: our lives and thoughts are, at every turn, shaped by a rising global civilization. But the current international order is a Babel of unrepresentative institutions, whose structures are amorphous and whose authorities are ill defined. Few of us have a say in the international political order. While the most natural scale of human organization increasingly appears global, we repeatedly turn to impotent and outmoded national remedies in meeting the global challenges that dominate public discourse. While the authority of the nation-state is steadily eroded by a backlog of issues best impacted through international cooperation, humanity has paused at the brink of global government. A global government could be the most oppressive force in human history, whose internal corruption and inefficiency would necessarily go unchecked by outside challengers to power. The risk of such an order ever arising has given many would be supporters of global government pause. And yet, to truly confront the global challenges we now face, we must move beyond our current anarchic order.[17,18] How we will break the impasse is perhaps the most important political dilemma of the twenty-first century. And we cannot begin to grapple with it without global consciousness. Its consideration throws us headlong into a study of international law and international relations.

Over the past decade and a half a virtual cottage industry has arisen amongst economists and some sociologists writing on the subject of globalization. Most of these writers have focused on the growth of international trade, telecommunications, and immigration. Mastering such a wide array of academic disciplines would take a team of scholars. But alas, a team of scholars is difficult to come by, tough to fund, and wearisome to organize. Hence the task of elucidating the significance of global consciousness tends to fall to generalists. The problem with generalists is we often get the details wrong. And we tend to suffer from many of the maladies that have long troubled philosophers: a heightened sense of grandiosity, a tendency to mistake theory for fact, and an annoying habit of creating castles in the sky. But if generalists are often wrong and sometimes awkward, we have a nose for meaning. For in understanding the whole, we can better recognize the significance of its parts. It is not the scrambling about of a private that is of historical interest but rather his part in the battle; not the battle that is most significant but rather its role in the war; not even the war that is meaningful but the way it transforms individuals and the world.

To comprehend the world as an integral whole, we must understand its many working parts. Few can integrate so much knowledge, and yet, if we fail to do so, we will remain impotent in the face of an ever-wider array of global threats and challenges. Such conundrums are typical of any leap to a higher level of integrated complexity. One system cannot be built because it rests on a matrix of other systems. Newly developing nations routinely confront such double binds. They need infrastructure to develop industry, but without the industry they will lack the revenue needed to develop infrastructure. Business cannot thrive without the rule of law, but this is expensive and its funding tends to rely on the revenue generated by a thriving business sector.[19] Like the developing nation, struggling to pull itself up by its own bootstraps, global consciousness challenges us to adapt to a global civilization that is still in the making.

As the wave of conservatism, known as the Reagan Revolution, first swept through America amidst the waning liberalism of the late seventies, my own idealism was just awakening. With all the delicacy of a rambunctious child, and all the determination of a suicide bomber, I argued endlessly with my skeptical parents that we can change the world. Of course, even a Napoleon or Alexander the Great cannot alter certain fundamental truths concerning the human condition. So, in that sense, my parent's were right that my desire to change the world was that of a narcissistic child. But there was another sense in which they could not have been more wrong. There is no act, no thought, no feeling, that cannot but help change the world. Everything in the world is pushing and pulling it in several directions at once, so everything matters. This recognition is key to global consciousness. That we framed the argument in terms of changing the world is revealing. Generation X was perhaps the first generation ever in the history of the world to almost fully conceive of its civic duties in terms of global responsibilities. That an ordinary child might believe himself an heir to such grandiose responsibilities was more than just a revelation of latent narcissism. A generational tsunami was churning on the horizon.

On the eve of the new millennium, demonstrators converged on Seattle from across the globe to protest the injustices of the World Trade Organization. For many, November 10, 1999 marked the birth of the anti-globalization movement. Farmers and small business owners, union workers and environmentalists, church groups and hunger advocates, media critics and civil libertarians, linked arms in solidarity, braving batons and tear gas, to effectively shut down a major gathering of one of the world's most powerful institutions. The movement was propelled by a concern for global injustice, organized through global networks, and led by global organizations. If not for global consciousness, it would have been impossible. Both the globalists and the anti-globalists were changing the world: two sides of the same coin, each propelled by global concerns, global forces, and an emerging global consciousness to present a rival vision of the next world order. The dialectic between the two, and countless other pressure groups, is transforming global debate. Somehow the ability to change the world has fallen within reach.

The story of global consciousness is one of increasing awareness of the world. The first manifestation of this awareness is often spiritual or environmental.[20,21,23,24] Spiritual practice provides the wideness of view needed to think and feel for every living being. And the realization that we are living on a finite planet with limited resources challenges us to think in global terms. When we first awaken to global consciousness, we awaken to a vast and fuzzy world of possibilities. But mature global consciousness integrates spiritual and environmental awareness into the recognition of deeper socio-economic and technological forces. The reason we know enough about planetary ecological conditions to be concerned is because we are wealthy enough to fund scientific studies and economically developed enough to broadcast their findings. Part of the reason we care is because we can afford to travel, to explore, to learn, and to take risks expanding the circle of ethical concern. Far from being too comprehensive in scope, spiritual inspiration and environmental visions tend to be not nearly comprehensive enough. If environmentalists ignore the way technological and economic development contribute to global consciousness, then their efforts may culminate in opposing the very forces upon which global consciousness rests. Hence, the study of global consciousness must be comprehensive and multidisciplinary if it is to matter. Not only must the "Teamsters and Turtleheads Unite," as the saying went in Seattle; they must join forces with the corporate CEOs and the chief economists of the World Bank.

And yet as the economist Pankaj Ghemewat points out, both the globalizers and the anti-globalizers tend to exaggerate the extent of actual globalization. According to Ghemewat, only about 1 percent of snail mail and 2 percent of all telephone calling minutes cross national borders. Only about 2 percent of all university students the world over are foreign, and just 3 percent of the global population consists of first generation immigrants. Internet traffic is more global in scope, but between 2006 and 2008 only 17-18 percent was routed across borders. News is also more international in scope. But while 21 percent of U.S. news coverage is international, about half of this deals with U.S. foreign affairs. Similarly, while about 38 percent of European news is international, half of these stories involve other European countries. Cross border trade in goods and services, where globalization would seem to really count, is also a bit higher - but not nearly as much as most of us tend to think. After hitting an all time high of 29 percent in 2008, it dropped to 23 percent in 2009.[25]

Such figures might suggest a work like this is overblown. If the actual extent of globalization has been exaggerated, then the need to adjust to a now globalized environment has likewise been played up. But climate change is entirely global in scope as would be a thermo-nuclear war. All wars between states are by definition international as are global pandemic diseases and the exhaustion of oceanic life. While the actual extent of cross border activities may be small, their significance is great. This may explain why global concerns are at one and the same time so exaggerated and yet so salient. It seems the most globalized phenomena are those most threatening to life on earth. And we are beginning to organize our minds and identities around their existence.

We should not assume the capacity to think globally. Since it is impossible to take in the whole world at a sweep, thinking globally requires that we first be able to think abstractly. But the pre-eminent theorist of cognitive development, Jean Piaget, noted this capacity is only arrived at after a long series of cognitive developments, sometime between adolescence and early adulthood.[26] Not everyone achieves this ability to think abstractly. Of those who do, the ability often remains partially developed or dormant. Most of us continually revert back to thinking in concrete terms, of the things we can see and touch and feel. Global thinking usually requires that we not only think abstractly but that we break the world down into statistics. We do not usually see the rainforests being destroyed, and even when we do, we can only see a part. Making sense of the destruction of rainforests requires that we consult the statistics regarding how much has been destroyed, over how much time, and for what purposes. These questions cannot usually be answered without reversion to statistics. But as the Nobel Laureate economist, Daniel Khaneman notes, most people lack the ability to think statistically.[27]

To think meaningfully about the world as a whole requires further capacities, like the ability to think systemically and to weigh one paradigm of thought against another. Technological advances have allowed us to exploit the natural resources and carbon sinks whose use now threatens the destruction of higher civilization through catastrophic climate change, and yet the development of a sustainable global civilization will probably require massive technological advances. Economic development has led to the mass destruction of non-human life, but protecting that life from overpopulation and exploitation may require further development. Sorting through paradoxes like these involves sifting through massive amounts of data and perspectives, weighing the merits of simplicity versus complexity, active engagement versus passive surrender, hierarchy versus equality. Each of these ideals has a role to play in the development of a sustainable global civilization. But if we lack the ability to prioritize their benefits with equanimity and intelligence, we may prove unable to sort through the complexities of the global challenges we now face.

For this reason, the American developmental philosopher Ken Wilber, suggests that perhaps the most vital challenge of the coming century will be that of taking as many people as possible to the developmental stage of global consciousness.[28] It is just this thought that inspired me to write this book. But while Wilber has written admirably about how global consciousness is achieved psychologically and why achieving it is important, we will be exploring how in the world we might begin to make sense of something so vast as the world itself.

Global consciousness can be overwhelming. The first chapter introduces some of the mental and emotional challenges to thinking globally, while the rest of the first section focuses on the material conditions leading to the development of global consciousness. Trade and imperialism have each played a substantial role in its development, but global consciousness really began to grow when humanity acquired the ability to annihilate itself with thermo-nuclear weapons. The story of global consciousness has been largely technological. Thus, the second section explores how technological advances are breaking down some of the social impediments to thinking globally. But the Information Age developments that have allowed us to break down so many barriers to global trade and communication are also responsible for the sense of overwhelm that leads so many of us to seek refuge in small worlds of our own making. Hence, the fourth and fifth sections explore how some of these same technologies might be used to simplify our lives and minds and how we might begin to integrate the complexity involved in living in a globalized environment.

The globalization of mind is a process of thinking our way into the farthest corners of the world. To truly understand how others live, we must develop the empathy needed to see the world through 7 billion pairs of eyes. Thus, the fifth section focuses on the nature of empathy and why it will be needed for a wide diversity of peoples the world over to cooperate in solving global challenges like climate change. But perhaps the most neglected corner of the world has been that in which the poorest of the poor reside. Thus, the sixth section focuses on how they live, what they need, and our ethical obligations to them. Yet it is not only people who deserve our care. This section also explores how cultivating a love for all life can allow us to develop global consciousness with grace.

There is, after all, something spiritual about global consciousness, for thinking globally involves grasping the nature of innumerable interconnections, between individuals, peoples, species, and generations. The seventh section thus focuses on the religious response to globalization - the evolution of a more inclusive God, the emergence of more universal sects, the breakdown of spiritual practice into component parts that can be mixed and matched across religions, and how spiritual leaders can aid in the development of a new global ethic. The last section then applies the social contract tradition to the whole of the world and explores how America might pass the baton of global dominance not to another global superpower but rather to a set of global governance bodies.

Finally, the postscript explores how each of us might make sense of this dizzying turbulence we call the world. Making sense of the world is a meaningful endeavor. In identifying with a greater whole, we ourselves become more whole. In recognizing more of humanity, so also do we recognize more in ourselves. We are not just Americans and Indians and Germans; we are human beings, endowed with the ability to construct our own lives and goals and values. The recognition feels good, for it breaks the shackles of cultural inhibitions, and through it we might become united in spirit with the whole of humanity. Global consciousness involves an awakening to far more than the problems of the world. It is a developmental awakening, an awakening that many would call spiritual.[29]

New material is introduced throughout the book. You should feel free to skip sections and chapters. They loosely build on one another. But most people do not finish the books they begin, so it is better to go to what interests you most first and then go back. The material with which most people may be familiar is that found in the section on the globalization of technology. If you are one of these people, give it a look over but do not dwell on it. Technological developments are integral to the globalization of mind, so it is important to get a feel for how they are linked, but writing on these issues is simply not my forte. This book was written in reverse order: most chapters were put down on paper before they were researched, with the research providing a means of refining my thoughts and correcting my mistakes. This allowed me to draw from deeper sources - both from within myself and from a wider range of studies – as opposed to sticking closely to the most relevant sources. Such a process can result in strikingly original ideas and a deeper personal engagement with the material. But it has also meant that many of the references are only partial. The citations in this book refer to the ideas of the authors cited, to the original source of my own thinking on the matter, and to recommendations for further reading. Such citations are typically accompanied by endnotes, but extensive endnotes can thicken books and scare away readers, while often going unread. Best to keep it simple and leave it to the reader to explore on his or her own.

The book itself is for those who have developed the ability to think globally but have given more attention to the globalization of trade than to the globalization of mind. It is also for those who have developed the ability to think globally but have not given much thought to how this ability transforms the way we think and relate with one another. And this book was written for those as well who can think globally but whose heads tend to spin when they confront the complexity and the burden of responsibility involved in living in a globalized world. It is best treated as an intellectual contemplation on global consciousness. Many questions will be raised for which there is no definitive answer. Many problems will be set forth for which there is no guide for action. But it is my hope and goal that the very act of reading this book will deepen the globalization of mind about which the book is written.

It is my contention that much of the anxiety we so often feel when we confront global challenges stems from a sort of global immaturity. Most of us are still as yet children to a globalized world; if we cannot adapt our minds to the challenges at hand, we will forever feel ourselves inadequate to the world in which we now live. This book is about developing the global consciousness that is necessary to becoming a good global citizen. Like much maturation, the process of coming into global consciousness may not always easy, but through mastering the challenges at hand we may come to a newfound sense of peace and equanimity. But global consciousness is not just about feeling good. Nor is it merely about learning to function in an interconnected world. Global consciousness is vital to making global civilization work. If we cannot conceive of an integrated world, we can only impact it in fragments. But climate change and nuclear proliferation are global phenomenon and cannot be ameliorated without some measure of global consciousness.[30] And our work on such issues would be trivial without global cooperation. To make global civilization work we must shed local allegiances and work hand in hand across borders.

It is no easy task to comprehend the world in all its seemingly infinite and imponderable complexity. Like crafting a life, the task cannot be achieved through effort alone. Lives are comprised of a mysterious mixture of intention and contingency. But lives emerge, over time, piece by piece, until the child becomes an adult and the adult makes for herself a life. Global consciousness is like this. It emerges over time, through a million little shifts in attention, occurring on the margins of consciousness until out of the chaos grow new understandings and identities and values. While the forces bringing about global consciousness are often impersonal, it is in the end individuals who must remake their own lives so that together we can remake the world. The task can at times be daunting. But like most great tasks, it is a rewarding endeavor.

SECTION 1

THE GLOBALIZATION
OF MIND

Where were you when I planned the earth? Tell me, if you are so wise.
Do you know who took its dimensions, measuring its length with a
cord? What were its pillars built on? Who laid down its cornerstone,
while the morning stars burst out singing...

GOD TO JOB

MAJESTIC AND SUBLIME

When doctors first learned to treat cataracts, they ranged across Europe giving sight to the blind. Many of their patients had been blind from birth, so for the first time, it was possible to study the initial experience of sight. One might imagine the first glimpse of the world to be miraculous, a dappled flood of color and light, like in the paintings of Monet, or perhaps vivid and magical like in a lucid dream. The idea calls to mind myths of rebirth and the healings of Jesus. Instead, it was often a nightmare. The ones once blind who now could see glimpsed a world of grotesque distortions.

The Pulitzer Prize winning novelist and essayist, Annie Dillard, relates that prior to receiving their sight, the patients would tongue objects and roll them in their hands to get a sense of their form. Little changed when the lights were turned on. They continued, like spurned lovers crisscrossing the streets of memory. For many, the experience induced depression and a retreat from the world. One fifteen-year old boy begged to be taken back to the asylum in which he had been living, threatening to tear out his eyes. But many embraced the change, swimming in a stream of wonder and the sunshine of delight.[1]

Our lives are filled with phenomena we are ill equipped to handle. The information inundating our brains, the appointments and deadlines that fill our schedules, even the words our eyes peal from the page, as if by second nature. All of this is as foreign to the biological equipment of humanity as sight to the blind. While we may have the capacity to lead functional lives in an information economy, the effort wears and strains, for our nervous systems did not evolve to live in a post-industrial society. And the human capacity for empathy was never meant to be extended to millions of people. The world has become overwhelming, and it is revealing its contours as never before. The billion malnourished people, tracked and traced through a wide array of transnational institutions, the ever accelerating extinctions, happening so fast they cannot be recorded, the churnings of climate change, impossibly averaged through ten thousand temperature stations and millions of satellite readings daily - as veil after veil is torn away, and the natural and social sciences reveal a vast and variegated world of diversity, humanity oscillates between the poles of depression and joyful embrace. The world has revealed itself, and we don't know what to do.

It is like the climactic scene from the Indian Bhagavad-Gita. The warrior and disciple Arjuna asks Krishna, who has disguised himself as Arjuna's charioteer, to reveal his true form. Out of a sun spire of blinding light, Krishna explodes in a kaleidoscope of forms and amidst a shifting stream of phantasms, Krishna transmutates himself into the moon and stars, the Indus and Ganges, the beginning and end of all things, and all the armies of all the world, marching off to battle, only to meet their demise in the gnashing teeth of time. The physicist Oppenheimer is said to have quoted Krishna in the midst of this display, when he witnessed the explosion of the first atomic bomb. "Now I have become death." Like the formerly blind boy wanting to tear out his eyes, Arjuna begs Krishna to once more assume his earthly guise.[2]

The world is increasingly difficult to turn off. If it sometimes seems so impossible to comprehend, perhaps it is because we are finally seeing it in its entirety - the subtle majesty of this lonely sphere, along with the trillions of beings of which it is comprised. Immanuel Kant described the sublime as an aesthetic experience of overwhelming and almost terrifying beauty - the infinite and heaving waves of a turbulent ocean, the boundless firmament of the night sky. The sublime is an experience of awe and horror, blissful expansion and spine tingling wonder. In contrasting the limits of human perception with the vastness of the universe, the sublime offers us a chance to see beyond ourselves.[3] Perhaps our experience of the world itself has become such an occasion for awe. If there are many who now retreat in isolationism and horror - the terrorists, the romantics, the fundamentalists, and the morbidly apocalyptic - concealing themselves as if from Krishna's devouring jaws, there are others who marvel in the sublime sight of an integrated world.

Perhaps it was like this for the migrants from the countryside who first populated the ancient towns of Catal Hoyuk and Jericho, Sumer and Ur. Their senses must have been overwhelmed with the sights and smells of a strange and exotic new realm, the marketplace and temple, alleyway and palace. European peasants encountered something similar when they first migrated to the soot filled cities of Birmingham and Paris.[4] There is something sublime in the teeming masses of aggregated humanity. The mannerisms of city dwellers must have been bewildering, the norms incomprehensible, and the air unbearable.[5] And yet somehow they carved out lives in hell, and after some time transformed that hell into a home and a culture. It is always this way. Each leap to a more complex form of social organization requires a correspondent leap in consciousness.[6,7] The complexity that first overwhelms is later captured in new mental models and behavioral norms. But the interregnum between one paradigm and the next can be jarring.

Opening our eyes and ears to the world is overwhelming. We wrestle with what to prioritize, what to value, and how to empathize. We tussle with how to weigh the needs of a malnourished child in Mali, a jailed dissident in Iran, and a flooded villager in Pakistan. Few have figured out how to keep so many people, places, and issues in mind. And there seems little place in our hearts for the pain and suffering that are discovered upon opening our eyes. Like the warrior Arjuna or the boy with new sight, most of us who open our eyes in this way will seek at some point to turn the world off. And it is not just individuals who struggle.

At an international summit on climate change in 2008, where representatives of the Bush administration held up action, a representative of the tiny Papua New Guinea rallied the delegates. "If for some reason you are not willing to lead... please - get out of the way." The crowd roared, and the world applauded, but in the end little changed.[8] All too often, we possess the will but lack the means to collaborate on global challenges. Together we grope blindly for the stones with which to construct some global institutional architecture under which we might organize our activities. The world cries out for a new organizing principle. We do not yet know what form it will take, whether it will be a government, a network, or some series of overlapping international accords. And yet we nevertheless continue to lay down the foundation, like bees unconsciously building a hive.

Standing on the shoulders of giants, we can just make out, on the distant horizon of human consciousness, the faint contours of a global civilization.[9,10] Global events now reach the whole world simultaneously. Global elites now share the same networks of friends and acquaintances. Global issues shape national debates, and global institutions condition the scope of national decisions. Our clothes and computers are each increasingly produced in a multitude of places, while movies and novels are increasingly crafted in a diversity of nations. Friends and neighbors are now more than ever likely to come from a variety of continents, and each of us is likely to identify with an ever more exotic set of references.[11,12] As networks, organizations, and production chains are knit ever more tightly across the globe, identifying with the nation of one's birth and its people over that of others appears increasing senseless. Globalization is not merely an economic or even a political phenomenon. Human identity itself is being globalized, and like a deep gaze into the vast, night firmament, the experience is at one and the same time beautiful and terrifying.

Karl Marx once wrote that philosophers merely interpret the world; the point is to change it.[13] But Marx knew better than anyone that the world needs to be reinterpreted before it can be changed.

Without reinterpreting the world, the same mental models continually reproduce the same broken institutions and all of the hazards they
spawn.[14] Reframing problems provides an opportunity to approach
them from a fresh perspective, with new ideas, new solutions, and
potential new alliances. The world of human experience is a puzzle
we may spend our whole lives interpreting and reinterpreting and
still never come to completion. Even in times of social stability, it
is only the rare few that sustain the passion and the interest to arrive
at a coherent view of the world that can withstand even rudimentary
scrutiny; there are just too many pieces of the puzzle. Most people, in
most times and places, instead organize their lives according to conventions. But in times of rapid change, conventions cease to fit our
personal lives into the lives of those around us, and the times themselves can appear out of joint.

We must reinterpret the world for ourselves, determining for ourselves the significance of events and the sources of our own identity.
Anyone reading this book will be aware of the revolution in telecommunications, the growth in institutions of global governance, the rise
of the global environmental movement, and the increase in threats to
human civilization. Global forces permeate our lives. But few of us
have spent much time thinking about how this changes not just the
worlds we live in but the very sense of who we believe ourselves to
be. It is not just events and exchanges that are going global; like a
frog in slowly heating water, we are being cooked in a global stew
of relationships, prospects, and values. And few of us have grappled
with the meaning of this transformation.

Global threats are integral to the maturation of global consciousness. Take, for instance, climate change. The dangers are clear. Rising
global temperatures are already melting glaciers. But the Himalayan
glaciers alone are a primary source of water for the Yangtze, the Yellow, the Indus, the Brahmaputra, the Irrawaddy, and the Mekong Rivers. Together they feed billions. Rising temperatures endanger crop
yields from India to the Great Plains. Melting glaciers in Greenland

are poised to raise sea levels, thereby inundating low lying, highly populated nations like Belgium and Bangladesh. And plant and animal species in forest reserves the world over, that evolved to live under restricted climatic conditions, are slowly passing into extinction, incapable of surviving in their current locales and yet unable to migrate from one isolated forest reserve to another. While climate has always fluctuated, never in the course of human history have global temperatures risen so quickly, never has there been such a consensus amongst experts regarding the cause of changing temperatures, never have humans been responsible in such a clearly explicable manner, and never have we been so locked into the institutional complexes that will be impacted by climate change. While oscillations in climate may be an old story, our current predicament is indeed something new under the sun.

We are well aware of these dangers, but there is another side to climate change. Climate change makes us more aware of the living conditions of distant peoples, like the Micronesians and Mauritians, whose lives and nations are most threatened by rising tides. And it identifies the world's wealthiest with the poorest. Each of us faces the same threat, and climate change brings us together to solve it. By placing us all in the same boat, it challenges us to identify ourselves as part of one human family.[15] That sense of global identification, and the institutions arising from and sustaining it, will make us quicker to respond to the next global crisis. Efforts to stall climate change strengthen global organizations, both governmental organizations like the United Nations and non-governmental ones like Greenpeace. Whether the next challenge is a genocide, plague, war, or famine, citizens are more likely to concern themselves with it, organizations are more likely to mobilize around preventing it, and global institutions are more likely to have the power to stop it. The world's most daunting challenges are now a source of strength, for they develop our capacity to think and organize globally. Global crises tend to strengthen global consciousness, and all of them together fortify global institutions. Crisis is the fertilizer for a growing global civilization.

This book reinterprets the world – as so many other books do. But in reframing our relationship to the world, it should bring about within its readers a realignment. Reading is no mere passive activity. It has been transforming the human experience of the world since the advent of the written word. The mechanical printing press could be said to have launched both the Northern Renaissance and the Protestant Reformation. Newspapers knit together the populations of Europe into nation-states. And the great works of Enlightenment philosophy helped light the fuse that led to the American and French Revolutions. Indeed, it was through the written word that Marx came closer than anyone to disproving his own thesis of historical materialism: it is not material forces alone that change the world but also the force of thought. Through the written word, the dead Marx overthrew governments and turned not just his mentor Hegel but the world itself on its head. Reading allows us to break the world down into its constituent parts and to conceive of it anew. It is easy when thinking about big global challenges to become fixated on partial solutions and false limitations. This sort of misaligned thinking can limit the tools at our disposal and damage the sort of coalitions needed to grapple with wicked problems like climate change and world hunger.[16] When the point is to change the world, sometimes the most productive thing to do is change the way you think. The advent of global consciousness is a revolution in thinking, and it is transforming the world.

But few of us respond to the starving child we read about with the same degree of concern we give to the jobless countryman. While the issues, the news, and the powers that be are increasingly global in scope, most of us continue to identify with the nations into which we were born. We value the lives of individuals who happened to be born into those nations more than others who were not. We pay more attention to the deaths of our fellow countrymen and women and we invest more resources into improving their lives. And yet, when pressed on the point, the vast majority of us would profess to value all human life equally.[17] This contradiction is striking and noteworthy. Identification with the nations of our birth, for many of us, leads to profound moral contradictions.[18] The consequences are dire for the billion malnourished people, living on less than a dollar a day, whose lives could easily be improved if only those of us with more resources understood them better. But few of us living in the developed world understand much about the lives of the world's poorest, and it is largely because we identify with the people and places and concerns that are closest. Global consciousness is pivotal to the fate of billions.

There are good reasons to concern oneself more with the plight of the worlds' least well off. The least well off are more likely to live in Africa and Central Asia than in the U.S. or Europe, so it will take some effort for readers who were brought up in the rich world to understand how they live. Without concerning ourselves with them, we are unlikely to understand them, and this increases the chance that we will harm them through the products we purchase and the policies we support. The suffering of the world's poorest also tends to be greater than those who are better off. And it is easier to ameliorate. One unit of happiness - as measured in say a dollar, a bowl of rice, or a caring gesture – tends to benefit the least well off far more than the most privileged.[19] But perhaps the most poignant reason to concern ourselves with the plight of the least well off is that we do value their lives. Most of us now experience a sense of responsibility for the lives of every living person, a sense of responsibility that is often disproportionate to our actions, which tend to be far more focused on national concerns. The problem is that few of us have brought our knowledge of the world into accord with our values. And the discord between what we know and what we do is often experienced as a chasm of overwhelming guilt.

Concerns such as these are leading individuals to increasingly conceive of themselves as global citizens. More and more issues are now global in scope: terrorism and the drug trade, nuclear proliferation and

war, the depletion of ocean fisheries and climate change, overpopulation and world hunger. In a world of global challenges, a cosmopolitan
identity better captures many of our deepest passions, worries, and
commitments. By embracing the world as a whole, we cast a wide
net around our own disparate commitments, thereby drawing our own
variegated selves under one big tent. In this way, the development
of global consciousness can inspire greater psychological integration.

Global consciousness is an awareness of the world as an integral
whole, and there are numerous layers to this awareness. At the most
basic level, the earth is viewed impartially, merely one more body revolving around the sun. This astronomical perspective is now integral
to the worldview of any schoolchild in the developed world, as is the
idea of the world as a place comprised of various nation-states, each
with its own respective place on the map. Even the hardheaded political realist takes a global view of world affairs, seeing nation-states as
components of an ever-shifting global equilibrium. Global business
leaders and economists look upon a similar world of equilibrating
trade balances, wavering growth rates, and flowing exchanges, all
comprising a vast system of global trade. The political realist, the
businessman, the economist, and the meteorologist must all think
globally. Their viewpoints both express and contribute to a growing global consciousness. But this need not affect their identification
with their country or group of origin. While they see the plight of all
peoples, they privilege their own. This is global consciousness, to be
sure, but it is weak. Let us call it global consciousness light.

Human consciousness is often thought of as a sort of bare awareness, like a movie screen upon which images are projected. In this
sense, the moon and stars and rivers and trees all appear upon the
human screen of consciousness, but the screen of consciousness is
unaffected. It is merely a container, a receptacle upon which sensations, perceptions, and actions are experienced.[20] This is a lot like
global consciousness light. We are aware of the world as an integral
whole, nothing more. It is a perspective that can now be discerned

in the strategies of any major corporation and in the studies of any high school student. While the world may be recognized as an integral whole, its people remain divided by indissoluble national bonds, and the man of weak global consciousness identifies with his ethnic or religious or national group over that of all others. In global consciousness light, one's own group is privileged. Fellow citizens are given more consideration, their suffering is more meaningful, their concerns more salient.

But when we speak of consciousness we often mean not just bare awareness but also the unity of experience. A person is conscious because she is aware of herself as a distinctive being with a range of capacities and past experiences, woven together in a present that points toward the future. Her momentary and fleeting experiences are knit together into a narrative about who she is and what she is doing on the planet, and this narrative is imbued with meaning. Strong global consciousness is similar. It involves not just an awareness of the world as an integral whole but an identification with it. In strong global consciousness one's personal narrative becomes enmeshed in the narrative of the world. We are members of a common humanity and our fate is entangled with that of all others.

When the revolutionary armies of Giuseppe Mazzini passed through the villages of the Italian peninsula in the mid-nineteenth shouting "Viva Italia," sharing neither a common tongue nor a culture, the peasants believed the soldiers to be praising some princess and joined in the chants. At the time, Italian was the mother tongue of only about 2 percent off the population.[21] There was no state of Italy, and until there was a state, there were no Italians. It was the same for the Americans, Iraqis, and Indians. More often than not the nation-state has been a marriage of convenience and a feat of the imagination. Individuals might group themselves around a common language, a shared religion, a set of customs, or a territory. Whether they group together to overthrow a monarchy and defend against some outside threat, the groupings tend to be opportunistic. But once grouped together, they identify with one another and mythologize their origins. Throughout the nineteenth and twentieth centuries, as the nation-state became ubiquitous, individuals discovered themselves to be Germans and Italians, Israelis and Egyptians.[22,23,24] And when there was little else to give meaning to their lives, they embraced their nationality as a badge of honor. Changing conditions are once again drawing those identities into question.

The sources of loyalty vary from time to time and place to place. People group together and identify with a vast range of characteristics and activities: armies and nations, races and religions, villages and families, hairstyles and music. There is nothing innate about the attachment to tribe or the love of country.[25] And there is little reason loyalty might not be transferred from the nation to the world. In a globalizing world like that of today, there is something arbitrary about identifying with one's country of origin. I am no more familiar, after all, with the face of a random Bostonian than I am with that of a Botswanan. It is quite likely the Bostonian and I are of different races, different ethnicities, and different religions. Even if we shared all of these traits in common, we still might be fierce political opponents, one a liberal the other a conservative, one a nationalist the other a globalist. And the Boston traffic is more likely to make of us honking rivals than cooperative comrades. Meanwhile, the Botswanan might share my concerns over world hunger, climate change, overpopulation, and rich-world agricultural subsidies. If it is often easier to identify with the individuals of another nation than with one's fellow countrymen, perhaps it is because the nation-state is a human construction. Its boundaries tend to be arbitrary, its origins imagined, and its suzerainty exaggerated. But the world itself has unequivocal boundaries and there is something definitive about strong global consciousness.

The earth is one and indivisible. It can neither grow nor shrink. Ruling out alien invasion, it cannot be impinged upon by an invading army nor split into pieces through emigration. The technologies and mores of another civilization cannot sweep through and disrupt its stability. And there is no other system or institutional complex, of which people might now partake, that is not enveloped in the atmosphere of the planet. The earth stands forth, solitary and sublime, stately and majestic, from a universe of seemingly infinite darkness, possessed with aesthetic appeal and the quiet capacity to transform human allegiance through just a glimpse. Once we think of the earth as the primary locus of human organization, it is difficult to dream up a wider authority to which we might transfer loyalty. This lends remarkable stability to the strong global consciousness of identity with the world, a stability only strengthened by ethical imperatives. It is difficult to justify giving more attention, more care, and more resources to members of one's own group over those of others, and yet it is increasingly difficult to distinguish between the two. Strong global consciousness breaks the cycle of ethical contradictions that almost always come coupled with allegiance to a particular tribe.

But ethical responsibilities are rarely simple. Ethics is an attempt to capture a seemingly random array of duties, concerns, and moral impulses under basic principles like the Categorical Imperative. Ethical principles not only group the things we intuit to be right under common principles but through those principles our commitments are extended.[26] The problem is that ethical principles have a way of yielding counter-intuitive results. We may conclude that each of us has an ethical obligation to help other individuals, when it is no skin off our backs, and the good we can do is great. And this makes sense when the commitment is to a friend or family member, maybe even to the homeless man who sleeps on your street. But do we really believe we should, or even could, respond to every appeal for a desperately malnourished child flashed before us on the TV screen? Somehow the principle that tells us to give when asked must account for the fact that the more we give the more we will be asked.[27] The philosopher Michael Sandel suggests that it is in the dissonance between proclivity and principle, that grey area where the principles we formulate to express our commitments break down in contradiction, that the impulse to philosophize arises.[28] But few of us possess the inclination and the moral intelligence to reason through such dilemmas. Moreover, philosophers merely interpret the world; the point is to change it. For those of us who do not wish to philosophize our lives away, we must somehow find balance between interpretation and action. We can begin by exploring the meaning of the commitments we now possess.

The circle of ethical commitment is growing.[29,30,31] Our moral horizons tend to be limited by that which we can see and feel, and by the communities in which we find ourselves embedded. From band to clan to village to nation, that circle has been growing. Now the scope of those communities is becoming increasingly global. And we increasingly saddle ourselves with the ethical commitments of global citizens. Somehow we must adjust our worldviews and actions to who we are becoming.

Global consciousness is growing, and the end of its growth is nowhere in sight. We do not know how local concerns will be integrated into a broader global awareness. We do not know what will become of the current system of nation-states, whether they will remain in some weakened form, whether they will be subsumed like Illinois and Idaho into the larger United States of America, whether the nations of the world will whither away, melting into a global government like the provinces of some empire, or whether nationalists will organize a backlash in an effort to halt the development of strong global consciousness.

What we do know is that the things we are aware of change us. They change our identities and they change our commitments. This is as true for the planet as it is for the nation. Nationalism arose for many reasons, but one of the most important was that individuals became for the first time capable of conceiving of the nation as an integral whole capable of grouping under the administration of a single state. The ability was tied to the development of common languages and shared news sources. Identities were fused through common administrative units and common sources of information. These preconditions of nation-states parallel our current awareness of the world and the ease with which we now communicate across borders. Global consciousness is growing thicker and stronger, because each of us is becoming more and more enmeshed in global systems. If we ignore these changes we will not only fail to develop institutions capable of responding effectively to global crises, we may fail to develop bonds with those for whom we feel, and we may fail to feel our full humanity.

HISTORIES OF CONSCIOUSNESS

...And I have felt
A presence that disturbs me with the joy
Of elevated thoughts; a sense sublime
Of something far more deeply interfused,
Whose dwelling is the light of setting suns,
And the round ocean, and the living air,
And in the blue sky, and in the mind of man;
A motion and a spirit, that impels
All thinking things, all objects of thought,
And rolls through all things.
WILLIAM WORDSWORTH

From ten thousand miles out, the earth appears a luminous, blue-green orb, swathed in swirling white clouds – a solitary sphere, hanging in darkness. It hovers - still, stark and desolate upon a background of radiant blackness. Grinding along its invisible arc, revolving through the eons on an unseen axis, its solitude is one of stillness – and yet it moves. Upon closer approach, the earth looms and magnetizes, an overwhelming force of churning mists and sublime azure. At least one contemporary science writer has suggested there is music to this sphere, inaudible to the human ear, too low for our apprehension.[1] Yet, we sense it pulsing and throbbing like the *Rite of Spring or Beethoven's Fifth*, beckoning from afar, drawing us in. Dabbled in a palette of verdant green, mocha, sea-blue, and ice, the earth comes alive to our senses. The imprint of coastline and eco-tones, mountains and deserts, demarcate the likely limits of human habitation, the invisible boundaries of human identity that we call nations. And from this vantage we might glimpse the past and present footprint of humanity

– the lights of some great city like New York or Mumbai, the fragmented remains of the Great Wall; or perhaps the liquid veins that so often sprout civilizations – the Nile, Yangtze, Euphrates, or Congo.

Perhaps the most interesting element of this sketch is that we can conceive of it at all. How is it that someone who has never been to the moon can write poetic prose of the experience? And how is it I can trust that many will find such a depiction of the earth moving? To a Homer, writing in the eighth century before Christ, the world was an enchanted sea of Gods and Goddesses, mysteries and monstrosities.[2] To the ancient Hebrews it was a hollow terrain of adversaries whose extinction might be commanded by a jealous God and then glorified in scripture.[3] If for the Greek Hesiod, a Goddess named Gaia personified the earth,[4] this was not the earth we now inhabit. In fact, the world in which we now live is far more fertile and teaming with mysterious organisms.

The Information Age bestowed a great gift to humanity for which we seldom express our gratitude - the ability of ordinary people to comprehend the world as an integrated and meaningful whole. Global consciousness is a relatively recent phenomenon in the history of the world. The capacity to survey the planet, in all its living color and vivid detail, would have been impossible for any but the most visionary geniuses of ages past.[5] Blocking their path would have been vast gaps in knowledge, of the peoples and places of the planet, gaps that could only be filled through immense leaps of the imagination,[6] metaphysical speculations, painstaking research, or the formal extensions of logic.[7] Such substitutes for genuine knowledge often signified great leaps in the evolution of human consciousness. Yet, they tended to be intimately woven into the prejudices and distortions that characterized so much past understanding of the world as well. Hence, the finest philosophy up to modern times bubbles over with the impossible speculations of Plato's *Republic*,[8] Rousseau's state of nature,[9] or Hegel's *Philosophy of History*. The lives and cultures of distant lands were plastered over with the whitewash of the imagination. And so the "Chinamen," "Hindoos," "Musselmen," and "savages"[10] that first surfaced from out of the darkness of the western unconscious, appeared more as exotic apparitions than real people. Their needs and aspirations were as unknown as they were unstudied. Now after several decades of exponentially mounting information and studies, we are beginning to inhabit one known world. The Internet, cell phones, and affordable air travel have made contact across that world ever-simpler, of course. But an increase in the number and size of global institutions has also made such contacts a necessity. Global institutions everywhere are growing in prominence: NGO's, multinationals, alliances, and associations.[11] With their growth, as well as a rise in aid, trade, and migration, more and more people are becoming functional citizens of the world, able to work and flourish in strange and distant lands.

So also, as the number of educated people across the world rises, more individuals know more about more of the planet. An increasing number of journals, websites, television networks, and citizen groups challenge us to think globally. Thus, conversations about the state of the world are becoming more informed and relevant. An increase of planetary threats like global warming, nuclear proliferation, pandemic disease, and terrorism have also challenged concerned citizens and politicians alike to think globally or to become irrelevant. And as the social sciences and international institutions keep cranking out increasingly accurate studies of the peoples and places of the planet, it is becoming easier to conceive of what life is like on the other side of it. This convergence of views is leading to what economists call economic "convergence." The idea is that it is easier to grow an economy at a faster rate in the earlier stages of development. But once the right institutions have been put in place, once wages start to rise, and once the population starts to age, and there are less tax paying wage earners and more old people to support, it becomes more difficult to sustain high rates of growth. The theory suggests that because of the differential rates of growth between developed and developing economies, there is a tendency for these economies to converge around a common level of development. The theory is a yet unfulfilled promise to the poorest parts of sub-Saharan Africa and Central Asia. But it explains a lot in the convergence between the rich world and emerging markets, like Brazil, China, India, Indonesia, Malaysia, and Turkey.

Francis Fukuyama highlighted, in *The End of History*, something deeper at work in economic convergence. *The End of History* is like many classics far more often cited than actually read, so if you have not actually read the book you would do well to ignore what you have thus far heard about it, because it is likely to be inaccurate. The idea is not that the train of history has stopped, as the title suggests; rather history has ended insofar as the great ideological conflicts of humanity have been settled in favor of liberal democracy. While there may still be Maoist guerillas fighting for power in Nepal, and while the Islamic Republic of Iran, and other such groups, might maintain or even gain power in a few scattered places, they are neither a functional nor an ideological match for markets and democracy, according to Fukuyama. Rather, humanity is now all travelling in the same direction, with the major differences being differences in development. Some of us are in the lead cars, some further behind, but everyone will pass through the same stops.[12] The markets of China and India will evolve their own unique contours, just as did the markets of Scandinavia, America, and the Asian Tigers. But however unique, these are market economies, and we can bet comfortably they will all pass through recognizable stages of development.[13]

Perhaps what Tolstoy once wrote of families could be better applied to socio-economic systems: every well adjusted socio-economic system is alike; every malfunctioning system is different in its own way.[14] This may overstate the case, for the differences between Sweden, Italy, Japan, Canada, and America are noteworthy. But unlike those between Iran, Kyrgyzstan, Bolivia, and Zimbabwe, they are bridgeable divides. Sweden might implement an upper tax bracket reaching as high as 90 percent, while America implements a flat tax. Denmark might publicly fund a proportionally representative electoral system, while Japan develops a primarily corporate funded two-party system. Such differences can appear radical from within a liberal democracy. But viewed from a more historical and global vantage, they are familial differences of little note. Little in these differences will keep their governments from being able to work together and for their citizens to be able to continue relating with one another. While economic development can bring about extraordinary lifestyle differences, it almost always comes coupled with a greater capacity for tolerance and understanding that make integrating differences relatively easy. And it is this sense of rising social complexity and inclusivity that perhaps best characterizes higher development. China may ultimately prove the thesis incorrect, but there are good reasons to believe that they too are on track for convergence and that, while democratization may be delayed due to the logistics of its size, it will begin to appear as soon as the low-hanging fruits of development have been seized and economic development begins to slow.

The path of development appears convergent, for numerous reasons. Nations tend to become more alike as they develop. Their citizens tend to share the same educational attainments, the same technologies, and the same pace of life. They have access to the same news sources, are affected by the same economic trends, and face the same life pressures. There is also an institutional convergence. A global consensus is emerging about the range of governance and economic institutions that work, and as they acquire the resources needed for effective governance, newly developed nations tend to adopt this basic set of institutions: democratic governance, free markets, constitutions, private property, freedom of speech, freedom of association, progressive taxation, social security, universal health insurance, and the list goes on. Barring the exceptional oil monarchies of the Middle East and China, almost every developed state is a democratic state. And all of them are more or less market economies. As Fareed Zakaria has noted, the path of development has quickly become a bullet train with published schedules.[15]

This convergence is not always a good thing. Exotic expressions of indigenous life are disappearing along with the thousands of ancient languages housed only in the libraries of dying minds. Moreover, development is destructive, not only of plants and wildlife but also of the peace of mind that comes coupled with social stability. What's more, the global consensus is hard to buck. Many homegrown institutions, say the communal landholdings of Mexican, Mayans or the infant industries of industrializing South America, have been dismantled so as to conform to the expectations of global investors. Since each nation is unique, and since investors tend to expect the institutions of their own nations to be just as effective in South Korea as they are in the United States, adherence to the global norm can unnecessarily disrupt cultural and even economic development.[16,17] The homogeneity makes for less experimentation; we cannot say where the next great innovation in democratic governance or economic cooperation might arise. Yet, global institutional norms make such innovations more and more unlikely to occur at all.

Still, if the world of today is far more homogenous, it is also far freer, far better fed, and vastly more educated.[18] While Freedom House counted just over 50 "fully free nations" in 1979, today there are over 90.[19] And with the freedom has come peace. While the U.S. did orchestrate the overthrow of Presidents in Iran, Chile, and Guatemala through covert operations at the height of the Cold War,[20,21] no stable democracy has ever waged a full on war with another stable democracy.[22] This principle hinges on definitions,[23] so that a change in the definition of what constitutes a democracy or a war can overturn the principle. But even if it proves only partially correct, it is remarkable nevertheless. National borders, the world over, are arguably more secure today than at any point in human history. In understanding one another better, we have become better able to work together. And in working together in multinational corporations, in non-governmental organizations, and in multilateral institutions, many have come to think of themselves as citizens of the world.

EVOLUTIONS OF ATLAS

Blessed be you, mighty matter, irresistible march of evolution,
reality ever newborn; you who, by constantly shattering
our mental categories, force us to go ever further and further
in our pursuit of the truth.
PIERRE TEILHARD DE CHARDIN

When astronauts returned from the moon in 1969, they brought
home with them photos of the earth. Not only did this make possible
the mass production of color images of the world, but ordinary people could also imagine themselves as those same astronauts reveling
in the sublime sight of our blue-green planet. There is a sense in
which those photos represented humanity's first glimpse of itself in
the mirror. For it was the first time we saw the world in all its splendor and constraints. And the frailty and beauty, the starkness and
improbability, of that image spoke to us out of the vast firmament
of emptiness.

But globes have been around for millennia now. History dates the
first to the Greek scholar, Crates of Mallus, around 150 BCE.[1] By
that point Herodotus, the so-called "father of history," had provided
a study of the history and myths of the peoples of the Mediterranean
and the ancient Near East. The problem was that the history and myths
he reported were often difficult to distinguish from one another. For
instance, the Phoenicians were said to have rounded the southern tip
of Africa, but what this meant and whether or not it was true were
not altogether clear.[2] This wasn't his fault. People simply lacked the
ability at that time to clear up these sorts of issues. And because they
lacked this ability, they didn't tend to take these sorts of truth claims

all that seriously. It would take a good couple of thousand years or so more before some of these questions were straightened out.

The oldest globe we now possess was made in Germany in the great historical pivot of 1492 C.E.[3] At that moment there came to be a pressing need for globes, as traders and explorers fanned out across the oceans. But it was not as if a skilled carpenter of the fifteenth century could just carve away at a block of wood until a sphere emerged, then glue a map on it. The whole Western Hemisphere and much of Africa were not even recognized by the most educated Europeans of the time, and they had mapped far less than this with any recognizable degree of accuracy. Of the terrain that had been charted, it is difficult to imagine that it held much meaning. It may have been exotic and alluring perhaps, but it would have remained a curiously unpeopled image.

Rather humanity came to know the earth by degrees, blindly piecing together a puzzle for which no image yet existed. The circumference had to be calculated and a means of mapping longitude discovered,[4] then the explorations and re-explorations that gave us our maps,[5] then the fighting over the boundaries of those maps. It was not until hundreds of years later that something approaching the globes so many of us grew up with came into being. For hundreds of years more, our globes remained strikingly inaccurate. At about the same time the 1890 census declared the closing of the American frontier, the final explorations of the source of the Nile were just being completed.[6,7,8] Meanwhile, the whole interior of Papua New Guinea, with its two thousand languages and fifty thousand inhabitants, living in orderly terraced farming villages dating to the stone age, was not even discovered by outsiders until airplanes flew over it in 1938.[9]

The earth as it was imagined just a couple of hundred years ago must have appeared more like a billiard ball than a bright blue marble. For it would have been barren of detail, like the abstractions of Newtonian physics and classical economics. And while it is primarily through the literary imagination that we might conceive of how the world as a whole was experienced throughout the modern era, it is revealing to note how seldom some depiction of the earth as a whole actually appeared in literature. Somehow a map or globe in the library may have been enough to move the imagination to the glories of exploration, like Marlow blindly placing a finger on the map to fix upon his destination in the Congo of Conrad's, *Heart of Darkness*.[10] But the spinning of globes was rarely enough to move the heart to a love for the planet.

Yet there was a change of heart in the late sixties. In certain eco-spiritual subcultures, it is common to hear people suggest that the photos of the moon,[11,12,13] or perhaps LSD, first awakened a love for the planet in mass culture. But this misses completely the magnitude of so many historical events of this era. In fact, the photos of the planet, and even the voyage from which they came, were merely a by-product of much deeper concerns. The Apollo space project, after all, was part of a competition with the Soviets, whose first manned satellite and its implications of superior rocket technology, represented an existential threat to the whole of the world. The newfound capacity to destroy the earth was so worrisome that it prompted the scientists who created the bomb to reverse course immediately after WWII was complete and to publish a critical book of essays, *"One World or None."*[14] Leading nuclear scientists like Andrei Sakharov in the USSR.[15] and Robert Oppenheimer in the US[16] became the first anti-nuclear activists. When having risen through the Soviet ranks under Stalin, Nikita Khrushchev finally came to power and learned of the destructive potential of the Soviet nuclear arsenal in the mid-fifties, it so disturbed him that he could not sleep for several days.[17] If the photos of the earth moved us in 1969, it seems more likely it was because the destruction of the planet through thermo-nuclear war appeared so immanent.

That impending sense of global peril, so accelerated and exacerbated by the Cold War, strengthened the role of post-war institutions like the United Nations, the World Bank, and the International Monetary Fund. For it was the purpose of these institutions to stabilize the international order, so as the threat intensified, they tended to become more active. These institutions grew in both size and importance as the post-war colonial empires rapidly disbanded and fragmented into states. During this time we saw the creation of the states of sub-Saharan Africa, India, Pakistan, Israel, and much of the Caribbean. Development became a priority for both the U.S. and the USSR, as they competed for influence in the once forgotten corners of the globe. This competition brought proxy, and sometimes real, wars to remote lands like Guatemala, Angola, Zaire, Afghanistan, and Vietnam.[18,19,20] Needless to say, these wars, and their potential for escalation, were a major concern to other nations. And for the first time, ordinary citizens began to conceive of a very concrete process through which the world as a whole might be destroyed.

Thus, the United Nations came to matter more and more, as international treaties and declarations initiated a slow build up to an international system. It was during this time that the world ceased to consist of exotic place names on maps and became a meaningful conglomeration of sovereign nation-states with unique cultures, economies, and institutions, all demanding attention. Educated people the world over came to understand them better, to be sure. But the ungoverned territories of the world also came to be consolidated under the management of states. It is remarkable the extent to which the post-colonial boundaries held. Somehow, the rising peoples and knowledge of the world had made every inch of this tiny sphere, spinning in a sea of darkness, matter.

Writing from the thick of this milieu, the legendary theologian and biologist, Pierre Teilard de Chardin, believed that as the human population rose, consciousness would swell with it and fold in on itself in mass introspection. And thus our awareness would seep from the mounting motion of the world and rise like dew to look in from afar on our frail endeavors. As humanity grew in proximity to itself, through increasing population and urbanization, our awareness of the human condition and the limitations of our world would accelerate. Somehow we would learn to step outside of ourselves and comprehend the human predicament from afar.[21] The meaning of such a vision is still enigmatic and can easily slip away like water from the grasp. Yet, shortly after he began his musings, we reached the moon and the atmosphere became peopled with satellites.

Our view of the earth is increasingly Olympian. From the middle stratosphere, the mountains ripple like waves across a sea of land, crenellations of a castle in demise. The discord of the Gods once echoed from these heights; they resolved their differences, became one God, then that one too began to vanish. Now sweeping vistas spread like patchwork from aloft the clouds: woodland, valley, summit, and plain – the blue-green hills of earth awake. Through the buckling peaks of Alps and Andes, Himalaya and Kush, white glaciers commence their retreat, liquid eons of ice abating, as the great rivers of the world gorge and narrow. They will make their way to the sea and be gone. Through a kingdom of clouds and heavenly billows, the living air reverberates with activity from beneath. Chocolate swathes of spreading desert, ochre seas, and burning jade, the ebb and flow of living and dying. This is our world, with all its wonder and implicit worries.

And the threats to this planet are being traced in ever-finer detail. The conditions are catalogued through an array of technologies only decades old. Satellites track weather along with the rise and decline of glaciation, desertification, and deforestation. Recent monitoring can even catch the emergence of pandemic disease and the changing conditions on farms. Through the analysis of particulate matter in ancient ice cores and tree rings we can trace the rise and fall of temperatures across the ages, climatic causes for the decline of empires and the fall of species.[22,23,24] With this information we can model scenarios for the future. And out in the ethers of the World Wide Web, we can glide through the landscapes of the planet, seeing the world in vivid and even historical detail on Google Earth. Perhaps it is testimony to the pace of technological development that seldom do these small miracles evoke a sense of wonder anymore.

A trillion points of extrasensory perception now illuminate the world. Satellites and monitors, readings and recordings, increasingly mediate our experience, as the surface of the planet comes to resonate with awareness.[25] It is not just that the world is being experienced through billions of human eyes and ears, along with the senses of trillions of other living beings. This animate house of mirrors, in which so many viewpoints reflect off of one another and grow in depth, is awe inspiring enough if we but pause to give it our attention. But throughout the twentieth century, and increasingly with each passing year, we are coming to perceive the world through technological prosthetics: the echolocation of radar and sonar, microscopic and telescopic vision, heat sensors, magnetic resonance imagery, and more. It was not so long ago that we knew the world only through our eyes and ears, taste, touch, and smell. Now we know the world through a wide and ever growing catalogue of overlapping sensorium.

The telecommunications networks that now link us together are not unlike a global nervous system. Data is transferred through countless nodes in both cases. And new information is accumulated, organized, and transferred out again. Data can now be mined through tracking the movements of cell phones. Hence, we can follow the whereabouts of masses of people as they work and shop and live. Of course, marketers will use this information to bring consumers and goods ever closer to one another, thereby connecting more and more of our lives to the marketplace. The legal and moral implications for the invasion of privacy here are serious, and the most cutting edge ethicists have only just begun to grapple with the implications. But that same information will also allow us to better organize our cities, trace the patterns of emergent disease, and put us in contact with others traveling along similar unseen trails in life.[26] As in the case of our web searches and surveys, there is an increasing variety of means through which individuals can group with other similar individuals.

Whether this be for good or ill, it is all bringing us closer together. And it is changing the very nature of our social systems.

Humanity once grouped itself along rivers and roads and coastlines. Now we organize along invisible channels of information: websites, blogs, social networks, and Twitter. The channels are openly accessible, global, and non-zero sum. Unlike a river basin or coastal port, there is no limit to the number of people that can belong to a social network and the number of networks to which one might belong. Thus, we can organize ourselves into larger groups with neither the conflict that accompanies competition for scarce goods nor the force required to coordinate prodigious sums of people. Larger and freer and more efficient means of social organization have always been available. But humanity has rarely made use of these economies of scale. The spread of ideas and technologies, knowledge and development, has been held in check by local prejudices: tribes engaged in constant warfare, ancient cities rife with ethnic and religious tensions, and industrial era nation-states, beset with bellicose nationalism. The result for the vast majority of human history has been frequent famine, chronic malnourishment, and socio-economic underdevelopment.

The human horizon has been limited, by a river valley or mountain chain and by the simple inability just to get along. It was not until the emergence of the railroad, with its shortening of distance and mingling of classes, that the nation-state really came into its own. The railroad spread ideas and goods over wider distances, broadening horizons, and transforming life prospects.[27,28] Unlike the empires of old, the nation-state tended to be participatory and democratic. But even the nation-state set people at odds with one another, this time over even greater distances, with the differences fought out through larger armies, with more powerful weapons.

The World Wide Web and advances in telecommunications are breaking the shackles that once bound humanity to its tiny enclaves. Regular intercourse with people on the other side of the world only became possible for most people in the last couple of decade. Until this time, world literature and news were barely accessible even for the elites. And it took massive resources to form a global organization. Now the world through which we interact is increasingly integrated and whole. The most natural scale for business and political organization is more often than not global. Ethical concerns range across the world. And the human field of consciousness is thus increasingly global. Our lives may be less cosmopolitan than we tend to think, but we are rapidly developing an infrastructure for the globalization of mind.

THE DIALECTIC OF DEVELOPMENT

He that wrestles with us strengthens our nerves and sharpens
our skills. Our antagonist is our helper.
EDMUND BURKE

Even if you have never read Thoreau, you have probably heard of his time in the wilderness. And like many, you may imagine he spent decades in self-reliant solitude. Generations of Americans have been brought up on the myth that he renounced civilization to live self-sufficiently in isolation from humanity. The reality is that *Walden* lay on the property of Ralph Waldo Emerson, a good friend of Thoreau's. It was just a couple of miles from his hometown of Concord, and Thoreau stayed there for just a couple of years. While he was there he spent much of his time reading and writing. He regularly entertained guests (20 to 30 of them on at least one occasion), visited his mother, and watched the pond's ice cut into and shipped away to warmer climates. He complained of train whistles and wondered at the intelligence of the simpler folk he met in the woods.[1] In a recent visit to Walden Pond, I walked through a replica of his cabin, more a cozy little house, with a bed, a desk, some chairs, and a wood-burning stove.

The now classic Walden is part naturalism, part contemplation, and part sand in the gears of perpetual progress. Anything but a spontaneous stream of consciousness, it was not until several years after leaving Walden Pond that Thoreau completed his finely crafted masterpiece. Later in life, after having taken over his family's pencil making enterprise, Thoreau would become a businessman.[2] Thoreau did not believe in the deep divide between humans and nature so prevalent amongst many of today's enemies of progress. He went to nature for moral alignment and stayed close to town for a more cosmopolitan edification. The global consciousness he pioneered came from contemplating the plant and animal diversity he discovered in the wild and the human diversity he found in books. And it emerged out of his study of world scriptures, inspired by the Transcendentalist movement to which he was both student and leading voice. Contrast this with a more common narrative of how he and others awoke to global consciousness.

The story of global consciousness usually begins in a forest on the edge of civilization. Some icon like Henry David Thoreau or John Muir sets out to slay the dragons of civilization, like a mythical hero, with a pen for sword and the simple truth that appears from within. In the solitude of the wilderness, these modern day nature mystics realize the beauty of creation and the sacredness of the planet. Having come down off the mountain, they set out to save the world, literally. John Muir founds the Sierra Club; David Brower founds Friends of the Earth; and Aldo Leopold founds the Wilderness Society. Their organizations then awaken the rest of us to the quickening pace of environmental destruction and the frailty of the planet. Nature mystic is here transmuted into global prophet, like Jesus returning from his fast in the desert, to proclaim the coming ecopalypse. While such stories tend to exaggerate the impact of these environmental prophets, they are mostly true. But they are too easily mythologized into Manichean struggles of good versus evil.

The mythologized awakening through nature, with its attendant return to a corrupted civilization, is a variation of several mythological motifs: the time in the wilderness, the struggle with inner demons, the mission commanded by God, the return of the hero. It is part of a long environmental tradition. The tradition comes complete with its own revered thinkers and men and women of action, its own great battles, and its end time eschatology. As we will see, the environmental tradition both arises from and propagates myths of global consciousness. The environmental movements that comprise this tradition are mostly responsible for the legislation that has cleaned up the air and water in developed countries and for the survival of innumerable species. Seminal thinkers who are a part of this tradition helped alert us to the destruction of the rain forests, the hole in the ozone layer, and the threat of global warming. The environmental tradition can claim to have inspired a greater sensitivity to the intrinsic value of life. And in the end, the movement that emerged from this tradition may prove responsible for the survival of human civilization.

But there is another way to tell the story of global consciousness, and it may account for deeper truths and inspire more effective action. The world cannot be seen from a forest or a mountain. Rather, it is constructed from billions of impressions, distant images and statistics, knit into a coherent whole in our brains. The planet lives and breathes only in the mind's eye, for it is only the mind that can conceive of something so vast as a world; remember all of those books Thoreau took to the woods. The world is far too immense to be sensed from the ground, and so feelings for the earth must first be filtered through the mind. We must construct in our minds not just a lonely planet, spinning in space, or some mythologized humanity fighting to save the earth. Rather we must conceive of a real world with real peoples, concrete places, and living species, all requiring certain definite inputs of resources, without which they would perish, a world of finite resources, whose existence must be measured and charted if we are to make sense of our impact upon it - a world, in short, in which the human mind, and all its most complex technologies, exist together in harmony with nature, as both outgrowth and culmination of nature.

Writing in the first half of the nineteenth century, most of this knowledge would have been unavailable to Thoreau. He might exhibit an environmental awareness that later proves crucial to the flowering of global consciousness, but however many books he carried with him into the woods, he would have had a hard time thinking globally in any way recognizable to us today. The natural sciences were not developed enough for him to grasp what we were doing to the planet: the species that had already perished and the atmospheric equilibrium we were just beginning to disrupt. And the social sciences were not nearly developed enough for him to make sense of distant civilizations.[3] The sort of global consciousness we now take for granted was in the time of Thoreau still inchoate and amorphous. Once we begin to treat global consciousness as a mental capacity, and the globalization of mind as a highly complex construction that is as much an outgrowth of as a challenge to civilization, a new story of global consciousness might begin to emerge. Global consciousness is not some sort of alternative to rationality but rather the culmination of reason. And it is not just a challenge to development as we have known it but also an outgrowth of that same process of economic growth. This manner of looking at global consciousness may be jarring for some environmentalists, who have good reason to worry about the calculating mind.

This story of global consciousness upends some of the most sacrosanct myths of what I have been referring to as the environmental tradition. While environmentalists have often been at the forefront of global thinking, environmental awareness is not necessarily global. Its allegiances and commitments are often limited to a local grove or stream, whose invocation may flood the mind with memories and feelings, but whose defense can require efforts vastly disproportionate to the goods preserved. One finds this sort of sentimental attachment to place in Wordsworth's *Tintern Abbey*. Here the return to a favored forest becomes a chance to return to oneself, and thus to measure one's growth in relation to the wild. Wordsworth treats nature as both a locus of spiritual transcendence and a source of personal development.[4] Aldo Leopold also writes of a relationship to nature in *A Sand County Almanac*, only this time it is a meditation on the destruction others have inflicted upon nature and a reflection upon his own work to restore it.[5] Such writings can cultivate in us a sense of the sacredness of all life and an appreciation for the ways nature might transform humanity. Hence, it is a morally edifying literature that might deepen our concern for each and every living thing. However, Wordsworth, Leopold, and Thoreau each tend to write about specific places. And many environmentalists come away from their writings having learned the lesson that they should narrow their field of concern to that which is near, and this is reflected in some of the issues most dear to their hearts.

Consider the localization of food. While buying locally produced food can inspire a greater sense of connection to local communities and environments, the net benefits of eating locally produced food tend to be marginal at best. Since locally produced food is often brought to market in small quantities, in gas-guzzling pick-up trucks, some studies suggest the greenhouse gas emissions of locally produced food differ little from food produced further away in greater economies of scale.[6] But let us say the local production of food does bring about a net decline in global warming pollution and that it also improves soil quality, and that it encourages healthier eating and thus a more efficient use of food, as proponents assert. Even under the best of conditions, the local production of food yields marginal environmental benefits relative to the work involved in creating local food markets. A single march on Washington, organized by all of the farmers and activists who keep local food markets running, and comprised of all the Americans attending farmers markets on any given summer weekend, would arguably garner enough attention to pass breakthrough legislation to reduce greenhouse gas emissions. And yet, week after week, year after year, they spend their time instead promoting and purchasing locally produced food. Of course, it is not the point of farmers markets to reduce greenhouse gas emissions. They are beautiful and good in their own right. But a significant percentage of the activists who believe global warming to be the single greatest threat to humanity have made the local production of food their signature issue. Somehow the highest values of some of the most motivated members of a generation have come to dictate merely that we should eat locally and organically. Add a little blue-grass music to the market, and this literally amounts to fiddling while the world burns.

Localized environmental allegiances are often at odds with the values emerging from a more systematic global consciousness.[7,8,9] Environmental allegiances often appear quasi-religious. The sense of the sacred that infuses a love for nature can inspire a greater sensitivity and care for all life.[10,11,12,13] As we will see in later chapters, cultivating a love for all life may be the single greatest thing we can do to improve the lot of all life on earth. But the experience of nature is easily reified, that is, the idea of nature is hardened into a category, rigidly opposed to that which is human.[14] When nature and humanity are thus opposed to one another, the human is all too often cast as polluted and profane. Here the mind and civilization must necessarily be alienated from the body and nature. Thus, the thinker is set at war with his own thoughts, the environmental movement with the civilization it seeks to preserve.[15] Nature is here pure and free, while a sort of original sin, which runs far deeper than anything propagated by the Catholic Church, corrupts humanity.[16] The problem here is that hating your own mind is not a good recipe for putting it to good use. The quest for sustainable technologies tends to appear here a fruitless stopgap measure, destined for failure, and so destined because the human must necessarily conflict with the natural. Thus, the best humanity can do is to get out of the way. The only problem is that there are too many of us for that solution to work at this stage in history.

If humanity will make the planet unlivable in the near future because of some flaw intrinsic to the species, and we can only live sustainably with drastically reduced numbers, responsible people will think hard about how to reduce human numbers. Population control can benefit almost every major global challenge,[17] but it is not at all unusual to hear even highly educated and sensitive environmentalists talk about the need to resist the urge to try to feed the poorest billion hungry people. Never mind that it is the poorest portions of humanity who populate the fastest. Since we cannot help imposing ourselves on a nature that is otherwise pure, there is a strong tendency amongst less sophisticated thinkers in the environmental tradition to hope for cataclysms that might ultimately cull the herd of humanity. There is something fascistic[18] and even genocidal in this logic. Of course, we almost never hear this sort of talk from environmental leaders, and environmentalists tend to be sensitive people, so this logic is usually mitigated by the respect for life that is inspired by the same environmental tradition. The point here is that spiritual environmentalism has a rather nasty shadow that under the wrong circumstances can be very dangerous.[19]

The environmental movement often appears extreme not simply because it is bringing new values to the world but rather because those values tend to breed so many unresolved tensions.[20] Consider the case of genetic engineering, often dismissed out-of-hand by environmentalists as a sort of blight on nature. Environmentalists tend to complain of anti-science climate skeptics who refuse to heed the findings of the Intergovernmental Panel on Climate Change, yet most environmentalists ignore the findings of the scientific establishment on genetic engineering. The National Academy of Sciences, the World Health Organization, the U.N. Food and Agriculture Organization, the American Medical Association, and the Royal Society of London, along with virtually every other major world scientific body commenting on the issue, have proclaimed the current generation of genetically engineered foods safe for human consumption.[21] Of course, this does not mean that every genetically engineered food is safe. After all, many non-genetically engineered foods are not safe for certain people and in certain quantities.[22] Rather, according to the world's most respected scientific organizations, there is nothing inherently dangerous about a genetically modified food relative to a non-engineered food. For the process of domesticating crops has always involved genetic changes. It may be reasonable to wonder whether respected scientists sitting on respected scientific panels hold the same standards of food safety as you do. But to paraphrase the now rene-gade environmental leader, Stewart Brand, those who know the most about climate change are the most worried while those who know the most about genetic engineering are the least worried.[23]

Current genetic science focuses on breeding low-till crops that are pest resistant. The development of such crops would be, all other things being equal, a great boon to the environment. Since the tilling of soil emits CO^2 and causes soil erosion, low-till crops would di-minish greenhouse gases emitted through reducing the tillage of soil and through halting the opening of new lands to agriculture. Insofar as famers could diminish their use of pesticides, herbicides, and fun-gicides, emissions would be further diminished. These are all major goals of the environmental movement.[24] Further, according to agri-cultural economist Robert Paarlberg, environmental advocacy against genetic engineering has been highly successful in keeping GMOs out of Africa.[25] To the extent he is right, and to the extent this has held back the productivity of African agriculture, the environmental tra-dition may be able to count among its achievements not just cleaner air and water and a safer ozone layer but also keeping vast numbers of Africans malnourished.[26] Since hungry farmers tend, amongst oth-ers things, to have more children, anti-GMO advocates may be re-sponsible for some population growth in Africa as well. Given the overwhelming scientific support for genetically modified food, and the potential boons it might bring on several environmental and social fronts, one would expect environmentalists to at least be open to a rea-soned debate on the issue. Instead, they tend more often to speak in the hyperbole of religious dogmatism. Once again, we may be witnessing a case of environmental values damaging environmental causes.[27]

If humanity is to avoid destroying the world's wild places, we are likely to require a wide array of highly potent technologies to mitigate global warming and to feed the couple billion more people who are likely to inhabit the planet before population is expected to decline around mid-century. The use of these technologies will often impinge upon the world's remaining wild places. Even wind and solar farms will require the destruction of vast areas of wilderness if they are ever to comprise a significant portion of humanity's energy profile. The trade-offs will be complex, and often painful, and they must be sorted through rationally.[28] Doing so will require an advanced global consciousness, capable of weighing a wide array of concerns one against the other. Insofar as the environmental tradition inspires a greater allegiance to an unspoiled localized nature, to the exclusion of more distant peoples and places, it will tend to advocate some of the least efficient solutions.

Leading environmental thinkers like Steward Brand and James Lovelock have begun to talk about saving the world from the environmentalists. While this wake up call seems necessary, it also seems to denigrate the immensely important work of so many environmentalists who regularly sacrifice their own well being so as to make our lives better.[29,30,31,32] Both Lovelock and Brand, along with leading climate scientist James Hanson, are pro-nuclear power and believe that nuclear power will be necessary to mitigate the worst impacts of global warming. They argue that, when government subsidies are not included, both solar and wind energy are still far too expensive for mass appeal. Further, bringing these energy sources to scale will require vast swathes of land and that the use of this land will be increasingly opposed by nature lovers and property owners, as they come to realize the extent to which the countryside will need to be industrialized in order to meet human energy needs. Other environmental leaders, like Al Gore, still have concerns with the cost of nuclear power, the ability to quickly bring nuclear plants to scale, and the proliferation of nuclear weapons.[33]

The point is not to advocate for nuclear energy or even the genetic modification of food. A serious exploration of these issues is well beyond the scope of this book. The point here is simply to hint at the trade-offs involved in several environmental issues and to point out that when these trade-offs are taken seriously, several issues that environmentalists long considered settled will be reopened for debate. This debate is important, for the environmental movement, which has done so much to inspire our love for the planet, and which has alerted us to the precariousness of human civilization, might also prevent the implementation of the only solutions capable of sustaining civilization.[34,35] And if this occurs, it will be because of a failure to think globally.

The environmental movement needs a new story, one that embraces our humanity in such a way as to inspire the sort of strong action that will be necessary to preserve the world's remaining wild places. It needs a story that includes more of who we are so that we might galvanize a wider array of forces in grappling with ecological disturbances.[36] This movement that has done so much to expand our idea of what it means to be human, and of what matters most, must evolve to include the calculating mind and its many tools and technologies. The heroes of the environmental tradition have bequeathed several strands, but still an incomplete weaving, of the tapestry of global consciousness.

The story of how the world came to reside in our minds, as much as we reside in the world, is a chronicle perhaps as tied to economic development as to the discovery of nature. Trade has been bringing isolated groups of people into contact with one another ever since some ancient tribe of proto-humans first realized their local monopoly on flint might be traded for the papayas in some neighboring valley. Greater contact has almost always brought greater understanding and with it a widening circle of moral concern, from clan to tribe, nation to humanity.[37] Peoples who trade together are often laid waste to together, for through trade, their destinies are intertwined. Hence, economic discourse is often a prelude to political discourse. Peoples who trade together often form families and states, and thus they stay together.

To be sure, the story of economic globalization is also a tale of exploitation, in which an ever-widening sphere of goods and services and experiences is commodified.[38] Increased trade tends to quicken the destruction of nature. The mind of the merchant and that of the statesman are both too often preoccupied with the rational control of that which rests beneath their imperial gaze.[39] But both merchant and statesman must occupy themselves with a widening sphere of concerns. And as the imperial mind widens in scope, it will sooner or later be led to take in the world. Thus, the development of the most exploitative dimensions of economic globalization constitute a precondition for the globalization of mind.

Commerce is not just imperial but also spurs global consciousness from below. Economic development provides the tax dollars needed to bring about full universal literacy and to build a system of higher education. And through this education, we learn how our actions impact others. Through literature and history, we learn about the lives of people who otherwise might not matter. We learn about how they go about their days, the events that influence their destiny, and the forces that forge their feelings. Through the study of politics and economics we come to see ourselves as related to others in vast networks of governance and exchange. The same issues that might upend our own lives are often just as monumental to our supposed enemies. Hence, through learning about the world, we discover a deeper relationship to it, and through seeing how we are related, we become sensitized to a wider sphere of humanity. In this sense, education tends to involve moral cultivation. Through learning about the lives of others we widen our circle of moral concern. [40] And we would never learn to care for so much more but through an education that is dependent upon surplus wealth. For many this will appear a paradox.

Economic development tends to breed individuals who are not only more globally conscious but also more self-conscious. A growing economy does not always produce greater economic security, but it will almost always produce a greater diversity of occupational roles. Individual must somehow be fitted to job role, and with growing development the process tends to require an increasingly finer fit.[41] Thus, a social system that gives greater latitude to individuals in their choice of career will, other things being equal, tend to be more productive. As individuals are forced to choose amongst a diversity of occupations, they will tend to think more about their own life paths. They will dream and explore, join organizations and read books, go to therapy and take classes, all so that they might choose a career that gives ample scope to their own peculiar proclivities. In the process of these explorations, they will not only learn about themselves but also about those who took the paths they chose not to travel. Anyone reading a book like this will be deeply familiar with this process, for it is a condition of postmodern life. Insofar as this sort of career development encourages individuals to know themselves well enough to choose the right career, it inspires self-awareness. Insofar as it produces individuals better suited to their jobs, it spurs economic development. Hence, economic development and self-actualization each contribute to one another.[42]

Economic development will usually provide the sort of leisure and security needed for individuals to take the time to think about what they really want in life. It is normal in a developed economy to expect this sort of freedom, and when it is lacking we tend to think that something has gone wrong. Hence, when people living in developed economies encounter others who lack this freedom to make for themselves a life, they often respond as if they are witnessing an injustice, as if some wrong has been committed. We feel this way for loved ones and fellow citizens but also for farm animals, for human fetuses, and for yet unborn generations. In crafting the lives we truly wish to lead, we become sensitized to the thousand subtle insults to dignity to which all conscious beings are exposed. We not only expect that a life should be free to unfold in its own special way, we are sensitive to what it might be like for such an unfolding to be obstructed.

Economic security not only makes possible the education through which we might become aware of the plight of distant others, it also makes it far less risky to intervene to improve their lives. We feel free to intervene because our own lives are more secure, and this is a direct result of economic development. But we also often feel compelled to intervene, because through higher education and deeper self-awareness, we learn to feel more fully the suffering of others. For these reasons environmental movements are usually strongest where per capita GDP is highest, places like the United States, Scandinavia, Germany, and England.[43] But it is not just environmental movements that are strongest in these places. Human rights, animals rights, disability rights, and gay rights movements all tend to make their appearance at a certain stage of economic development.[44] That advanced economies are usually also democracies, where organizing such movements is an accepted part of citizenship, only underscores the point that economic development tends to breed moral development.

That the most exploitative economies also produce the widest circle of ethical concern will remain to many an irritating paradox, irritating because it suggests that something so crass as an ever-expanding process of commodification might produce something so elevated as a widening sphere of ethical concern. The association makes me uncomfortable as well, for it seems to justify the abuses so often incurred in the process of development. And corporate parties often use these same arguments to justify cutting social and environmental programs. Yet, economic development seems a necessary but nevertheless insufficient condition for the birth of environmentalism. After all, it is difficult to imagine a contemporary environmental movement that did not pay homage to Muir and Thoreau, Leopold and Brower. Somehow we need to explain why the strongest movements for human rights, animal rights, and the environment all tend to arise in the most developed places. And the environmental tradition routinely fails to answer this question.[45]

Perhaps it is not until a certain stage of economic development has been reached that these environmental thinkers can even articulate their thoughts and not until a certain stage of industrial advance that we yearn to hear their messages. Thinkers like Leopold and Muir may represent as much a culmination of as a challenge to modernity. They seem to study as often as they revel in nature, and this is a wholly modern way of being in nature. Rachel Carson, whom many suggest launched the environmental movement with Silent Spring in 1961, was also a scientist. Contemporary writers like E.O. Wilson and Farley Mowat are similarly scientists, often writing about their grant-funded research in nature. We read their writings, which they have only written because science has advanced to the point of studying the underlying mechanisms of life. But science would never have reached this stage of development but for an abundance of surplus wealth that might be spent on such research projects. Bearing all of this in mind, the environmental tradition appears as much an outgrowth as a challenge to modern industrial society. But if the environmental tradition is to make its message heard by a post-industrial global society, it must give more attention to the economic conditions that allowed it to flourish. And it must embrace the mental capacities that are required to think globally.

Global consciousness evolves dialectically, from technologies and trade that were never intended to transform our minds. The Onion, America's best faux news source, put it well in their satirical account of the inventor of Twitter, responding to talk of a Twitter Revolution in the Iranian uprising of June 2009. "Twitter was intended to be a way for vacant, self-absorbed egotists to share their most banal and idiotic thoughts with anyone pathetic enough to read them... When I heard how Iranians were using my beloved creation for their own means—such as organizing a political movement and informing the outside world of the actions of a repressive regime—I couldn't believe they'd ruined something so beautiful, simple, and absolutely pointless."[46] Technologies are regularly put to uses their inventors never intended. When Alfred Einhorn invented Novocain in 1905, he initially intended it to be used as a surgical drug. As Novocain came to be increasingly used in dental procedures, Einhorn was offended and spent the rest of his life arguing for its surgical utility.[47]

Fostering global consciousness tends to be an after thought for business leaders orchestrating multi-national expansions. But global awareness grows as employees and executives learn about the cultures they have been thrown into. It wells up as they befriend foreigners and travel the world in pursuit of profit. As their interests become intertwined with the Chinese or Indians in whose countries they have located, these business leaders come to read from their same news sources, partake of their same vicissitudes, and share in their hopes and dreams. And when we seek out a book on China or India or solutions to climate change, the authors are often these same later day Marco Polo's, pioneers on the cutting edge of a new world.

Human rights and environmental activists also owe a good deal of their global consciousness to the work of these multi-national corporations. Challenging the abuses of multinational corporations carries them across the world. With the technologies developed by some of the very corporations they are fighting, activists organize themselves in transnational networks. And like the business leaders, they come to stand in solidarity with the peoples of far-flung places. Activists read their news, fight their fights, and share their dreams. Through work with the peoples of the world, activists begin to think of themselves as citizens of the world.[48]

The development of global consciousness is dialectical. International institutions, international studies programs, the environmental movement, and much of humanity's concern for the planet, in general, are a flowering of economic development as well as a means of redressing its fallout. Environmentalism is as much a product of as a challenge to economic development. And it is sustained by, as much as it now sustains, economic development. The great economist John Maynard Keynes once wrote that, "practical men, who believe themselves to be quite exempt from any intellectual influences, are usually the slaves of some defunct economist."[49] Perhaps we could say the same of some global thinkers and environmentalists. Their love for the planet rests to a great extent on a developmental process that is now all too often destroying the earth.

SECTION 2

GLOBALIZATION OF COMMUNICATION

Modern bourgeois society with its relations of production, of exchange and of property, a society that has conjured up such gigantic means of production and exchange, is like a sorcerer, who is no longer able to control the powers of the nether world which he has called up by his spells.

KARL MARX

CONJURING DREAMS

In the 1938 classic *The Sorcerer's Apprentice*, Mickey Mouse plays apprentice to a great wizard. Attempting to imitate the sorcery of his master, Mickey rouses a broom to life and rests as it performs his chores. As the broom fetches water from a well and drains it into a stone basin in the wizard's laboratory, Mickey falls asleep and dreams that he himself is a great wizard, commanding the waves below and the dome of stars above. He awakens to a basin near full, yet the broom carries on without cease. After repeatedly endeavoring to immobilize the broom, Mickey panics, takes an axe, and smashes the broom to pieces. Yet each piece stirs to life, becoming scores of new brooms, and all of the brooms together resume their task, until from each of their labors they raise to life a swelling flood.

Human innovations have this tendency to overpower their makers. At times, this is dramatic, say the weapons of war or revolutions gone astray. But more often than not technology overwhelms us in mundane ways. We call forth the powers of our sorcery, enlist the facilities of nature in the service of invention, adapt ourselves to our creations, and somehow believe that we are still in charge. As the systems theorist Francisco Varela has noted, "we lay down a path in walking."[1] We construct worlds for ourselves that we then inhabit, as if those worlds had arisen organically, free of human artifice. We do this with technologies and businesses and political systems, molding ourselves to the furniture of a human-built world.[2] It is a handy trick that appears intrinsic to the human mind. Born into indeterminate worlds, subject to the powers of creation and destruction, humans have evolved to be a paragon of adaptation. But sometimes we find ourselves unable to adapt to our own creations, and they sweep us away with their awesome force. We become less paragons of adaptation and more like clever mice, racing through the labyrinth of our own fantasies.

It is not just one or another innovation that overwhelms, for one technology calls forth another and another, until a system of technologies lords over us like Mickey's army of brooms. The automobile brought forth the interstate highways; the highways brought about the need for big-box stores; and the cars, the highways, and the big-box stores were custom fitted to life in suburbia, where atomized individuals came to devote an increasing portion of their spare time to television viewing. Together these technologies came to comprise a human-built world, which shaped American culture in the late twentieth century. The pattern is typical. We mold our movements to those of the machine, cramp our bodies and minds into school desks and classrooms, pace our synapses to those of the computer. We morph into servants of our own inventions, subjects to an army of our own creation. And it is not just individuals who are so regimented. Technological systems transform social, economic, legal, and political realities. The whole of our worlds are brought into line. If we are to understand the role of information technologies in bringing about global consciousness, we must recognize how global consciousness is an integral component of fiber-optic webs.

Here the concept of a mode of production can be illuminating. The idea comes from Karl Marx, and while overly deterministic, illustrates the way new technologies and productive processes bring into being new life worlds. Marx was interested in how social systems, and the people of which they are comprised, develop in conjunction with productive capacities. A concept that could demonstrate this relationship between social and economic systems would allow him to criticize capitalism as not just an exploitative economic system but also as an alienating social system. Through capitalism, Marx believed, people became the slaves of their own inventions, and in their slavery shackled their bodies and minds to the rhythms and pace of the machine.[3] But it was not only the machines to which Marx believed individuals were shackled, for the machines brought forth entire new worlds. Though it was core to his corpus of written material, Marx never actually defined a mode of production, and there is a perennial debate about what exactly he meant.[4] The idea suggests stages of economic development. Social scientists often refer to hunter-gatherer, horticultural, agricultural, industrial, and post-industrial societies. Recognizing that one stage is almost always prior to the next and that there are rarely reverses, the stages are taken as sequential: first hunting and gathering, then horticulture, agriculture, and industrialization. And since the prior stages are simpler and the later ones more complex, as measured by any number of variables ranging from the number of artifacts to the degree of differentiation in the division of labor,[5] the stages are often viewed hierarchically, with each later stage representing an advanced state of integral complexity.[6] Developmental economists since at least the time of Adam Smith[7] have tended to be acutely aware of these stages, integrating them into their models of economic development. Sociologists and anthropologists, on the other hand, have had a more conflicted relationship to the idea of development, sometimes detailing the different stages and sometimes deconstructing the motives of those promoting these models. Marx integrated the anthropological interest in the integrity of social systems into the economists preoccupation with stages of development, demonstrating how each stage of development consists of a mutually reinforcing web of institutions and beliefs, animated by a system of technology.[8]

Technology is central to any mode of production, as Marx would have it. "The hand-mill gives you society with the feudal lord, the steam-mill society with the industrial capitalist."[9] Technology shapes the possibilities and limitations of productive capacities. And the organization of the productive process circumscribes the nature of job roles within it, whether they are creative or monotonous, self-motivated or collective, physical or intellectual. The productive process orients the way working hours are spent and hence how work shapes the mind and body. The scoliosis of primitive farm laborers, the carpel tunnel syndrome of office workers, and the stubby fingers of early factory workers are illustrative of the potential malformations. But this shaping of the self through work goes much deeper, conditioning mental models, molding personas and perceptions and the very way we seek release from tension. Neural networks are wired through work, muscle fibers reinforced, bones aligned. And insofar as the educational system prepares people for work, it conditions when we speak, when we listen, how we sit, and what we know. In a society of factories, students sit in rows, respond to bells, and conform to expectations;[10] in a post-industrial school they are taught to play nice, to be creative, and to think for themselves. For Marx, it is not the university that shapes the mind but rather the work that will later be required of students that determines the curriculum of universities. In this way, economic activity conditions our perceptions, shapes our values, and constrains our prospects. In short, it makes us who we are.

The productive process also shapes the nature of ownership. While it usually takes family wealth to finance a plantation, it takes entrepreneurial zeal to fund a factory. And it usually takes a public corporation, organized through a stock exchange, to finance a multinational corporation. Managing these respective entities calls for varying skill sets and temperaments. The plantation, the factory, and the mega-corporation each bring to power different personality types, with a range of drives, values, and aversions to risk. Hence, from one mode of production to the next, the class of owners varies, from risk-averse feudal lords to driven entrepreneurs. And like the laborers, the bodies and minds of the owners are also shaped by the nature of the work in which they engage. Modes of production are in this way prisons from which even the wardens cannot break free.

Since there is almost always some correlation between wealth and political power, any shift in the organization of ownership brings a corresponding shift in the distribution of political power. Yet, each class of owners – whether landlords, capitalists, entrepreneurs, or tribal leaders – has its own perspective and political ideals. Strong middle classes tend to facilitate the transition to democracy; landed aristocracies strengthen monarchies. These are basic axioms of the social sciences. According to their ideals, and in their interests, the predominant classes alter the nature of property rights and hence much of the law. They privatize property, control it through the state, or share it through wikis. And the classes most suited to owning and managing the productive forces establish a political system suited to their needs and ideals. Thus, the mode of production is like a template of technologies that shapes productive processes, ownerships structures, class hierarchies, political power, and the consciousness of owners and workers.

Most important for this study, modes of production shape consciousness: the things of which we are aware, that which we think, and who we believe ourselves to be; whether we are members of a village, identified with one another through tradition and ethnicity or self-interested individuals, tied to others through the interests and laws of a nation-state; whether we are rational or gut thinkers, yin or yang - all of this is shaped by the mode of production into which we are born. The power of production to transform one's self-conception is important here, because as the mode of production shifts from industrial to information society, each of us is being transformed in ways that are both mundane and unusually difficult to fathom.

Human consciousness is undergoing a tectonic shift. Information technologies transform our sense of space and time, and this changes the peoples and places with which we most identify. Since information technologies are globally interconnected, using them brings global consciousness to maturity. It does this by uprooting us from our own locales while exposing us to the products, the news, and the creative productions of the world. We are uprooted through cell phones, cable television, and of course, the Internet. And it is not just individuals whose identities are transformed. The continual advance of information technologies deepens global production chains, strengthens business networks, and shores up financial markets. It makes it easier to organize communications amongst world leaders and their subordinates. And it strengthens global protest movements. The ability to think globally is now critical to financial, to political, and to social competence, for the arsenal of technologies now sweeping us into the future is globally integrated. The emerging system of production is reorganizing lives across the globe. The way we think, the things we value, the people with whom we identify, and the ways we do business are all being globalized. The Information Age is not only a technological phenomenon but a social one as well. And the consciousness this engenders transforms lives.

Humanity is now deluged with information and racing to keep up with the system of global production. The environmental hazards overflow like oil from a ruptured well that we know not how to contain. Like Mickey Mouse, we are struggling to keep up with nightmares that have sprung from our own cleverness. But in the process, we are learning to see further and deeper into the nature of things. This brings us back to the Sorcerer's Apprentice. Ultimately, Mickey was let off the hook: the wizard stepped in and laid the brooms to rest. Perhaps we will be so lucky. Man is the ape with the furrowed brow that somehow seems to muddle through. The forces we have conjured up through information society are like a Leviathan, a juggernaut threatening everything in its path. But the same forces that threaten our destruction are also making us globally conscious, and through global consciousness we are learning to cooperate.

WEAVING THE WEB

*In its essence, technology is something
that man does not control.*
MARTIN HEIDEGGER

Back in the eighties, Tim Berners-Lee had an idea, and it changed the world. "Suppose all the information stored on computers everywhere were linked." Now a lot of us had ideas around this time, some of them quite revolutionary. But few have ever had such an impact. Tim submitted a proposal to his superiors at the European Organization for Nuclear Research in 1989, describing what would later become the World Wide Web. His title, "Information Management: A Proposal," was about as stimulating as the response he got from his boss, "vague but exciting."[1] But ideas matter, and ideas like this one can fundamentally alter the human-life-world. The basic architecture of the Internet was built in the seventies at the Pentagon. Like nuclear weaponry and the awakening of global consciousness that the threat of a nuclear holocaust inspired, the Internet can thus be viewed as a spillover effect of the Cold War. But the networks it spawned were small and private; thanks to Tim Berners-Lee, the World Wide Web made the Internet accessible.

The World Wide Web is one of those rare inventions deliberately fostered to bring about fundamental social transformation. By providing addresses to each website, and making all of them easily accessible, it opened the Internet to anyone who cared to join. Like farming in the agricultural era and factories in the industrial, the Internet lies at the heart of Information Age infrastructure. It is used to buy, to sell, to work, and to manage. It is the means by which we transfer data, news, and goods. Through it we connect with friends and family and even find love. And it is a truly participatory medium through which we assemble, organize, and transfer information. "The web was designed so every user could be a contributor," notes Tim Berners- Lee. "That sort of participation was the whole idea and was there from the start." [2] Without the World Wide Web we would lead profoundly different lives. The Internet, of which the web is merely an organizing mechanism, is central to a new mode of production.

A single invention will occasionally transform the nexus of human concerns, but rarely is this intentional. Electricity, automobiles, television, and radio each came to define the twentieth century. And they transformed the nature of whole societies. Sometimes they regimented, sometimes exhilarated, sometimes degraded, and sometimes tranquilized. Everywhere they appeared, they were like barbarian invaders who sweep down from the wastelands, wiping the slate clean. The innovations brought change. Like the capital of which Marx wrote so passionately, for better or worse, the great inventions of the twentieth century first shattered and then rebuilt the human community. The freedom they made possible atomized individuals, fractured local communities, and paved the way for stronger nations. Such social transformations are often unleashed through innovation. The mechanical printing press facilitated the Protestant Reformation, the Northern Renaissance, and ultimately modernity. But there is little reason to believe that Johannes Gutenberg intended to unleash such sweeping changes. While he may have grasped the weightiness, one suspects he was blind to the significance of his project. For the potential impact of a new technology is seldom predictable and can often only be explained in hindsight.

But the web was woven to make an impact, and it has become a medium and a template for participatory change. What has come to be called net neutrality, the principle that all Internet traffic should be treated equally, with no second-class websites and prohibitive commercial fees, was fostered and protected from the start. [3] The blog movement is an open challenge to political authorities the world over. Coupled with Twitter and Facebook, and under conditions ripe for revolution, it may prove critical to subverting some of the world's most malicious rulers. Similarly, by providing small time entrepreneurs and innovators access to the same software used by major corporations, open source software subverts established business hierarchies. YouTube exposes corrupt and abusive politicians, criminals, bosses, and cops. And by integrating a profusion of perspectives, Wikipedia makes a mockery of academic authorities whose narrow concerns can constrict and even squelch dialogue. Both the medium and the message are subversive. The World Wide Web is a magnet for social and political renegades. And it allows them to organize with ease. The contributors to the web are often motivated by the same desire as Berners-Lee: to remake the world from the ground up.

The Internet simplifies and facilitates social organizing by connecting people in ways previously unimaginable. It not only changes what we are capable of achieving, it changes who talks to whom and under what conditions. It changes how we work together and the sorts of entertainment we share. All of this revolutionizes human relations, which groups are most powerful, which institutions most salient, which organizations most influential, and which people matter most. Never before have individuals had such control over their social lives. It is not simply that we have greater freedom to choose amongst various interests, say what we do for entertainment or edification. We now have the second-order ability to shape the space and time through which we interact, whether online or in person, real time or virtual. We choose between text and phone, Twitter, Facebook, and blogs. And we expect an increasing level of control over who joins the conversation. This second-order governance of our lives gives us the capacity to shape the social conditions through which our interests emerge and develop. We do not just choose what we want; we also choose the things we want to shape our choices. And this lends to our social lives a vastly greater degree of autonomy.

Manual labor has always been a burden, weighing on the shoulders of humanity like a heavy yoke. While industrialization eased the burden of farming, it replaced it with the harness of sweatshops and stockyards. But the information economy is largely ephemeral. Computerization has transmuted a world of objects into one of bits. Information is easier to manipulate than products and services. With each computer connected to all others through the web, virtually anyone can cut, paste, compile, and transfer information. This has led to an increase in the number of knowledge workers, the people who work primarily with information. Knowledge work may be a lighter physiological burden than farm or factory work, but the freedom involved in such work can be stressful. Individuals are more and more the authors of their own work, the creators of plans and procedures and programs.[4] This increases autonomy and self-motivation in the workplace, changing the office from a place in which people are trained to conform to one where they learn self-expression. Knowledge workers are at their best when they add value to information through its reorganization. And this changes the very nature of work.

Increases in the differentiation of labor have long characterized economic development, but the current subdivision of job roles is less like a tree and more like the roots of grass, branches within branches within branches, forever fracturing, twisting, multiplying, and folding in on themselves. By bringing more pieces of information to bear on any given going concern, the Information Age inspires the constant growth of new niches of expertise. As new areas of expertise appear, new job roles likewise emerge. Since many of these jobs involve the mastery of little known fields of knowledge, managers must relinquish control to underlings. Since most jobs involve working with increasing amounts of information, ordinary line workers come to appear more and more like specialists, masters of their own tiny domains. Postmodernity may prove to be the graveyard to hierarchy. Modernity rigidified rank as human relations came to be structured according to the dictates of machines. While a decent manager might eventually learn how to spot good lawyers or accountants, it is far more difficult to discern what makes a good restoration ecologist or data management systems specialist.

While the dissolution of hierarchies may at times appear ubiquitous, it is far from a foregone conclusion. New information technologies tend to shatter monopolies of information only to see control reasserted at new levels.[5] The printing press, the telegraph, and the television each inspired a concomitant breakdown and reassertion of authority. And something similar may happen with the Internet. But we are still in the heyday of the revolution. State controlled media in non-democratic nations must now compete with bloggers, YouTube, and satellite TV. Even if they can arrest a blogger here and there, they can rarely match the explosion of expression from below. Advertising departments must now account for bad ratings and reviews, and they increasingly withdraw into insubstantial entertainment, as if in submission to a public that does not want to be manipulated. In one domain after another, we see the nature and scope of authority circumscribed. A time may indeed come when "the empire strikes back," but authoritarian tides continue to roll away.

How all of this will really play out is at this stage still indeterminate. What is at this stage clear is that the information revolution consists of such a wide array of battles still being waged, that much like the second decade of the War on Terror, most of us have lost track of where they are being waged and why. The deluge of information is flooding over proprietary walls. A whole generation has grown to adulthood utilizing and contributing to a common stock of information, sharing music and video games, blog posts and reviews, software and applications. The property rights established by previous generations now criminalize the most ordinary online activity. But the Millennial Generation expects to get their music, their news, their movies, and their software for free. They have grown up in an era in which the guarded self-interest of previous generations has come to threaten the economy, the environment, and their very futures. As they attain to power in coming decades, their experiences will inform the legislation they pass and their willingness to enforce old laws. We should not expect them to honor what came before. While it may take generations, and while our prognostications may ultimately be wide of the mark, we can count on the Information Age to bring about some gradual revolution in the nature of property.[6]

Change the mode of production and there will be a corresponding change in the nature of property; this was axiomatic for Marx.[7] Everywhere industrialization left its sooty mark, private property rights were clarified and fortified by the state.[8] From the commons in England to the hunting grounds of the Sioux, industrialization obliterated the common ownership of land.[9] Meanwhile, it brought forth the public corporation.[10,11] Whatever the law might state, we are today witnessing a similar mutation in the nature of property. Skills and abilities have ceased to be guarded like valuable pieces of real estate, and are instead poured like wine into political campaigns and blogs, charitable work and free promotions. The non-profit sector and philanthropy are growing and have been on the rise for decades.[12] And it has become normal to contribute, anonymously and with little hope of reward, online reviews, software, and personal advice.

While the average American wage earner has experienced little if any real increase in wages for the past several decades, leisure time, as measured over the course of a lifetime and per capita education levels, have nevertheless grown. This makes it easier to find the time and the skills needed to give freely.[13] By making it easier to share information and to organize, the Internet has brought about an organizational revolution, thereby increasing the number of venues through which individuals can serve and give. Insofar as it awards reputation and recognition to those who participate most, the hyper competition of the digital age provides further incentive to give work away for free. It is an irony of history that the dissolution of industrial society would only be accomplished when the specter of communism was finally chased from the scene and the far more ephemeral force of the

Internet took over the task of revolution.

We are in the throes of a multi-generational shift in the mode of production.[14,15,16,17,18] And since the changes we can expect to see will often be gradual and piecemeal, these changes will be accompanied by many false prophets, proclaiming radical transformations where there are but passing trends. The complexity of the web will make these sorts of judgment calls commonplace, and it is almost certain that my own analysis will contain many an error. With so much happening, it is easy to find only what you wish to see. Moreover, the powers that be have a way of coming back from the grave, to forever haunt us like some Terminator. You smash him into a thousand pieces, and somehow the pieces reconstitute, and come back stronger, this time in the guise of a Governator. But while the speculations can appear sophomoric, like the belabored efforts to declare a major, they are a necessary part of growing into the future.

The Internet is a bit like the radio, which facilitated so much freedom of expression in the West but was also used to indoctrinate fascists and to organize killing squads in Rwanda.[19,20] The information economy has come coupled with the breakdown of the welfare state and a massive rise in income inequalities. And it is so constituted as to allow for, and even facilitate, the emergence of an ever growing number of apparently natural monopolies: Google and Facebook, YouTube and Flickr. As local hierarchies are smashed to bits, new hierarchies reconstitute themselves at higher levels. Even as Facebook provides for the easy organization of friends and family, and the fluid expression of interests, it is perhaps the largest accumulation of personal information ever in the history of the world, more than the CIA, the KGB, the MI5, and the Mossad together could ever have hoped to acquire. There is always the risk that this information will be used for the purposes of oppression by some massive monopoly with something to sell. The collection of personal information by the National Security Administration may prove in the end to be an early kink in the informational architecture that is later tamed; or else, it may signal the coming of a new era of centralized power. The information revolution may either inspire freedom or allow for the consolidation of greater centralized command. It is a revolution still in the making: the jury is still out, the barricades are still peopled. It is always difficult to predict the social impact of a technology that is still maturing. And the question is really beyond the scope of this work.

But if Google comes to rule the world, the information it uses to control our lives will be filtered from the bottom up, and it will be not an American or a Chinese but rather a global Google. The collapse of proprietary firewalls echoes the fading of cultural barriers. Digital technologies transport us from the material world. While the websites we visit online may be primarily the products of American organizations, while they may require the support of buildings full of staff, located in real nations with real interests, we nevertheless imagine the web and its websites to exist in the ethers. This is significant. Since the Internet is global in scope, and since users are free to move from site to site at will, participation online can feel like traveling through a transporter. As the pace of information flows increase, the space of the world appears to decrease. Online participation frees us from the encumbrances of localized identities, and this transforms the sense of who we believe ourselves to be. When we go online, we become citizens of the world. Digital technologies alter the sense of distance for both real and imaginary reasons. Not only does the Internet bind us closer together through real social and trade networks, but also more important for our purposes, the web makes us feel closer to all of humanity. The result is an ever-increasing identification with the peoples of distant places and an ever-stronger sense of global consciousness.

THE NEW CLASS

Instead of capitalists and proletarians, the classes of the
post-capitalist society are knowledge workers and service workers.
PETER DRUCKER,
"THE GODFATHER OF MODERN MANAGEMENT THEORY"

Creativity has come to be valued - and systems have evolved to
encourage and harness it - because new technologies, new industries,
new wealth, and all other good economic things flow from it.
RICHARD FLORIDA,
ECONOMIST AND AUTHOR OF "THE RISE OF THE CREATIVE CLASS"

Upon witnessing the motivated and disciplined forces of revolutionary France at the battle of Valmy, the poet Goethe is reputed to have
exclaimed, "from here and now begins a new epoch of history." Such
proclamations tend to be overwrought, and this one itself is probably a fiction. Had the utterance actually issued from the mouth of
Goethe, the statement itself would nevertheless ring false, for the
forces that launch an historical epoch are legion. Yet, one might have
been tempted to murmur something similar in surmising the victory
of President Obama's disciplined and motivated legions on election
night in 2008. A new generation flooded the streets as if in celebration of some great historical turning. This was for many their first
experience of mass politics, and at the time it seemed as if everything
would change. Obama's supporters were empowered not just by their
victory but also by the social media and telecommunications that
brought them to power with such stunning effect. Just as the militias
of revolutionary France were a mere expression of the modern age,
the victory of President Obama was a political inauguration of the

Information Age. After decades of preparation, the world's wealthiest and most powerful nation had elected an Information Age President.

Jesus almost got it right: while the meek have rarely gotten their fair shake, the geeks have inherited the earth. Just as the industrial capitalists dominated politics through the early industrial era and the corporate CEOs through the age of consumer capitalism, knowledge workers dominate the Information Age. The category of knowledge worker includes people whose primary job is thinking: programmers, web designers, administrators, educators, entrepreneurs, scientists, and writers.[1,2,3] Their preferences pervade the political scene. Their methods and viewpoints dominate public discourse. They educate our children, run our institutions, write our books, and produce our films. And they increasingly comprise the bulk of the upper-classes.[4,5,6] Their numbers have been growing since the 1950s, and they are beginning to exert a significant influence over political priorities. Just as the rise of political parties and the development of citizen's special interest groups each transformed public participation in their own ages, Internet campaigns are transforming the political landscape of today.

When John F. Kennedy assembled the best and brightest for his core team of advisors, he was quick to snap up Robert McNamara, the slick young President of Ford, regardless of his lack of qualifications for Secretary of Defense. In their day, Ford and Chrysler, General Electric and Westinghouse, were giants. Schools readied children to work in their factories and unions sprang from their floors to fight them in epic political battles. But those days are over. General Electric is now synonymous with old; Ford broke down at the roadside years ago. Wind and solar have stolen their thunder, taken the high ground, and threaten to bury them in carbon taxes.[7,8] There is a vast redistribution of political power taking place before our eyes. It is not that the Peabody Coal Company is obsolete; there is still a demand for their product, and their profits may grow with the coming years. They may even use their lobbying power to distort the nature of the

American economy for some time to come. But they have ceased to command our attention. Few care what they or the CEO of General Motors thinks. Their technologies, their management, their ideas, and their brands appear to younger generations musty, fusty, dirty, and corrupt. To make a comeback, the auto and coal industries must reinvent their business models and transform their reputations. In short, they must grow up and enter the Information Age

It is axiomatic of human social and economic development that the lower stages tend to be subsumed in the higher, like a foundation that once lain can be later forgotten.[9] After the child learns the alphabet, she goes on to spelling, sentence construction, and writing essays; after the village learns to farm, they can forget about farming and build a civilization. What we are witnessing today is the great going-under of industrial civilization.[10] Aging industries like auto, oil, coal, and insurance stagger as their strength drains and evaporates. Massive and hierarchical, these dinosaurs once shaped American society but now lay deep beneath the soils where new economic life germinates. The American economy will probably continue to make use of these industries into the foreseeable future. But industrial era processes and companies will increasingly come to appear as outmoded as farming is today.

The power-shift that is now taking place involves far more than the rise and fall of economic sectors. To the extent that demography is destiny, the American Right can be expected to gradually weaken. Demographic groups who tend to vote Republican, like white men, uneducated women, and suburban residents, are all decreasing; meanwhile, traditionally Democratic voters like Hispanics, blacks, educated women, and urban residents are on the rise.[11] This is no coincidence. Liberals are embracing the new era as conservatives fight the river. Right wing reactivity to climate science, to higher education, to universal health care, and to the increasing reliance on soft power, may represent not the appearance of a fierce new movement but rather the last throws of a dying beast. Like the industries of the industrial era, both the truths and the constituencies of conservative politicians are being buried by the complexity of a new epoch. It may be just a matter of time before they are swept under.

John Stuart Mill once suggested that while conservatives are not necessarily stupid, most stupid people are conservative. That American Republicans all too often appear to fulfill this Millian tenet, a century and a half later and an ocean away, cannot simply be chocked up to a vast left-wing conspiracy. Insofar as they are the opponents of progress, conservatives are the standard bearers of simple-mindedness. But for problems as varied as raising a child, running a business, and administering a municipality, the complexity of the Information Age makes all but flexible and sophisticated solutions obsolete. It takes a sophisticated mind to navigate a highly complex milieu. Those whose strengths lie in "common-sense" solutions, who make a virtue of concrete thinking and "straight-shooting," will increasingly miss the mark. But there is no monopoly on simple-mindedness in American politics, and these things have a way of changing over time. American political parties are if anything opportunistic, and tend to shift with the tides, picking up a few votes here and a constituency there until the party that freed the slaves becomes the one that filibusters civil-rights legislation.[12] So perhaps it is best to say that whichever party is willing to sort through the complexity, embracing interpretations and solutions that account for the complications arising from an infinitely intertwined environment, will increasingly gain power in an infinitely complex world.

As political parties go to battle, money and influence continues to accumulate in the high-tech sector. It is Google not General Motors, shaping America's relationship to China, Bill Gates not Lee Iacocca, leading Africa out of poverty. High tech promises to transform the world, oil and coal to destroy it. Spawning a vast array of start-ups and innovations, the high tech sector is far from monolithic. It includes up and coming industries like bio-tech, nano-tech, and green-tech, industries which grab headlines with solutions to our most pressing problems. But it also includes the financial sector and health insurers, which often make their money shifting about other people's money. Some are sharks, some are dolphins, some are mere phytoplankton, but they all swim in the same swirling sea of complexity. As the inventions of today become the consumer products of tomorrow, and as the firms that produce those products and services grow in size and strength, the nexus of political power will continue to shift to these rising industries. But it is not only the industry and its firms that are influential: so are its people.

The technologically savvy possess the hard power of skills and resources. Their ability to network, to organize, to publicize, and to innovate is vastly more efficient than that of the technologically illiterate. They have built the Amazons, Googles, and IBMs of the world and invented the Facebooks, Twitters, and smart phones through which we lend shape to our lives. Their skills and resources are vital to disseminating information, winning political campaigns, and organizing pressure groups. The best hope for democratizing China may rest on the shoulders of a handful of bloggers. If they can outwit the censors, encrypt their identities with cheap and easy-to-install software, and share their views with a growing coterie of readers, then the Middle-Kingdom might become the center for twenty-first century democratization. The same battles have become commonplace the world over, and the authoritarians just might win, using information technology to exercise ever greater powers of surveillance over ever more vulnerable populations. But whichever side wins the battle it will be the knowledge workers who generate the strategies that win the war.

Knowledge workers possess not just hard power, but the soft power that is needed to co-opt and attract. People want to emulate and be associated with the technologically savvy, because however mediocre they may appear, these "geeks" have the power to navigate an overwhelming technological matrix. Those who cannot speak their language and utilize their tools are at a severe social and economic disadvantage, handicapped in their communications, and hobbled in their work roles. Information architecture has gotten so complex that even skilled programmers cannot unravel the component parts of the code with which they program. Even as individuals become more familiar with information technologies, the software and hardware alike is increasingly imbued with magical qualities. We fetishize the latest technological developments, taking the iPhone and iPad as talismans, possessed with unlimited and inexplicable powers, as if their possession, nay their very touch, has the power to transform. Their lines and curves are suffused with sex appeal, and the glow rubs off on the latter-day sorcerers whom we entrust with their translation. We crawl to these wizards in meltdowns and seek through their wisdom the power to transmute the dross of bits to bars of gold. Just as feudal lords set the agenda for the Middle Ages and industrial capitalists for the industrial age, knowledge workers are shaping the Information Age. They dominate the schools and the entertainment industry and maintain the technologies that give structure to our lives. Information technologies rewire our brains, altering the way we perceive, think, and relate.[13,14] It is little wonder American conservatives tend to lash out so haphazardly, at the politicians, the schools, the drugs, the entertainment. Their enemies are everywhere[15] - the ambiguous and sophisticated, the vague and complex - and their enemies lurk not least in the corners of their own uncharted minds. Each of us is dyed in the colors of the Information Age, soaked in its stresses, and permeated by its dreams and illusions. And while knowledge workers are no exception, for them the culture is more likely to make sense. And it is a rare fish that has trouble breathing in the sea in which it was born.

The Information Age self is every inch the new man and new woman revolutionaries are so fond of proclaiming. Like the operating system of a computer, the self is increasingly seen as a sort of blank screen that contains the features of a life, like so much software. Whatever fate you are born into, whatever race or sex, sexual orientation or country of origin, is inconsequential when you comment on a blog, make a purchase, or design a website for someone on the other side of the world. The Information Age self has been pealed away from its local environment and left to float in a sea of information. Far more important are the things you know, the places you visit, the people you associate with, and the tasks you can perform. These can be added and subtracted over time, like so many accessories.

Trading the security of the probable for the indeterminacy of the possible is rarely easy, for new freedoms tend to come coupled with new restraints. The Information Age self may be free but it can also be fragile, for the self is seldom as mutable as we tend to think. The information age self can lack integrity, character, and the kinds of relationships that only thrive in the fertile soils of time.[16,17,18] We co-evolve with our career paths and life partnerships, making the sort of adjustments that build character, as the growth of self and other flower together along a shared continuum. Such relationships cannot simply be substituted one for another like so many articles of clothing. To attempt such exchanges tears at the fabric of a meaningful life. There is always a danger than in the process of altering so many features of the self, we will in the end discover our lives to be denuded of meaning. Still the range of life options now available to the average individual allows the Information Age self, which is in many ways also the cosmopolitan self, to throw off social straightjackets and construct a life of her choosing.[19] The web will always favor the speculative, the provisional, and the indeterminate. Even if the nature of the web were to change from a place of anonymity to one of ubiquitous exposure, birth-based identities would continue to matter little. And as the local features of identity fall away - the inherited traits, the social obligations, and the burdens of one's past - the self is freed up to participate in more global systems.

The Information Age self is globally conscious. Birth-based identities, which so often limit the scope of ethical commitments, are losing relevance. With them may dissolve some of the prejudices and rivalries that pit one society against another. With them may dissolve some of the shackles that bind consciousness to the nations and ethnicities of our birth. The hierarchies of power that so often demand obedience are losing their authority. Perhaps they will adjust so as to preserve some of that authority. But if they do adjust, it will be to a world that is in its nature and concerns global. The dominant class is now more educated and globally conscious than ever before. Their corporations, their non-governmental organizations, and their networks of friends and colleagues are all increasingly global. Much of the newfound strength of moneyed elites comes from their ability to organize themselves globally. And the global consciousness that has become emblematic of their subculture of wealth cannot help but influence the rest of us. As we will see, this is not an unmitigated good. The new global elite is wealthy and powerful, and global inequalities are extreme when compared to those of say, the United States. It is for this reason, amongst others, that we will focus substantial attention on global poverty in later chapters. But if the next class of elites holds an uncomfortable share of global power, they are often most conscious of the global challenges that threaten us all.

SECTION 3

GLOBALIZATION OF INFORMATION

It was the hour before the Gods awake.
Across the path of the divine Event
The huge foreboding mind of Night, alone
In her unlit temple of eternity,
Lay stretched immobile upon Silence' marge.
Almost one felt, opaque, impenetrable,
In the somber symbol of her eyeless muse
The abysm of the unbodied Infinite.
SRI AUROBINDO, INDIAN ACTIVIST AND MYSTIC

OCEANS OF EXPERIENCE

Every moment of every day, the human brain is showered with sensation. We live in information rich environments, trees and clouds alive with data, light and shadow growing from the primordial ferment of raw sensation. The sights and sounds, feelings and smells of a verdant forest, its dappled canopy of broken light, its shifting patterns of browns and greens; even the denuded spaces of a city skyscape, with its shimmering glass and incomprehensible geometry, impossible logic and broken rhythms, overwhelm the human capacity to process information. We are deluged by a tsunami of reference points. The brain races to calculate distances, the lacunae between objects, the interval between events, lending to experience the subtle sense of space and time. Out of this stockpile of impressions the brain constructs an integrated world.

We can only infer the nature of the actual world. Sensory perceptions inundate the floodgates of mind. But the primordial experience of the world is of an ever-shifting flux of sensation, restless waves of dizzying ambiguity, engulfing the self at every turn.[1] The intermingling of all things constantly erodes the boundaries between self and other, one object and the next.[2] We are more like waves than floating ships, more like the sky than the sparkling sun. The brain fabricates the boundaries of a world in flux, constructs representations upon which it acts. Simulating a snapshot of the world is challenging. The brain must distinguish figure from ground, value from dross. But the brain also pieces together representations over time, assembling images and impressions into patterns, purporting relationships, concocting narratives, and lending to the world a sense of meaning. Scattered memories and impressions are synthesized along an imaginary time continuum into the unified catalogue of experiences we call a life.[3] This is the nature of the human life world.

The actual world is more akin to the vast void that once lay before God. It runs together like water colors in the rain. It melts together like dripping wax. But the brain discerns form in a stream of colors, and makes of those colors a complete picture. It molds waxen images into shapes. The world appears to us in a code that the brain is uniquely evolved to decrypt. How exactly the raw representations are assembled by the brain is still debatable and is beyond the scope of this work. What is important here is that the job is overwhelmingly complex and somewhat arbitrary, yet human beings are predisposed to experience an objective reality that is remarkably consistent across cultures.

Other beings experience the objective world differently. Trees must somehow sense the nitrogen and phosphorous they seek in the soil as well as the carbon dioxide they filter from the air. Without this ability they could not function. What mechanism they use to perceive these chemicals and what this feels like from inside the tree, we can only infer. There is little reason to believe trees evolved to experience anything like the sense of self possessed by a mammal. But the tree must somehow, in its own enigmatic and arboreal fashion, organize its perceptions into meaningful patterns to seek out what it needs to survive. Bats experience the world largely through echolocation; they make high pitched sounds, inaudible to the human ear, which reverberate off of moths that may be dozens of feet away. By listening to these echoes they can detect the type of object, its location, and the direction in which it is moving.

The radical divergence in perceptions between sentient beings highlights the arbitrariness of human perception. Humans play film producer to an ocean of experiences. Random perceptions and feelings, thoughts and beliefs, memories and traumas, are shaped into meaningful stories.[4] Since we have neither the space in the brain nor the powers of mind to retain so much data, the experiences are edited for storage, framed for the sake of clarity, and classified for ease of access.[5] Limited spatial and processing capacities require experiences to be organized, like books in a library or photos in an album. These experiences must be organized with limited brain and nervous tissue and made accessible to the mind at the moment of recall. Thus, the brain prioritizes, links, categorizes, and ultimately, distorts perception.

Snapshots and models of the world are always an approximation, like the paintings of an inexperienced artist or the fumbling notes of a rookie reporter. We spin stories and milk meaning from life experiences. But the raw data is beyond reach. Instead of recalling specific sense data, we refer to rules of thumb, theories, and prejudices. These are simplifications of a vast and complex puzzle of perception: maps upon maps upon maps. Hemmed in by the spatial constraints of the brain and the processing power of the mind, we economize on memory, on attention, on nerves, and on time. Since brains are limited in capacity, so also are its depictions. Somehow we must fit the novel of an experience into the short film of memory. And this ultimately involves distortions. This is certainly a problem for the man who seeks to comprehend his own little corner of the world. Amidst the constant string of misperceptions, he can usually somehow muddle through. But the problem becomes increasingly insurmountable as the little corner grows to be an entire world, with its vast diversity of species, cultures, events, and concerns. Each of us will construct our perceptions of the world in a different way, and these differences can threaten the stability of the social order.[6]

Social complexity always comes coupled with the prospect of collapse.[7] One reason for this is that highly complex social systems are difficult to control. There is always a danger that some missing nail might unhinge the ship. But there is also the danger that increasing social complexity tends to come coupled with a growing estrangement.[8] Since distortions arise at every stage of abstraction, as the number of abstractions needed to understand a social system increases, the resulting distortions will likewise multiply. People in complex societies often experience the world in such radically divergent ways that they lose the ability to communicate with one another.[9] They are divided by occupation, by class, by subculture, and by disposition.

But the world itself is in our minds one vast abstraction. We only experience it in tiny fragments, like the scattered shards of a great civilization with which archeologists construct historical narratives. Their stories are difficult to believe, and endlessly diverge, because they are premised on so little. It is similar with making sense of our own worlds. As each group brings to the table a different narrative, the likelihood of divergence grows. And like Babel, a city that ultimately collapses due to its complexity, there is a danger that our images of the world will become like mutually incomprehensible tongues. Perhaps we will all one day become globally conscious, not of the same blue-green marble, but rather of a radically divergent global kaleidoscope, speaking mutually incomprehensible tongues around a common table.

And still, like the world itself, through which we are each materially and perceptually interlinked, each of us is tied to all others by a commonly shared anatomy and physiology. Human sense organs and brains share the same basic architecture. Each of us is predisposed to see, to hear, and to feel a common set of objects and gestalts. The prototypical human body consists of two arms, two legs, and ten fingers. This provides for a common set of abilities, the ability to craft and manipulate artifacts, the ability to walk and run, the ability to point, to gesticulate, and to scratch your ass. The capacities are so common that providing the means to their attainment whenever possible is quickly being seen as a basic right for those who do not possess the prototypical set of body parts. Out of these abilities, we craft our technologies, shape our cultures, and tell our tales of what it means to be human.

Having been exposed to a multitude of exotic practices, found in obscure indigenous cultures, we are prone to overemphasize the differences amongst humans. A pre-colonial, Sioux Indian would have experienced an altogether different world than that of the post-industrial, urban Manhattanite. Yet the differences tend to be exaggerated. Both groups speak in words and trade in goods, raise families and eat meals, work and make treaties, live in lodgings and govern themselves according to complex political procedures. Separated from one another by over ten millennia, the civilizations of both the old and the new worlds lighted upon the domestication of crops and animals, the construction of cities and empires, the rule of kingship and the centrality of religion.[10] Somehow the whirlwind of experience is beat into the patterns of a common code, recognizable across vast distances of space and time, and emblematic of our common humanity.

Anthropologists speak of human universals, hundreds of experiences shared by humans across each and every culture: dancing, music, smiling, hunger, clothing, ornamentation, meal times, and the avoidance of incest, to name just a few.[11,12] While the actual world may remain in the final analysis a surging sea of mystery, the inner world of experience converges. Immanuel Kant noted, two and a half centuries ago, that all humans experience a world in three dimensions, in a continuum from past to future, comprised of discreet objects, perceived in gestalts, and with a sense of the totality. While Kant wrote prior to the array of advances in cognitive science and may have thus mystified the origins and nature of human experience, his observations are still useful. Barring injuries to the brain, all of human experience is organized according to a common set of what he called categories: space, time, unity, totality, etc.[13] These categories, into which experiences are assembled, bring order to perception and therefore make it easier to act in the world. Instead of seeing a swirl of colors and roar of noise, we perceive discreet objects, interacting with one another in space, whose actions occur in linear time. Objects appear to us amongst other objects as part of a total reality. While physicists would agree with Kant that the world we assemble into these categories is not the actual world, few if any would claim the

ability to climb out of their own minds and experience some primordial reality. The categories are prior to experience, an innate heuristic
with which we simplify experience into manageable chunks.

But the commonality of experience is shattered when we move
from the realm of fundamental sense experience to that of understanding. Beliefs differ on fundamental questions like the nature of
the good life and the extent of free will. Values run the gamut from
hedonism to asceticism to moderation. And conceptions of the nature
of the world range from the magical to the mythic to the scientific.
The diversity of values and beliefs is great across cultures and even
greater across modes of production.[14] Few are prepared to bridge the
spans necessary to travel from one island of experience to another in
this marshland of human societies.

As global consciousness continues to develop over the next several decades, it is possible that each of us will come to experience the
world as an integral whole and yet our experiences of it will diverge.
In a single tribe or a village the range of experiences do differ. One
girl is born under challenging circumstances to loving parents, who
tend to her every need, in a time of war; and yet, her younger brother
is ignored by his now traumatized father and rejected by his lover
even though he was born in peace time and possesses a remarkable
memory. Each will develop their own distinctive personalities and
life paths. Even in the most rudimentary units of human society, individuals develop varying traits out of divergent experiences over
the course of their lives. Still, in a village or tribe, individuals share
common experiences of the climate and environment, language and
customs, overall social order and levels of violence. Thus, the range
of experience is limited.

Increase the scope of possible experience to that of an industrialized nation-state, with its millions of citizens, endless divisions of
labor, and blooming subcultures, and experiences will diverge still
further, like stars flying away from one another in an expanding universe. Individuals develop not just different personality styles but

different values, beliefs, and ideological persuasions. Individuals develop along different lines because their experiences differ, often radically. Some are born into wealth, others poverty; some are brought up liberal, others conservative; some are taught to strive hard, others to surrender. Whatever they are taught and whatever they may experience as children, once they begin working, each will enter his or her own private universe of techniques and norms and life lessons, each inhabiting a universe veiled from fellow citizens in layers of occupational obscurity. Postmodern life paths tend to be divergent, for we are molded and shaped by the confluence of events that make up our careers, all of the compromises and decisions and stresses that shape our values and give meaning to our life. And still, the democratic states into which we are born manage to knit us together in institutions, socialize us into a thin set of norms that are a prerequisite for the normal functioning of any advanced society.[15] Somehow the center holds – just.

When the unit of human organization increases to that of the whole world, the differences amongst people are further exacerbated. They are separated by linguistic, historical, economic, political, and cultural differences. Thus, many of the forces that would bind together a nation are absent from the world stage. The barriers to a global civilization can thus appear insurmountable. While the number of human universals is prodigious, they may be too abstract to bind us together into a common global civilization. While the people of all human societies share meals, each shares them according to its own set of rules, norms, and patterns of behavior. While all societies use language, and perhaps even a language based on universal laws of syntax,[16] each language is laden with subtle nuances and metaphorical structures that are often untranslatable.[17] That humans experience a world of objects familiar across cultures is in many ways a wonder. That we can bind together individuals whose lives and values differ markedly is an institutional feat. But few of us attain to an integral comprehension of global processes. Thus, many would assert that the idea of uniting our fates into a common global destiny is a dream. But they would be wrong.

Humanity is bound together by a common set of inescapable contingencies. We share the same oceans, rely on the same atmosphere. A recession, a drought, a civil war, state failure – none of these are halted at the borders of one nation but rather overflow into the domains of all others, like waves rolling over a reef. The drug trade and global terrorism are wholly global in nature and in scope. While there might be some nexus, like Afghanistan, out of which they arise, it is the impotence of state authority and the irrelevance of borders that makes these places significant. Nuclear devastation or catastrophic climate change would affect an atmosphere shared by us all. While a particular nation state might be responsible for any given catastrophe, the means of prevention and the manner of clean up are all-too-often global. Global trade and technological development pour over trade barriers like waves over pebbles. Whether it is in the form of films or novels that artistic productions grapple with the ambiguous identities of émigrés and immigrants, the productions themselves journey from their countries of origin to make their rounds across the globe. In a similar manner, we have long ago ceased to identify most technologies with their country of origin.

The global civilization that we share is shaped by a common set of technologies. The information that molds our views travels fast and freely around the world. The leaders that unite us are an emerging class of global representatives and the functionaries of global institutions; the laws too are increasingly global, as is our sense of justice and the people whom we believe to deserve our care. The language through which humanity might communicate is neither English nor French, nor some new kid on the block like Mandarin or Hindi, rather it is the same language that has always knit citizens together into a common unit of governance: that of a common destiny. Moreover, advances in telecommunications are annually bringing us closer to the day when the art of translation will become obsolete in person-to-person communications. While each of us experiences our interconnection with the rest of the human species to a greater or lesser extent, the influences continue to wash over us, threatening the sense of who we are and the relevance of any limited conception of identity. The vast panoply of human differences is fast converging around a common set of concerns. It is this that makes common experience possible.

The question of how we might make sense of this wide world of seemingly infinite variety is the same question that confronts humanity at every level of organization. The individual, the tribe, the nation, the world, must each edit, classify, and organize the raw datum of experience. Experiences are worked over like the raw footage of a film and crafted into narratives, for individuals and nations alike. The ability to shape the basic data of sense experience is just as much a wonder as the ability of states to unite seemingly diverse peoples into common nation-states. There is little reason humanity cannot shape for itself a story of its global destiny. Still, with each unit of increasing complexity, humanity confronts new challenges. While there may be a need for some stronger notion of global civilization, while there may be good reason to believe such a higher unit of organization is being advanced and can ultimately be achieved, the informational challenge remains unsettled and unsettling. Somehow we must make sense of the fabric of the world into which we are rapidly discovering ourselves to be knit.

MAPPING THE WORLD OUTSIDE

In that Empire, the Art of Cartography attained such Perfection
that the map of a single Province occupied the entirety of a City,
and the map of the Empire, the entirety of a Province.
In time, those Unconscionable Maps no longer satisfied, and the
Cartographers Guilds struck a Map of the Empire whose size
was that of the Empire, and which coincided point for point with it.
The following Generations, who were not so fond of the Study
of Cartography as their Forebears had been, saw that that vast
Map was Useless, and not without some Pitilessness was it, that they
delivered it up to the Inclemencies of Sun and Winters. In the
Deserts of the West, still today, there are Tattered Ruins of that Map,
inhabited by Animals and Beggars; in all the Land there is no other
Relic of the Disciplines of Geography.

JORGE LUIS BORGES

The Argentine novelist, Jorge Luis Borges, was extremely well read. His novels soared across space and time, drawing from the Muslim philosophers of the Middle Ages, probing into the ferment of Latin American history. Reading vast sums of information and perspectives can provide a compendium of overlapping maps, with each book charting its own little portion of the world. The ambitious are often tempted to synthesize these maps into one comprehensive philosophy that might explain the reason for all things under the sun. Perhaps this dream of philosophical dominion was present to Borges as he wrote his tale of the scaled map in 1946.

Marathon reading can help make sense of the world. The pondering of literature and philosophy, poetry and politics, reveals to us the inner world of human experience and the outer world through which experience is organized. Through prolonged and impassioned study, we might discover how our personal lives and those of others fit together. We might discern the influences of biology, psychology, culture, and economics, how each influences our lives and which hold the greatest sway over human experience. The widely read can also attain a measure of self-knowledge, recognizing their own unborn reason in the thoughts of others. Hence, through reading we might begin to makes sense of the world in which we live.

This too is a kind of global consciousness. Trace the impact of any thought or action far enough, and it will tend to ripple to the earth's far corners. Trace those ripples day in and day out over the course of a lifetime of reading and you will tend to attain something like a map of the human-life-world. There is little need to leave your room. While the journalists and travellers who crisscross the world will often develop a sense of tolerance and appreciation for difference, rarely do their travels produce something we might call wisdom. And while good social scientists are usually well travelled, seldom are the well-travelled natural social scientists. The musings of world travellers might nevertheless constitute a sizable portion of the reader's repertoire. But if you want to develop global consciousness, it is far more important to develop a good map of the human-life-world, and this is a task for which the perennial reader is peculiarly suited. So, a well-rounded humanistic education can go a long way toward developing global consciousness. Such an educational path has played a great part in fostering my own global consciousness. The only problem is that few have the time to read widely, and those of us who do must confront another set of problems nicely framed by Borges' map.

Since the map is scaled to the territory, it covers and thus includes everything in that territory. If you want to know about a place, you have to travel there. It is like taking a trip to the library for a map with directions to the library. But maps should save us from precisely this trouble. Borges' map obscures more of the actual world than it reveals by papering over it, literally covering it with paper. Bookworms often have this problem. Our studies can obscure as much of the real world as they reveal. By focusing on the written word, the bookworm often misses the meaning of what is staring him in the face. However precise and insightful, words are mere maps to the subtleties of reality. Thus, while marathon readers often develop global consciousness, their maps tend to be inaccurate and incomplete.

Contrast this with Borges' map, scaled to include everything. A scaled map of a table will, by definition, cover that table, perhaps like a cheap vinyl film, but a film that is fitting. A scaled map of the world is more problematic. Each hilltop, each building, must be dusted over with map. The map must include travelers, journeying to lands so as to learn of their lay. It must include cartographers who place the travelers on their now revised maps, and still more cartographers, mapping the cartographers, mapping the viewers, in an infinite regression.[1] The map can serve as a poignant metaphor to human society. Academics, scientists, editors, and the news media are a lot like the cartographers; they are a part of the world, but they make their mark on the world largely through their study of it. They are a part of the world that transforms the world, so they must also take account of one another in their maps.

This makes my brilliant philosopher friend who has never heard of Glenn Beck a bit like the Amazonian tribesman who has never seen a newspaper or television. If you want to understand the American political system, you need to study more than just legislation and election results. You also need to study how commentators alter the political landscape. Though Beck is a strikingly inaccurate commentator, his bulldozing of mountains and papering over of yawning chasms is nevertheless a vital part of the American political landscape. Columnists and editors and political scientists each alter the political landscape every time they tramp across the world to make their mark on the map. To ignore the influence of even a Glenn Beck is to make oneself willfully ignorant.

Maps and mapmakers are always part of the world and must therefore be included in their own maps. But as the maps include more, they become ever more unwieldy. Eventually, only the cartographers can comprehend their maps, and at their peak of accuracy, like the works of some great philosopher, who has to coin new terms to make his meaning clear, only their maker can decipher their meaning. Sooner or later, the maps cannot be maintained. Thus, "in the Deserts of the West, still today, there are Tattered Ruins of that Map, inhabited by Animals and Beggars; in all the Land there is no other Relic of the Disciplines of Geography." Somehow we must find a way to construct highly inclusive maps that are manageable. And if you think we have strayed from the important business of global consciousness, think again.

One of the greatest challenges we must confront in the globalization of mind is the sense that the world is too vast for any one person to comprehend. After all, the exponential rise in information concerning just the United States makes grasping the issues that matter a full time job. One of the many reasons politics has become so polarized in recent years is because there are so few issues in which enough of us are fully informed to have a good exchange of views. And the world is a lot bigger than just a single country. Most Americans know the lay of the American political landscape. We know at least a smattering of American history and the issues that matter. And even an alert high school student can weigh in on at least a few of these issues. Developing global consciousness means doing this for the world, and with it a whole new set of issues that matter. Somehow we need to access more things with the same limited brain tissue. For if we cannot make sense of the wider world of which we are a part, we will tend to retreat into smaller worlds, even as global challenges loom ever larger. But making sense of something so vast as the world will require better maps.

The Internet now allows us to add what for all practical purposes is an infinite degree of specificity to our maps. Not only can we view, let us say, the Parthenon, in fine detail on Google Earth, but we can view it over time, speculating on artistic renditions, reading about the impressions of its viewers in different historical periods. In fact, it is theoretically possible to access so much information on the Parthenon that if the information were stored on paper it would fill not just the Parthenon but all of the buildings on all of the streets leading to it as well. That we can imagine such a wasteland of information is both a sad commentary on the uselessness of many doctoral dissertations and a sign of the times. The Internet makes Borges' map that once covered the earth passé. Like so much postmodern philosophy, it portrays a level of complexity that is purported to be unmanageable but which information technologies have managed to integrate into our lives. A map like Borges' can now be stored in a tiny thumb drive, and it wouldn't get in the way at all. So the Internet may solve at least a portion of the mapping problem simply by being able to store more information.

Stretch your mind a little and you might imagine a map that contains not only the entire world in infinite detail, but also all of the details of every moment leading up to the present, all stored in some supercomputer in Utah and accessible online. If we could somehow keep free will from mucking up its forecasts, such a computer might allow us to predict the future. Certainly it would do wonders for forecasting, if only we could figure out how to organize all of the information it contains. Of course, such a computer would probably never exist anywhere but in the imagination. But the idea of such a computer highlights some of the challenges of climate models. Climate scientists are forever seeking more powerful computers through which they might run models of future climate scenarios.

While it is settled science that increasing levels of CO_2 in the atmosphere will heat the planet, the extent of this heating is still up for question. The problem is that there are so many positive feedback mechanisms in which a little heating causes a little more heating, and we simply do not understand how they will impact one another. As warmer temperatures melt arctic ice, the darker Arctic Ocean will absorb heat that would otherwise be reflected by the ice, and this will raise global temperatures. But if we cannot predict how fast the arctic ice will melt, we will not be able to predict how fast this heating will occur. The same goes for the arctic permafrost, which when melted will release methane, a powerful greenhouse gas that will cause further heating. Warmer temperatures will also cause many forest fires, how many we cannot say. But the burning forests will release still more CO_2, thereby further heating the planet. The thought that each of these feedback loops will act upon one another in runaway global warming is the kind of thing that keeps some climate scientists tossing and turning into the night.[2,3]

Climate scientists can get an idea of how future changes in climate will play out through studying past changes. Over the course of the past few decades, they have devised multiple means of determining the history of the earth's changing climate. The most common techniques involve studying the decay rate of Carbon-14, a unique carbon molecule, in ancient ice cores, trees rings, coral reefs, and fossilized plants and animals. By studying patterns of growth and decay, they have been able to construct a reasonably accurate climate history stretching back hundreds of thousands of years. This past history allows them to test the assumptions they program into their current computer models; when they run their forecasting programs backward and their assumptions match up with the real history of climate change, then they can feel more confident that the programs will be just as efficient at predicting future changes in climate. The problem is that we don't only lack information about the past, but also the computing power to predict future changes. Weather forecasting and climate science have actually played a leading role in driving increases in computing for just these reasons.[4] But climate scientists are now challenged to integrate more data than ever before, with the future of life on earth often seeming to hang in the balance. The problem is there are just so many factors influencing climate change, not the least of which is that most unpredictable of animals, homo sapiens. But as computing power increases, we will acquire a better grasp of the impact of our actions on future generations, and this will help us to feel more confident about the decisions we make today. While we might never achieve omniscience concerning the human condition, the further integration of vast patterns of information, through previously unimagined computing power, can allow us to collectively plan on a global scale and with relative precision for crises that might not occur for centuries.

While climate scientists need more data if they are to do a better job of keeping the world running smoothly, most of us are inundated by information. The Internet is like a closet overflowing with clothes. Seldom is it worth sorting through the mess to get to what we want. Most of us will, most of the time, just opt for what lies at the top of the search. This is an organizational problem that search engines make easier. With each passing year, search engines take us to the information we are seeking with greater and greater accuracy. But there is another problem that lies prior to the search: with so many choices and so much information, we had better know what we want to find. Otherwise, we might lose ourselves in a closet full of mismatched clothing. This is not simply a practical, but also an existential, conundrum. As we are flooded with options in the quest to discover what we truly want, there is a danger we will be overwhelmed with choices[5] and simply immerse ourselves in miscellany. When we spend less time seeking and more time running searches, we might discover what we want, but what we want might not be worth finding. A look at the most popular videos on YouTube drives the point home that people who do the most searching do not tend to seek that which is most meaningful.

Old-school maps told us what to look for – cities, rivers, roads, etc. Some person or group determined the things readers would find most useful and constructed their maps accordingly. Religious teachers scribbled their maps in the margins of scripture; philosophers mapped the world of the mind. In each instant, it was an authority external to our own minds that decided what we needed to know. Anyone who has ever made use of a road map can attest to the benefits. With the main roads, the gas stations, and the restaurants all included, you have everything you need to get across the country. But most everything else that mattered was missing, so it was easier to stay on track. As we come to make our own maps, we have to figure out for ourselves what to look for: the things we value, the things we need, and the things we favor. Maybe this will be the rivers and the roads as charted on the old maps. But it might just as well be the altitude, the wiring of the electric grid, or a listing of 24-hour gay-bars. The point is that the authorities can no longer know nor tell us what we want without looking foolish.

If the computer were merely a device for accessing Wikipedia, we would probably still all possess one and marvel at the ability to voluntarily assemble and cooperatively compile so much information. But Wikipedia accounts for only a tiny portion of the information on the web and just the surface of voluntary cooperation. This cooperative accumulation of information is the Library of Alexandria of this generation. There is something sublime in all of this data and code, so varied and seemingly limitless. The thought of finding what we want in the subterranean depths of these mountains calls to mind imagery from the Buddha: the turtle that swimming through the ocean randomly places its neck through a hoop, or the bird that carrying a silk scarf flies over a great mountain once every thousand years and slowly wears it away. It is worth pausing every now and then to recognize the marvel of what is so often a source of anxiety. The information we have accumulated can seem as immeasurable and vast as the universe is incomprehensible. A microcosm of global complexity lies dormant in each of our computers. And every time we turn them on, we are made conscious, if only faintly, of the vastness of the globe.

Day to day, this expanse tends to be experienced as information-overload. We struggle to keep up with a world that any mature adult might have grasped with alacrity just as couple of decades ago. Now commitments slip by and messages go unreturned by even the most responsible among us. The information that has been amassed piles up in our lives like so many papers on the desk – projects left unfinished, websites that will never be explored. Along with our to-do lists, anxiety accumulates, the nagging sense that there is not enough time or that we have somehow forgotten something along the way. We are like that formerly blind boy who now stands blinking before a world of overwhelming complexity, and the urge for regression can loom heavy.

We are losing the ability to access the things we truly want to find. There is just too much noise obscuring what really matters. And this has left all too many lost and rudderless. Order has evaporated in both personal lives and in the social organism just as we have come to need it most. Lifetimes of information pile on top of our heads, to which no meaning or sense of priority is attached. And on top of it all, thinkers like myself push and prod with new moral imperatives and unanswerable concerns, to take on yet more, to learn more, and to find more meaning. When the events impinging on our lives are more distant, and the causal connections more intertwined, we need to either concern ourselves with this broader circle of concerns or be prepared for the whole social mechanism to become unhinged. The primal scream that appears to lie just beneath the surface of so much terrorism and talk radio seems due in part to this pressure to comprehend a world that is simply overwhelming. Like Arjuna before the true face of Krishna, or Job before the sublimity of God, we are dumbfounded. But organizing information has always been a challenge, which humanity has often overcome. And retreat does not seem to be a viable option.

When Melvil Dewey set about creating the Dewey Decimal System in 1876, each library classified its books in accord with its own idiosyncratic system: some alphabetically, others topically, still others aesthetically. Of course, this made inter-library loans an organizational nightmare. But it also made the task of sifting through mountains of books in a large library comparable in magnitude to some labor of Hercules. Dewey set about bringing order to the disarray that was so characteristic of knowledge in his day right after he left college. First, he set down an outline of all fields of knowledge. Then he attached a number to each field, with the subsections denoted through a series of decimals that could be endlessly extended. And like God, dividing the heavens from the earth, and so also the land from the sea, Dewey set forth his creation and proclaimed it good. This was the sort of enlightenment era project that served us well throughout the twentieth century, as we combed the libraries of the world for what now can seem a naïve and meager corpus of knowledge.

The technological philosopher, David Weinberger, points out that we have a limited amount of space in which to store things in the real world. So organizational protocols like those of the Dewey Decimal System will always be necessary. Whether the space at issue is that of a library, a closet, or an office supply store, we have to prioritize and organize concrete objects that occupy space.[6] This doesn't always work as smoothly as the Deweys of the world might like. Consider how a librarian, held captive by Dewey's universal systematization, might classify "The Crusades as Seen Through Muslim Eyes." It might fit equally well under the section on Islam, Christianity, history, or war. But Dewey's librarian has to choose. He also has to choose where to put each of these sections in the library. And some sections can be highly inaccessible - on the fifth floor, of the tiny spillover library building, on the other side of the campus. So this problem of organization can become a political problem of who and what gets featured, and we encounter it every time we open a newspaper, turn on the radio, or watch a political debate. When space is limited, access is a zero-sum game. And to get headlines, people will pay top dollar, organize marches on Washington, and even strap bombs to their bellies and blow up busloads of children. The problem with a universal system of classification like Dewey's is that eventually subsections will overtake main sections of the library in both size and importance, as the importance of disciplines rises and declines over time: microbiology will come to dominate biology, cognitive science to dominate psychology. Eventually, the system will come to lack order, as old subjects become irrelevant, new ones come into being, and society severs and fuses the links between each subject, redefining the boundaries of the known world.[7] There is, simply put, no natural order to knowledge but only an ever-shifting flux of mentally constructed categories that matter. And all of the problems involved in classifying books apply equally well to classifying information in our own minds.

It is different in the world of cyberspace, where things are immaterial and therefore lack spatial dimensions. Here we can store things under numerous headings. The crusades book can be cross-referenced under Islam, under Christianity, and under history. It could show up under books you might like and books bought by people who bought what you bought. It could be listed under bestselling non-fiction, best books on the crusades, and books to give to your Islamophobic relatives. The point is that it can be listed under all of these things simultaneously.[8]

Weinberger further illustrates his point with the shift to digital photos. Previously, a family might divide its most cherished photographs amongst various members scattered across the country, in numerous albums, each with its own theme – baby pictures, weddings, the trip to Antarctica, etc. Now they can list their photos by date, place, theme, and chronology, all of them. They need not choose. And each photo can be made accessible to everyone. This can certainly make things easier to find in a world in which the number of digital photos seems to be growing in rough proportion to all other forms of information. This is really quite revolutionary. While we may not be able to fit any more information into our brains, or even our libraries, the Internet can store most of the information we need. And it can make that information more accessible as well, and not through some obscure card catalogue, the use of which must be taught in school, but in ways that are easy and intuitive to grasp. Finding what we want to find need not be as improbable as the randomly swimming turtle poking its head up into the hoop.

With the ability to access things more easily, we are able to store more things as well. Perhaps the Internet itself illustrates this phenomenon best. For in many ways, it is a vast library of information. If the information on it were stored in any one place, it would take a massive federal agency, with its own internal transportation network and army of employees, to organize and manage. However, we can now carry it around with us on a handheld phone and access everything through a simple search engine. This does not mean we have settled the challenge of how we might make sense of something so vast as a world. But it does suggest the problem may not be nearly so overwhelming as we at first believed. If one of the impediments to global consciousness is the difficulty of managing a world of information, we at least have a few piecemeal solutions to the problem and perhaps a sense of how we might develop a few more. Somehow we have found a way to store in our pockets and access at will a world too vast for the human mind to comprehend.

MAPPING THE WORLD INSIDE

I know well what I am fleeing from but not what I am in search of.
MICHEL DE MONTAIGNE, RENAISSANCE PHILOSOPHER

There is nothing quite so useless, as doing with great efficiency,
that which should not be done at all.
PETER F. DRUCKER

Borges' driver would have had to drive him to where he wanted to go in order to point to it on the map. But Google takes us there with a simple command. This allows us to race through mountains of information with a single click. The only problem is that Google often fails to get us where we want to go with any degree of accuracy, like one of those time machines that always overshoots the mark. Right now our searches tend to yield rough approximations of what we want to find based on the popularity of sites related to those searches. This will change. The Semantic Web promises, amongst other things, to hone the searches and take us right where we want to go.

And still it is possible to imagine Internet searches not only taking us where know we want to go but also where we did not know we wanted to go, drawing out our emerging and inchoate aspirations, like an incisive psychologist shepherding us through the subterranean depths of our minds. Refined searches can mine previous searches, purchases, friendships, and affiliations in a hunt for patterns of interest. Algorithms can link and integrate these patterns to reveal deeper internal drives. The searches might synthesize personality style, level of education, and political orientation. And value-based surveys could help prioritize the findings. In this sense, our computers would come to know us better than we know ourselves, leading us to sites that not only peak our interests but integrate our values. We can get a hint of the potential by considering the way we are often more grabbed by the personalized recommendations on iTunes and Amazon. Of course, the same knowledge can be put toward manipulating our attention and selling worthless trinkets. It can be used to track our political affiliations and personal contacts. And it will probably be used to stamp out the cinders of some incipient democratic movements. Just because there is some good in personalized search engines, does not mean it is all for the best.

Whatever its ultimate merits, this search capacity presents extraordinary opportunities for the self to break ties with local affiliations and develop more according to its own internal logic. This would not be the first time technology proved an aid to self-discovery. The printing press aids self-discovery every time we find our own submerged thoughts in the lines of a great philosopher or our own suppressed emotions in some character in a novel. This simple technology in many ways allowed the early Protestants to discover their own consciences. Through solitary readings of the Bible, they forged personal relationships with Jesus. New consumer choices usually provide new venues for expression. Squirt guns and tool sets, spam filters and day-planners, all help us to do things we could not have done without them. And as we have seen, a system of technologies can fundamentally alter the way we think and the things we want. Insofar as refined search engines take us closer to things we truly want, they promise more than just easy access; they aid us in partaking of the worlds we truly wish to inhabit, and in so doing they transformation us. Refined search engines free us from much of the static of extraneous information. We can link ourselves to networks more suited to our tastes, open doorways to and explore spaces that previously lay undisclosed. Enhanced search engines can help us become alert to our own subjectivity and less subject to the authority of others. And they can further free us to write the novels of our own lives.

But the human psyche is riddled with contradictions and unpredictable drives. And often the things we most desire are the greatest fragmenting forces in our lives. So, while Internet searches can aid in self-discovery and psychological integration, they can also do the opposite. Social theorists have long argued that the individualism of the passive consumer is largely an illusion, masking over the inner discord and shallowness of desires.[1,2] Consumerism is less a means of expressing one's deeper drives than of channeling those drives into a limited set of prepackaged goods and services. While enhanced search engines promise to increase our options, there is no guarantee the things we light upon will touch us deeply. But the Internet is not merely some giant Sears catalogue: through it we gain access to products and services, of course, but we also gain access to participatory communities. And it is through our dialogue with the communities we value most that we discover for ourselves the things that most matter. While Facebook might not fulfill my own need for sustained inquiry, reading through the highlights of scattered friend and family members' days strikes me as far more meaningful than say watching television or discussing baseball at the corner bar.

Yet it is often argued that the closer search engines take us to the communities we truly cherish, the more all communities run the risk of balkanization. As each of us becomes more autonomous, our interests tend to diverge one from another, and the groups and norms that once bound us together lose their sway. In this sense, personal integration and social fragmentation are linked through the same causal mechanism: as the individual grows stronger, the social bonds amongst all selves fracture. This has long been a complaint about the modern condition.[3] The means through which the self develops are often the same means through which communal bonds are destroyed.[4] While over the past two centuries liberal nation-states have developed a loose framework of rules and norms that allow for maximum personal expression, and minimal harm to others, that expression often comes at the expense of social cohesion and cooperation.

Cass Sunstein points out that as we refine our positions in isolation from others, it becomes ever more difficult to forge a social consensus. The problem is particularly acute in the clash of what he has termed cocoons.[5] Cocoons are websites where individuals draw hedges around themselves and strengthen their positions through the positive reinforcement of like-minded thinkers. Such cocoons can be wonderful places to learn more about why we believe the things we do. The problem with cocoons begins when we head for the door. Views formed in isolation tend to lack the disciplining force of dialogue.[6] They can lack clarity and consistency, and are often infused with mistrust. When intellectual opponents who neither comprehend nor trust one another enter the public sphere, debate can degenerate into a nexus of irreconcilable conflict. Views forged in the furnace of debate, on the other hand, tend to be more defensible and more refined.[7] This is one of the greatest benefits of participating in an open academic community. Here we are more likely to understand and respect the depth of opposing views and to integrate them into our own positions. Hence, our positions become more dynamic and resilient.

The problem of cocoons is nothing new, though. The United States, always a stew of religious and ethnic diversity, has long grappled with the problem of social divergence. Mormons and Jews, Quakers and Italians, have lived in their own neighborhoods, sent their children to their own schools, and voted for their own candidates. And while this has often strained the social compact, these once alien communities have come to form the bedrock of the nation. The differences were integrated through universal primary schools, bowling leagues, and business associations,[8] what the nineteenth century sociologist George Simmel referred to as the "web of group affiliations."[9]

But to look only to the nation is to miss the larger picture. For the nation, where citizens are indoctrinated in schools, conditioned by the law, and assimilated through the workplace, is itself a sort of cocoon. Whether or not American liberals and conservatives can get along may be inconsequential to world peace, world hunger, or the global environment. There are far bigger fish to fry. Far more serious are the misunderstandings between Christians and Confucians, Muslims and Jews, Chinese and Japanese, Americans and Iranians. These are age-old analogue, not digital, divides. And the result of these divides has all too often been not the administrative paralysis that so worries American commentators on the partisan divide but rather the far more serious case of degeneration into war. If cocoons erect barriers to the acculturation process in any given nation, they can also make us more receptive to extraterritorial cooperation. What we all too often forget is that local cocoons are often tied to global alliances. And these are far more transformational.

Communities of interest run the gamut from the political to the artistic to the scientific, and they drift across national borders like so many greenhouse gases. The New England Journal of Medicine is relevant to Americans, Saudis, and Chinese alike. So are news sites like The Economist and The New York Times. Never mind that they bring together only doctors or center-left cosmopolitans. The divide between American liberals and conservatives is petty compared to that between Americans and Iranians, Israelis and Egyptians. These are not the petty political squabbles of privileged American families but dangerous hatreds whose consequences might ignite global wars. While many cocoons will be places of ethnic and religious fanaticism, others provide the language and support needed to challenge that extremism and its attendant bigotries. Through using the Internet to nourish our incipient interests and thereby become more ourselves, we free ourselves from the most dangerous groups that are likely to demand our allegiance. By the most dangerous groups, I am not referring to the Animal Liberation Front, the Ku Klux Klan, or even Al Qaeda but rather the Americans, Chinese, Russians, and Israelis. The most dangerous sort of violence in our era is that perpetrated by states.

More important than the influence of fringe groups is the mainstream fanaticism of well-adjusted citizens. Over the course of the twentieth century, millions of otherwise normal citizens repeatedly murdered millions of other seemingly normal citizens in competing nations. The Nazis may have been fanatics, but the American GI's of the so-called Greatest Generation were not. They committed mass murder as a matter of course, regularly killing tens of thousands of Japanese and Germans a night in fire bombings. The war, of course, culminated in obliterating two Japanese cities with nuclear weapons. Yet the consciences of these soldiers, and of the nation, seemed to come out relatively unscathed. They were often unaware of the effects of their actions.

Perhaps the existence of isolated outposts of fanaticism will remain a permanent feature of the Information Age; perhaps religiously motivated terrorism is here to stay; there will always be some who choose regression in a world of overwhelming complexity. But it is difficult to imagine the reappearance of anything like the sort of mid-twentieth century conformity that made it so easy for naïve young men to kill tens of millions of people in two world wars.[10,11] This is a good thing, and it should be celebrated. By fracturing the cultural bulwarks of identity, the Internet opens venues for cross-cultural collaboration. Enhanced search engines only intensify these sorts of connections, as we become more and more unwilling to settle for the limits of birth-based identities. All of this weakens the sway of traditional political and religious authorities, and it raises the bar for any religious or ethnic campaign that might recruit us to their cause. To assert that the Internet fragments humanity is to narrow the scope of inquiry too tightly. The Internet provides a forum through which differences can be expressed. In fracturing the American consensus, it orients our attention toward the global. To focus on the petty and relatively fleeting differences in the American political spectrum is to complain about the broken dishes brought about by the rumblings of continents merging.

We have all become a bit like those sailors of old who traveled past the edges of the known world to that place on the maps where "here there be monsters." We are living in the liminal space between one age and the next, pioneers mapping the territory as it is discovered.[12] With so much to assimilate, we should not expect to map it all. But the faster we can search through the mountains of information, the more we can assimilate. The more we can process, the more we will be prepared for organization at a higher level of integrated complexity. Better search engines will not provide us with a map, but they can help us get to where we want to go. And in that sense, they are emblematic of the coming age. The world is far too big a place to know in full. But there are always ways of navigating the unknown.

We do not need to know everything, just enough. But most of us must know more than we currently do to function well in the Information Age. Good search engines can help. So can learning more about the right things. And the pressures can be mitigated through shifts in identity. By identifying with a wider nexus of relations, we are able to draw support from a wider range of sources. It is important to remember we are not alone, and the transformations that occur in our personal and social lives need not be conscious. Human societies have a way of muddling through changes that to even the most brilliant individuals appear daunting. If things are too complex, we find ourselves drawn to simplicity. We focus on a few friends, settle into our homes and jobs, and narrow our commitments. If they are overwhelming, we scale back, step away, or learn to cope. It is quite possible that Information Age societies will react to the problem of overwhelming complexity with a range of such simple solutions, even as we are widening other areas of focus. We need not name the solutions here. They need not yet even exist. For over the coming decades, the human urge to master the environment will continue to produce novel means of bringing order to chaos. A new order is taking shape in human civilization, and while we may not yet be able to trace its contours on a map, there is much we can do to find our place.

SECTION 4

GLOBALIZATION OF EMPATHY

However selfish soever man may be supposed, there are evidently some principles in his nature, which interest him in the fortune of others, and render their happiness necessary to him, though he derives nothing from it except the pleasure of seeing it.
ADAM SMITH

Think occasionally of the suffering of which you spare yourself the sight.
ALBERT SCHWEITZER, NOBEL LAUREATE

BINDING MINDS

When news of the Nazi concentration camps first filtered into America, Jewish groups sometimes self-censored their own reports. Reasoning that no one would believe them if they told the truth, they downplayed the numbers of the dead and detained. Since oppressed groups often exaggerate their own stories in order to garner support for their cause, Jewish groups needed to account for other's mistrust of their accounts. But there was a deeper more insidious reason the truth was muted. Few people know how to grapple with the kind of suffering brought about by mass tragedies like the Holocaust. If the full truth were told outright, there was a danger people would have simply put down the paper and turned off the radio. One should never underestimate the power of human denial.

The inability to empathize routinely leads us to close our eyes. Friends blunt the hard truths; reporters divert our attention. With little market for devastating and prolonged suffering, newscasters focus on electoral horse races instead of the death count in the Congo. People tend to look askance of severe suffering for good reason. We turn away, not because we do not care, but rather because we care so much, and we care so much because, as we will see, we are biologically programmed for the job. But in a world of suffering others, brought to us by books and blogs, television and film, our empathic capacities can quickly become strained. The victims of famines, natural disasters, hurricanes, wars, and ethnic cleansings wash across our screens in a flood of imagery. Unable to grapple with our feelings of empathy, we shut them down, and turn them off.

Empathy is the ability to understand and share the feelings of others. It is the ability to place oneself in another's skin - in their life, their family, and their culture. Empathy allows us to imagine ourselves living the life of another and to inhabit his world as if it were our own. We feel ourselves the Ethiopian with the distended belly, imagine ourselves the outspoken editor left to wither away in an Iranian prison. We carry his burdens and sympathize with his highest aspirations. And through his eyes, imagined in our own minds, we see into his world. Empathy allows us to think through the factors of another's logic: the financial pressures, the limits of home life, the dreams, the goals, and the obstacles that stand in her way. Empathy may be an emotional response, but it requires the ability to think oneself into another person's shoes. In revealing the terms and conditions upon which another's thoughts are premised, we can trace a path through his Byzantine logic.[1] Suddenly, we see the sense of the Ayatollah's Fatwa, the politician's compromise, the general's sacrifice of troops, however much we disagree. And in our seeing, we feel for our opponents, bringing humanity to our judgments and reason to the debate.

The study of empathy has become increasingly integral to the fields of primatology,[2] neuroscience,[3] evolutionary psychology,[4,5] and ethics,[6,7,8] and it has seen a recent surge in research.[9,10,11] Some of the most intriguing research centers on mirror neurons, a species of neuron that lights up when we view the experience of another.[12] When subjects witness the hands of other people being pricked, this species of neuron lights up in magnetic resonance imagery as if the same thing had happened to their own hand. Of course, there is a sense in which we have known all along that we can share the experiences of others.[13] Aristotle noted the tendency to share the trials and tribulations of protagonists in films and plays as if they were our own well over two millennia ago.[14] But there is something validating about understanding the mechanism through which empathy is generated. Not only does it allow us to situate the study of the softer emotions in the harder sciences, but it also demonstrates that if our sentimental imagination involves flights of fancy, then those journeys are nevertheless rooted in hard wiring.

The primatologist Frans De Waal has brought further validation to our everyday experience of care, demonstrating it to be pre-verbal and in many ways pre-cognitive. Through the systematic study of primates, he has shown that the experience of empathy predates humanity. Primates, whales, dogs, and other higher mammals share this experience. They respond intuitively to the suffering not only of members of their own species but sometimes even to that of other species as well, suggesting that empathy may be something far deeper than a genetically inscribed mechanism to encourage care for kin. De Waal writes of a chimpanzee tending to an injured bird, carrying it to the top of a tree, gently spreading its wings, and urging it to fly, and of a whale individually nestling each diver who helped it break free from entangled fishing lines.[15] A short romp through YouTube will reveal numerous instances of such interspecies love: the lion and gazelle who are inseparable friends, the elephant that went into morning when its best friend, who happened to be a dog, died unexpectedly. Tales of dolphins rescuing humans lost at sea have appeared consistently since ancient times. But explanations of interspecies love have rarely entered into the practice of hard science. Something revolutionary appears to be afoot. Perhaps we have become more aware of the feelings of others, because so many of us are so much more self-aware.

Empathy requires the sustained concentration of the heart, mind, and imagination. It is this ability to think ourselves into the exotic world of the Ayatollah, to imagine his frustrations, and to feel for his struggles, that allows us to make our own actions mutually comprehensible. Empathy gives us access to the emotional signals vital to building a relationship. Having established this connection, we can better communicate believable threats, attractive bargains, shared interests, and persuasive principles. It is for this reason that skilled diplomats tend to be better attuned to the feelings of others; through building cross-cultural relationships, they become better placed to achieve national objectives.

But empathy allows for something far more beautiful than the facilitation of self-interest. Through empathy we learn to appreciate the limitations and constraints under which another must operate, not just the circumstantial constraints but the psychological limitations as well. Through it we might more readily forgive inadequacies, build trust, and set aside differences so as to better accomplish mutually satisfying goals. Understanding changes everything. While we might not be able to grasp all the forces at work in the life of another (few can do this in their own), in our effort to sympathize, we stand shoulder to shoulder in common cause. The gesture can be powerful. It demonstrates a willingness to learn and an ability to share pain. And it defuses enmity. It is just such empathic gestures that opened the way for Nelson Mandela to unite South Africa. And many a time an American politician reaches across the aisle to forge a controversial piece of legislation, it is empathy that smoothes the way. Empathy allows us to share a common bond, and whatever good might be achieved through human bonding - the houses built, universities commenced, treaties forged, and institutions established - the human bond is a good in and of itself.

Achieving this kind of solidarity means throwing oneself headlong into the muddy waters of the life of another and feeling for the stones upon which he stands. This requires that we be "present" with others, alert to their momentary thoughts and feelings, for the present moment is the only moment in which experience occurs. And each moment of experience is laden with information: the thousand perceptions vying for attention, the score of emotions calling out for a name, the thoughts, the memories, and the relationships that make up a gestalt.[12,13] But empathy calls for much more than just attention to the present, for we bare on our backs the burdens of the past as we breast the currents of life into the future. The present moment is much like an eddy in which the momentum of circumstances gathers together before untangling into the future. It ripples with fading patterns and surging aspirations. Empathy demands of us that we don't just feel for another but that we think about the context and continuum of her point of view.

The human-life-world is an inheritance of experiences, stones of memory, laid down row upon row, and rising into the mists of the present. Empathy calls on us to locate the experiences of others along a continuum of time. The jogger has a purpose and we cannot understand her experience of the moment without knowing why she is running. The significance of two lovers fighting in public will be lost to us if we do not know why they are fighting and what that fight means to the future of their relationship. It is the same with each of us. Our experiences of the present are located on a trajectory. Tracing that trajectory means being not only attentive but also thoughtful, for truly understanding the feelings of another requires that we place their actions in the context of their lives. This ability is critical to feeling for the Chinese factory worker, the Lebanese merchant, the Egyptian protester. If we are to feel for their struggles, we must make sense of their actions. But to do this we need to understand their lives.

Empathy is a sort of mortar; it binds us together. It binds our hearts together through mutual sympathy; we can share in relationships because we can temper our actions in accord with others' feelings. Empathy binds our actions together by making them mutually comprehensible; we can share in work because we can communicate to one another our intentions. Our communication is understood because we can see the world, if only through a glass darkly, as if looking out from another's eyes. Human relationships and institutions are built upon this basis of shared understandings. And it is through these understandings that the world of humanity is constructed.

The psychologist Simon Baron-Cohen has demonstrated what happens when empathy is absent. His research suggests that several psychological maladies – psychopathy, borderline personality disorder, and narcissistic personality disorder - are merely varieties of a more general problem: an utter absence of empathy, what he has termed zero degrees of empathy. Baron-Cohen studied the physiology of the empathic response, isolating parts of the brain that become active when empathy is present and passive when it is absent. And he found that the parts of the brain associated with empathy in people suffering from these personality disorders were strikingly unaroused by the sight of other people's suffering, whereas the brains of others would become active at the sight of a smiling face or a crying toddler. The lack of empathy made it difficult for these subjects to read other people's nonverbal cues, their facial expressions and body language, to synch up with their behavior, and to share in lasting and meaningful relationships According to Baron-Cohen it is the lack of empathy that makes these personality styles disorders. For with the loss of empathy we lose a portion of our humanity. And this is bound to have an impact not only on our own lives, but also on the lives of others with whom we live and work.[14]

When our efforts to understand one another slacken, our social worlds begin to crumble. Projects are wrought with confusion, relationships plagued with misunderstandings. Under such circumstances, institutions can no longer function. The joints of communication are loosened, and the edifice of mutual understanding becomes unhinged. Without empathy actions appear like gusts of wind in a deep canyon, elusive in origin, strangers to the order of things. The absence of empathy paints people in the colors of darkness, black boxes of mystery, mute, void, and incomprehensible. And so we come to fear one another's unpredictability. Leaders appear irrational, institutions senseless. The world makes little sense because we are unable to understand why people do the things they do. Their behaviors are incomprehensible because their logic appears broken, like a movie glimpsed in still frames. Out of those snapshots we craft our own stories. And society shatters into a loose assemblage of impressions, interconnected like the geometric figures of a cubist design.

But empathy brings language to life, imbuing it with shades of meaning, the words of the heart that seldom find their way to the tongue. When Martin Luther King Jr. speaks of racism, he speaks to experiences that can be understood by not only his followers but also the closet racists. He speaks to the nation in the code of its highest dreams and aspirations.[15] The tapestry of culture is always woven in a fabric of mutual understandings. When that cultural fabric is tightly knit – say in a peasant village or amongst the followers of some marginalized sect - then there is less need for words, and the things that are spoken can be heard more deeply. Martin Luther King Jr. strengthened American culture by deepening our empathy. In so doing, he helped us to hear one another more fully.

Somehow the center continues to hold in a postmodern world of radical diversity. And empathy provides an explanation. Immersed in our several worlds of divergent languages, values, networks, and concerns, we somehow manage to share in a common sense of humanity. The social fabric is tempered by empathy at every turn. It aligns our interests, strengthens our bonds, and deepens our commitments. Through the unspoken bonds of empathy we are able to feel ourselves a part of the living society of which we are members. And through this feeling we learn to embrace not only our own fates but also those of fellow citizens. This deepens our sense of belonging. Empathy gives us the trust needed to carry out cooperative endeavors.[16] Actions can be synchronized and aspirations harmonized when we comprehend the conduct of our neighbors.[17] This helps us to burnish bonds of solidarity as we work together for a common cause. Empathy allows us to identify with others, thereby deepening dedication and inspiring commitment.

And just as it facilitates cooperation in any one culture, empathy opens a path to cooperation amongst cultures. When we understand the predominant values of a culture we can then see deeply into the hearts and minds of its members. A man's values are key to his thoughts and feelings, his hopes and dreams. When we grasp their structure, we can unlock his spirit. Values prioritize perceptions, what we read and with whom we speak, the tasks we perform and the goals to which we aspire. And they influence feelings by altering that which we hope for and fear. A change in government, the death of a loved one, and the loss of a job are each interpreted differently through the lens of different values. Genuine empathy always involves an effort to understand those values.

This understanding is of particular importance when attempting to understand another culture. Amongst other things, Americans tend to value freedom and efficiency,[18] the French leisure and security. These values are embedded in deep traditions and aspirations stretching back hundreds of years. They are inextricably linked to legal codes and structures of government.[19,20,21] Cultural values determine the importance attached to rank, to merit, to heritage, and to power. And they take us far in defining these two societies. Yet, there has never been one France[22] nor one America.[23,24,25,26,27,28] Never do the reigning values of a society go undisputed, and they are always changing.[29] But still they subsist, like a standing wave or ocean current, repeating their patterns across space and time. Each generation is faced with a similar set of incentives and disincentives, thereby producing an ever-shifting pattern of responses that constitute the heart of a culture. By understanding these patterns, we can empathize with not only individual persons but also with whole peoples. And by empathizing with a multiplicity of cultural values, we can empathize with multiple different peoples. Without such empathy global cooperation would be impossible.

Empathy pushes through the wall of statistics and academic studies to swim in the life stream of real human lives. It unravels the mystique of exotic mores by allowing us to recreate the world of the other within ourselves. We become the terrorist ground up in the gears of impotency, rage, and suicidal despair, ticking like clockwork in his short and anguished life; we experience the trauma and desperation of the Iraqi whose life has been shattered by civil war; and we sense the constraints of leaders at a loss as to how they might intervene. Empathy allows us to simultaneously stand above and within conflicts. Insofar as we can understand the values of the parties to a conflict, we can stand with those groups. But insofar as we understand those values to be contingent upon circumstances, we stand above the fray. Empathy provides the resources necessary to forge a consensus, and the ability to forge a consensus out of multiple competing values is vital to international cooperation.[29] Without empathy, our global consciousness is more akin to the philosophical musings of Hegel or Kant,[30],[31] distant abstractions of a more rich and variegated world, perhaps made concrete by the evidence of statistics, but nevertheless void of that human element, which allows us to share in relationships across borders, and to work together, in the words of Marcus Aurelius, "like the upper and lower rows of a man' teeth."[32] Empathy is what makes global consciousness come alive.

COOPERATIVE APES

If there be a knife of resentment in the heart or enduring rancor,
the mind will not attain precision; under fear and suspicion
it will not form sound judgment.
CONFUCIUS

While not yet thirty and with no real business experience, at the turn of the millennium and in America's health food Mecca of Boulder, Colorado, I launched an effort to open a cooperative, vegetarian health food store. The idea was that the health food movement had grown out of the cooperative movement and that, while fast disappearing, food co-ops were integral to the health food movement's sense of social and environmental responsibility. Without food co-ops, the high standards of this emerging industry might rapidly regress. Whereas public corporations are owned by their members on a one-share, one-vote basis, and are thus highly undemocratic in their governance, cooperatives are democratic. They are owned by their members, who each have an equal voice in how the organization is run.[1] They combine the collective purpose of socialism with the market discipline of capitalism. And because of their participatory nature, cooperatives tend to inspire deep commitments and a strong sense of community.[2] In smaller countries, with homogeneous populations and a supportive regulatory framework, like Denmark and Sweden, cooperatives have at times accounted for a major source of retail sales. They are difficult to get started, but once built, their success rate is high.[3]

Having surrounded myself with a board of experienced business people, who were each committed to the same cooperative ideals, leadership soon passed to a collective team. Over the course of three years we sold over three thousand memberships and raised over a million dollars in member and small bank loans, eventually accumulating enough funds to open a storefront. Few if any American food co-ops had ever begun so large and with so many members. But compared with the most successful Whole Foods in the country, which happened to be located just down the street, we were minuscule and underfunded. The lack of capital would later translate into a poorly paid, overworked staff, lacking the discipline of experienced management and established corporate practice. Since there were no food cooperatives approaching the size of our own for at least five hundred miles, and since the vast majority of the nation's larger food co-ops had grown, with little competition over the course of decades, from mere neighborhood food clubs, we needed to create an entirely new business model. We had to grow rapidly, with little capital, while inspiring a high level of dedication, so that members would not defect to the better-stocked and slicker health food chains. This called for high levels of commitment, which were sustained through community building and high ethical standards. Most important to me, we were vegetarian. We were also GMO free and sold only organic produce. In retrospect, I should have heeded the horoscope I found for myself in The Onion, America's top faux newspaper, in those first few weeks when we made the decision to open a storefront. To paraphrase from memory: "This is a terrible time to start a business; for Christ's sake, you know absolutely nothing about business."

All in all, the co-op lasted through five years of high staff turnover, under-stocked shelves, and desperate fundraising drives, culminating in a long and drawn-out death. It was beautiful while it lasted, exhibiting all of the warmth and idealism of a small group of thoughtful and committed citizens trying to change the world. The co-op provided a venue through which its community of members organized service projects and expressed their shared values. But like all too many idealistic endeavors, good will was ground down under the cumulative stress of real world constraints: overwork, infighting, and member defection. The failure was variously blamed on under-capitalization, poor board planning, insufficient staff discipline, and weak member commitment.

But each of these weaknesses could have been overcome through greater cooperation. Members could have given more money; the board could have worked harder to find common ground; staff could have provided better service and mutual support; and the community could have been more tolerant as the board and staff better learned to run a storefront. An organization whose members cannot trust one another will rarely last, and many a civilization has fallen due to civil war. Greater cooperation might have strengthened staff service and board volunteerism, decreased shopper defection and community in-fighting, and increased capital and fundraising drives. People who stand together in solidarity almost always fair better than those who stand alone. These lessons in cooperation apply quite well to the global challenges humanity faces in the twenty-first century.

The problem with widening the circle of cooperation to groups beyond family is that natural selection tends to select against sacrific-es to non-kin relations.[4] Up until just the last few years, there was a near consensus amongst evolutionary thinkers that since individuals who care for non-kin will sometimes lose their lives in the process, their genes will be selected against. Care for kin, on the other hand, is a gift that keeps on giving. A mother who sacrifices for her offspring is caring not just for an individual with whom she is close but also for her own genes. And this means that her granddaughters and great granddaughters are more likely than not to exhibit the same caring tendencies.[5] This does not rule out the possibility that sacrifices might also be made for non-kin. Higher mammals will often sacrifice their lives for others to whom they bear no close relationship. As we have seen, they will sometimes even do so for members of another spe-cies.[6] This may be because the empathy that evolved to encourage care for kin also has the spillover effect of inspiring care for non-kin.

Or perhaps the care that evolved to strengthen cooperation amongst near relations is imprecise and also inspires care for individuals who are unrelated but nevertheless close. While we appear biologically programmed to sacrifice more for close relations, and while this often translates into weak commitments to the larger groups of which we partake, biological programming can also be bypassed.[7]

Consider the musings of anthropologist and evolutionary psychologist Robin Dunbar.[8] Monkeys and apes tend to strengthen their bonds through mutual grooming. Hours spent picking lice off the fur of a friend amounts to hours spent in intimate communication and bonding. Mutual grooming can in some species of primates account for up to twenty percent of their time. The grooming is not limited to kin. And those who groom one another regularly sacrifice more than just the hours of their day. Mutual grooming is integral to coalition building, and primate coalitions will often defend one another in the case of attack. Species that spend longer grooming also tend to band together in larger groups. And larger groups are safer groups. They are more likely to detect and to confuse an attacking predator. And they are more likely to defend their territory against the rival groups of their own species. However, the ability to maintain larger groups of primates is constrained by the inability to devote sufficient time to grooming.[9]

Dunbar theorizes that the initial function of language may have been to increase human group sizes. Since verbal communication can take place amongst several individuals at once, and across greater distances than fur plucking, it would have allowed for the size of human groups to increase. Language would have allowed proto-humans to keep track of one another, to tend to their relations, to deepen their bonds, to increase cooperation, and to thereby strengthen their chances of survival. Dunbar suggests the magic number would probably have consisted of about 150 individuals.[10] He arrives at the number by correlating brain and group size among bats and primates. The larger the brain, the larger the group, and the larger the group, the

more time members of a species will tend to spend in mutual grooming. Based on the size of human brains, Dunbar hypothesizes that
proto-human groups would have consisted of between 130 to 170
individuals. This happens to be about the size of most clans in tribal
societies, the smallest units in European armies, the average individual's network of acquaintances, and numerous other carefully chosen
collective units. But such a large number of people cannot be held
together through mutual grooming alone.[11]

According to Dunbar, there is a well-established sociological
principle that suggests human groups of more than 150-200 individuals will become increasingly hierarchical. For cooperation to succeed
in larger groups, it must inspire strong commitments. But outside the
small group, misunderstandings tend to multiply. The misunderstandings can involve mutual misinterpretations of interests and intentions,
means and ends. And as the group size grows, opportunities for clarification tend to decrease. It is difficult to maintain personal contact
with a couple of hundred individuals, impossible with a couple of
million. Hence, larger groups must develop some means of clarifying
goals and intentions amongst their members. This will usually require some kind of regimentation. And without a hierarchy of power,
such regimentation is difficult to achieve. But regimentation requires
conformity and often stifles emotional and intellectual expression.
Hence, there is a strong tendency for members of regimented groups
to defect to smaller more inclusive groups. Sometimes this is impossible, as in the case of nations, where emigration is often too costly
to make defection practical. In such cases, members of hierarchical
and regimented groups often hold back their willingness to cooperate, even as they remain formal members of the these larger groups.
Hence, even as language has allowed human groups to increase in
size, and as larger groups are often capable of greater cooperation,
they often lose in commitment what they gain in extent.[12]

All of this poses massive challenges to international cooperation.
Collaboration is critical to cooperation amongst nations. It is inte-

gral to ending terrorism and to staunching the drug trade, to reversing climate change and to stopping the spread of nuclear weapons. But cross-cultural misconceptions are omnipresent in international affairs. While language allows a man to communicate with far more people than Dunbar's 150 acquaintances with whom he might regularly associate, it is an impersonal form of communication. And misunderstandings can run rampant in impersonal exchanges. There will be misunderstandings over etiquette, priorities, timing, values, intentions, and authority. The misunderstandings in the international arena arise largely because of language and cultural differences, to be sure. But in weekend meetings of thousands of participants, representing scores of states, and where agendas are tight, there tends to be little time or opportunity for clarification. The governance of a nation can be, if not always regimented, then at least systematized. The national leader delegates authority to cabinet members, and they in turn delegate tasks to their hierarchy of assistants. But any such attempt to regiment international organization in general would, at this moment in history, provoke a series of fast and fatal defections.

The Obama administration, like most American Presidential administrations, can fashion an agenda and stick to it because its members understand one another's goals and pressures and limitations. They understand one another because they share the same values, pursue the same objectives, and communicate with one another daily. This mutual understanding allows them to craft a message, communicate it to thousands of workers in dozens of departments, and to enact it through a legislative agenda. If the message is sometimes distorted and the agenda seldom implemented in its entirety, if the team members sometimes resent one another and jockey for power, this only illustrates the challenges involved in political collaboration. If even the best and the brightest of a single party, in a single nation, armed with a carefully crafted agenda, and the singular determination to achieve their goals, have trouble collaborating, then the challenges can only multiply in the international arena.

Productive work requires that mundane tasks like sending memos and e-mails, setting priorities, and making appointments be harmonized. Since there is only so much time for talking, a surprising amount of energy goes into interpreting gestures and mannerisms, the tone of voice, the odd hand gesture, the back handed compliment, the veiled attack. Analyzing these kinds of clues accounts for a sizable portion of gossip and news stories, and can sap the strength of an organization. Great teams tend to comprehend the meaning of one another's gestures intuitively, without the constant resort to gossip and all its attendant hazards. When a team of workers knows one another well, the constant interchange of signals and cues synchronizes tasks like the well-oiled parts of an efficient machine. This kind of synchronization requires empathy.

Comprehending the actions of rival groups and nations tends to require patient study of their culture, their government, their interests, and their values.[13,14,15] This takes time, and it takes sensitivity, and when misunderstandings do arise, rarely can the principle players come together to clarify their intentions. Meanings once mangled tend to remain malformed. Misconceptions are piled up over the decades, reverberating through the hopes and fears of everyday people, and echoing across the generations, until they all too often culminate in the build up of arms and the launching of wars. If we are to work together we must first understand one another, and to do so, we must break the causal sequence of miscommunication.

Without the shared understandings arising from empathy, everything needs to be made explicit as in a lawyer's contract. The mission has to be spelled out, the procedures specified. But even contracts require shared understandings.[16] They are based on common conceptions of language and ownership, intentionality and violation, terms for which the meaning is seldom questioned outside of a philosophy department but which differ markedly across cultures. Private property is not absolute, even in the relatively libertarian U.S., where property owners benefit from a multitude of protections. The legality of corporate personhood,[17,18,19] the extent of intellectual property rights,[20] shared land and water rights,[21] and legal obligations to animals[22,23] are all regularly disputed. But ordinary citizens rarely consider the limits of private property consciously. Instead, they are discovered through the experience of paying taxes, maneuvering code restrictions, suffering theft, and sharing in a marriage. It is through simply living in the world, in other words, that we discover what is meant by private property. But the meanings differ from one culture to the next.[24]

Shared work presents paradoxes that only empathy and the tolerance arising from empathy can resolve. If the rules are not made explicit, work is permeated by confusion. But if you multiply the rules efficiency can be stifled. If workers do not understand one another's motives, work will be derailed, but if they take the time to learn about one another, there is a danger they will spend their time socializing and clarifying what was meant by this or that gesture. Empathy transcends this double bind by aligning interests without having to resort to coercion. It allows people to feel understood without opening the floodgates of the mouth; it allows them to adjust their work to the needs and interests of others without having to constantly stop and explain themselves. Much of what we know about what is appropriate is gathered through simply paying attention to others. By remaining attentive to the experiences of others, we become better able to align and synchronize our shared work. In this way, empathy supports social equilibrium. When we understand one another's needs and aspirations we can work harmoniously toward common ends. And in so doing, our sentiments are slowly unified.

Empathy is integral to understanding the needs and interests of other peoples, and it is vital to global consciousness. It animates our expectations of distant cultures, bringing clarity and color to the inscrutable features of the Tibetans and the placid exterior of the Japanese. It fathoms the hands that shape human lives: the taboos, the inhibitions, and the social expectations that mold distinctive beings into members of a culture. Empathy encourages curiosity, thereby deepening understanding; through understanding, sensitivity is heightened. This humanizes interactions. And it lays a foundation of shared understandings vital to global culture. It is only by aligning ourselves with others that we are really able to work with them, to strive together to achieve common objectives. Empathy inspires people to discover the aspirations and concerns of both allies and enemies alike, thereby forging trust and mutual understanding and, most importantly, a shared sense of destiny. Empathy transforms identity; through it the small self grows to include the world; thus, the individual identifies herself with the collectivity of individuals. Through universal empathy, we are able to see ourselves as members of a species, and this deepens commitment to common human causes. This common purpose is vital to global problem solving, for global projects tend to be the most daunting.[25,26]

Climate change is perhaps the most complex issue ever faced by the international community of nations. The complexity begins with defining the scope of the problem. The matter here is scientific. Temperature readings must be taken daily in thousands of places across the planet: Santiago and Cincinnati, Greenland and the Gobi Desert, Timbuktu and Samarkand. But the temperature taking procedures need to be consistent over time. They cannot be taken on the rooftops one year and at street level the next, inside the city one year and in a forest the next, for this would skew the data. It would be like shoving a thermometer first in the mouth, then in the armpit, and then in the rectum and expecting to get the same temperature. Since temperatures vary from one position to the next, temperature stations need to remain fixed. Once the data is gathered, scientists from around the world must agree on how they will blend the data, which readings they will throw out, and which algorithms will best reflect the actual rise and fall of global temperatures.[27] The matter is not as easy as one might presume, for the notion of a global temperature is in the end an abstraction, and the potential combinations of data with which this abstraction is arrived at are endless. Scientists must decide how many temperature readings to use for Greenland, for the eastern seaboard of the U.S., and for the mid-Atlantic. The problem of arriving at an accurate number is compounded by the fact that some provinces have more resources than others to put toward scientific research.

But it is not as if some single group of climate scientists has merely discovered some anomalous trends in temperature readings and declared the coming apocalypse. The notion of the greenhouse effect is well over a century old. The idea that atmospheric carbon dioxide traps heat, and that an increase in carbon dioxide in the atmosphere will cause the earth to become hotter, can be cross-tested by comparing temperatures with atmospheric levels of CO_2. The correlations between rising levels of CO_2 and rising temperatures has held strongly for over half a million years. Multiple research teams, each approaching the question of climate history with their own unique sets of data and computer models, have arrived at some generally agreed upon conclusions. And while there are dozens of national and international scientific bodies that have made statements to the effect that global warming is happening, it is primarily caused by humans, and it is serious, none has challenged this consensus. Thus, the data has been checked and cross-checked, over and over again, through multiple overlapping methods, and through a multitude of different institutions.

The International Panel on Climate Change, the body charged with integrating this data, must coordinate the work of hundreds of scientists across the world, and they are under fire from all sides. Critics scour their work for the tiniest flaws, which might then be used in climate skeptic propaganda. Since the critics often acquire their funding and stature from the ignorant, the complacent, and the vested interests, they tend to frame their criticism so as to allow little room for scientific debate. Meanwhile, economists rely on the same calculations for projecting the economic impacts of climate change and climate legislation. And politicians use the data to justify their stands for and against action on climate change. Thus, variations in data are amplified, distorted, and echoed in endless loops. It is little wonder public opinion on the issue can appear so irrational. And it is easy to see why climate summits accomplish so little.

International accords seldom involve all of the world's 195 nations. But legislation to slow climate change impacts them all. Mongolia and Vietnam and Germany, and every other nation, must each consider the impact climate change will have on its own land and people and economy. They must consider future energy needs, the ability to regulate emissions, the impacts of temperature changes, and the consequences of inaction. The concerns are interrelated. The costs of climate change must be weighed against the costs of mitigation. And the conclusions must be justified both to home constituencies and the court of international opinion. Failure to do either leads to impasses. And with a couple hundred nations party to the agreement, there is ample room for such junctures to multiply. These are wicked problems of coordination, and they do not end here.

Home constituencies must be convinced of the fairness of the agreement, and for this they must understand the needs and interests of other nations and peoples. But since the needs and interests of so many parties are too much for even a scholar of international relations to grasp, education alone will not do the trick. Moreover, global warming will disproportionately impact the peoples of the world. While it is mostly caused by developed nations, it will mostly harm developing nations. The dryer parts of India and the African Sahel are likely to be hit the hardest. But these are already some of the poorest parts of the world. If we cannot understand what it is like to live in these places, and if we do not value the well being of people living there, we may find ourselves unable to muster the political will to mitigate the worst harms of global warming. The injustice of rich peoples inflicting such hazards on poor peoples has bred resentment, rooted in centuries of colonialism and enslavement, and the resentment has made climate negotiations highly contentious.[28]

It is transcendent values like love, understanding, solidarity, and empathy that can break the impasse. If there is little empathy, there will be little understanding of the sacrifices being made by each group, and cooperation will be strained. If there is little empathy, there will be little patience for the idiosyncratic needs of alien groups. Empathy deepens the capacity of disparate individuals to bond together in common purpose, and when there is little time to forge an agreement, a sense of common purpose can focus energies. It is just this kind of focus that is needed, just this kind of understanding and sense of camaraderie that will be necessary for the nations of the world to cooperate on issues ranging from the drug trade to terrorism, from climate change to protection of species.

Over the course of the nineteenth century humanity sketched in the still blank spaces of the globe, as we have seen. Throughout the twentieth century anthropologists, sociologists, political scientists, and historians filled in these territories with knowledge of the past and present. At the opening of the twenty-first century, we are challenged to empathize with the living people of these once exotic locales – to comprehend the richness of their inner worlds and to feel for them as brothers and sisters. Martin Luther King Jr. once noted, "We are bound together in a single garment of destiny." But our humanity only becomes common when we understand one another in the flesh and blood and spirit. It is through the development of empathy that we might actualize this vision and take hold of our shared destiny. But it is not only cultural differences we are challenged to overcome. It is one thing to imagine oneself living the life of a middle class Argentine or even a Turkish villager, both of whom are likely to share with the average reader of this work a sense of security and cultural continuity, adequate nutrition and freedom of expression. Perhaps the greatest divide lays not so much in the differences between these sorts of fairly affluent cultures, but rather in the far deeper chasm that separates both us and them from the poorest of the poor.

PUZZLING POVERTY

*As Prometheus, having stolen fire from heaven, begins to build
houses and to settle upon the earth, so philosophy, expanded
to be the whole world, turns against the world of appearance.*
KARL MARX

*We are in a sense trying to climb outside of our own minds,
an effort that some would regard as insane and that I regard as
philosophically fundamental.*
THOMAS NAGEL, PHILOSOPHER

There is an organic beauty to the settlements of destitute humanity
- dwellings tinged in hoary rust and soil - shacks strewn along the
sloping lay of land, tight knit, raw, and boundless - mazes that spring
from the earth and multiply in layers and labyrinths. Burgeoning civilizations bursting through the swollen refuse of the old - dark and
fertile, like hummus from the forest floor – putrid too and tinged in
decay. Perhaps the world has hidden some of its riddles here, deep in
the wrinkled grin of poverty, along termite trails of possibility – this
is the terra incognito that now mystifies our maps. And if we are ever
to make sense of the world, we must somehow come to understand
what is happening here.

Everywhere it seems, teeming cities overflow with life. The largest mass migration in history is taking place right before our eyes, as
hundreds of millions of Chinese drift into the coastal cities of eastern
China from farms and villages in the west.[1,2] Like a life raft that is
full, these mega-cities cannot contain any more people – and still the

masses keep arriving. The once rural Africa too is becoming urbanized at a breathtaking pace. By 2030, the urban population of Africa
is set to double to just over 50 percent.[3] Yet African cultures have
historically been rural. And even now many of the cities of Africa get
along largely without roads and sewers, electricity and police. Humans can ingeniously organize themselves into functioning communities even in the most inhospitable of places. So, we should not be
too quick to see a wasteland before we know what is happening here.
But how such places can keep expanding strains credulity. In Mumbai and Rio the slums are maturing.[4] So, here we might find models.
And yet, few of us consider the daily pattern and arc of life that flows
through these places. James Martin provides a chilling depiction with
which we might begin:

> Hopelessly overcrowded, people live in corrugated-metal
> shacks, rusted ship containers and junked cars. Most shan-
> tytowns have no electricity. The streets become one long
> puddle when it rains, clogged with dead rats, mosquitoes
> and garbage... There are malnourished potbellied children
> everywhere... It is difficult to get a sense of their magni-
> tude by viewing them from their edges. This sense hit me
> for the first time when I traveled over some of them to film
> them. Flying low, you could see the squalor of an utterly
> wrecked society; flying high, you could see the enormous
> size of them, shantycities stretching for miles and miles in
> all directions.[5]

About a billion people in the world now live on less than a dollar a day - roughly equivalent to the number of people living in the
developed world. I say "about a billion" because the number is often
in flux.[6] The amount of food a dollar can buy is always in flux. It is
impacted by the weather, by the price of oil, by the level of ethanol
subsidies, by fluctuations in the value of currencies, and by specula-

tion in agricultural commodities. Needless to say, living on a dollar a day is precarious. While most of the absolute poor live in rural areas, each day brings them in waves to the teeming slums of the emerging world. These urban poor are pivotal to the fate of the world, and since few of us have any idea how they live, few of us can truly empathize with them. There is also another reason to fixate on one well-rounded number: it is easy to remember. And in constantly remembering that there are roughly a billion people living in absolute poverty, some readers might come to be obsessed by it.

Comprehending the world's future means coming to grips with the plight of the world's poor. Our fate is intertwined with theirs through an intricate web of connections. It is here that the next AIDS or SARS might fester; here that the carrying capacity of the earth might come to be determined as the rising price of food erupts into the overthrow of governments; and here that the next movement of the militantly dispossessed might ferment in a stew of ideological fervor. Yet it is also within these slums that we might first glimpse the next wave of global development, as we add to the planet another billion or so consumers and entrepreneurs.[7,8,9] The fortune of these shantycities is critical to the fate of the world. Yet their destiny is still indeterminate.

Making sense of these shantycities is important because so many people live in them. More poignantly, the suffering there is vast. And by comprehending its nature we might better remedy the conditions leading to it. Moreover, these quarters present an array of challenges to the societies in which they are located. The challenges are infrastructural, political, epidemiological, developmental, and humanitarian. If states like India and Brazil cannot integrate their shantytowns into the wider cities of which they are a part, it is possible the development of these nations will stall[10] and possibly even reverse course. But the challenges affect us all. Their demographic and environmental conditions are central to the fate of the world. We may all pay a price in the spread of disease, the rising price of food, and the breakdown of states.

Comprehending the plight of the world's burgeoning shantycities is vital to the evolution of global consciousness. It is comparable to the efforts of a man who, seeking self-awareness, must probe his own grief and failures if he is ever to feel whole. It is buried beneath the urban refuse of the third world that we might best glimpse our own global shadow. There is a great likelihood and danger we will ignore these districts due to a lack of data and first hand accounts. Knowing their numbers, their levels of malnourishment, and how much money they live off of each day, is not nearly enough to comprehend the nature of the lives of the people within them. However, the personal anguish that so often comes coupled with our first insights into the conditions of desperate poverty can make a focus on these sectors difficult to sustain.

Statistics cannot do a very good job of revealing the role of trauma in shaping a life path; nor can they tell how the desperately poor live from decade to decade. Human lives and communities are not lived in segments but as organic wholes in which each part is related to all the others. The child leaves the farm to live in the shanties, learns the ways of a new world, and starts a business selling chapatti by the roadside. Perhaps he marries, perhaps he dies of disease; perhaps he lives hand to mouth for the rest of his days, perhaps the slum grows foundations and high rises and his nation toils its way out of poverty. The statistics can only tell snippets of such a story. Hence, there is a danger that the sorts of data most of us use to comprehend the lives of the most desperately poor paint for us a distorted picture of their experience. Empathy demands we take a closer look.

Movies like the Brazilian, *City of God* or *Captains of the Sand*, sketch an image of warm, tight knit neighborhoods, where broken lives are made bearable through care, where order emerges in the midst of chaos, and where good people are sometimes corrupted and sometimes stand together in solidarity. To be sure, there is danger and alienation and traumas, laid down one upon another like scars over scar tissue, in the kinds of patterns that can cripple a character and pervert a life path. But it is easy to imagine from the fictionalized accounts how one might construct a life for oneself and build a home in a third world slum. The picture is softened, to be sure, by the fact that literature and film cannot do a very good job of portraying the smell of raw sewage. But the BBC series, *Welcome to Lagos*, which chronicled, amongst other things, the personal lives of a community of garbage pickers in Nigeria's largest city, managed to highlight the filth without sacrificing the dignity and humanity of its central characters. There is a far greater problem here with the cinematic arts: while we might discern with some degree of accuracy its realism, it is much more difficult to discern the prevalence of what we find in its depictions. The series on Lagos, which was the most intimate portrait of this kind of poverty I have ever come across, was actually attacked by one of Nigeria's Nobel Laureates in literature, Wole Soyinka. He charged that the film painted a neo-colonialist caricature of noble savages, living in urban squalor. This seems an overly defensive position to me, as it erects too high a bar for outsiders seeking to understand what it is like to live in such places. Nineteenth century novels like *Oliver Twist* have left such a strong impression on readers that another Nobelist, Edmund Phelps (this time in economics), has suggested that we have completely misunderstood the process of early industrialization.[11] Like so many novelists documenting social ills, the period Dickens' chronicled was fleeting, relevant for but a generation or two, and the suffering he highlighted was largely limited to a select class, whose plight was rapidly improving. The arts provide venues through which to sharpen our empathy, but they do so in fragments. Again, I disagree with his reasoning, the point being that reasonable people, seeking to understand the conditions of the desperately poor, all too often do wind up in disagreement. After witnessing a thousand depictions of the desperately poor, learning to reconstruct their most intimate thoughts and feelings and patterns of life, we must still struggle with questions of context and prevalence: how often they are bound in solidarity, under which circumstances compassion prevails over self-seeking, and when the pressures become overwhelming and unbearable.

There is a pattern to the settlement of slums like everywhere else. People arrive, find work, build dwellings, and orient to a new environment.[12] Such patterns tell us much about the experience of a place. The problem is that few of us know much about the nature of life in third-world slums. We do not know whether people spend their whole lives there or eventually work their way out. We do not know what happens to them as the slums become neighborhoods and as infrastructure grows. Because their economies tend to be mostly under the table, we don't know much about the resources available to residents and how they are managed. And we know little of the stresses placed upon residents by the perpetual threats to their survival. Finally, the shantycities of the third-world are a relatively recent phenomenon. We can only forecast how trends like the growth in cell-phone usage, the spread of democracy, the ubiquity of micro-credit, as well as yet unforeseen innovations in compost toilets, solar financing, and online organizing, may transform the nature of life in the slums.

The absence of answers means the lives of residents must be painted in outline. Emotions appear to us in still frames, mute and momentary. We imagine the relationships amongst children in a photograph, the prevalence of crimes portrayed in a novel. Since the arc of life remains so impalpable, it is easy to imagine a people without history, as if the individuals we feel for are unable to grasp the continuum of their own lives. Thus, we project upon them our own hopes and fears and aspirations, empathizing with our own illusions, grappling with our alienation from them as if it were their own alienation. Empathy has its origins, as we have seen, in what psychologists call a Theory of Mind.[13,14] We can feel for others because we have come to believe that they can think and feel for themselves. It is difficult to feel for others when we cannot imagine what might be going on inside their heads. Our empathy will always remain stunted until we get the facts straight. And if we cannot empathize with such a significant portion of the world's people, our consciousness of the world will remain incomplete.

Of course, it is not as if academics have not already performed a substantial portion of the work that might help us to better understand the lives of the desperately poor. They have, and in great detail. An interested reader can begin to answer some of the questions raised in this chapter through the ground-breaking and fascinating *Voices of the Poor* trilogy, based on a World Bank survey of over 20,000 poor people in over 23 countries.[15,16,17] Such books are a good place to start, and a quick glance through the notes to this section will reveal numerous other excellent sources. But the questions I am raising are deeper, pointing to the vast gulf that separates our own subjective experience from that of others,[18] and the ways in which absolute poverty widens this gulf. The problem plagues every effort to comprehend the experiences of distant others, whether they be third-world slum dwellers or polar bears swimming through the ocean, searching for ice.

As noted above, about a billion people now live off a dollar a day. At first glance, this seems impossible. Clearly some of their financial shortfall is made up for in barter, scavenging, and self-sufficiency. But the levels of malnourishment in the world do match up pretty closely with the number of people living off a dollar a day. Hence, we can infer that the shortfall, while perhaps accounted for through under the table trade, is still associated in some way with malnourishment. While this can be inferred, the inference is not necessarily accurate. It is possible that the poorest are somehow able to meet their nutritional needs and that the most malnourished are not the poorest. It is also possible that the bodies of those whose caloric intake is restricted make better use of the calories they do consume, or that the malnourished, like so many nutrition-starved individuals in the wealthy world, do not experience themselves as malnourished.[19,20] These questions are important to bring out into the open because they are the sorts of questions we naturally tend to ask when we first begin working our minds into the lives of the desperately poor.

Being professionals in the art of the dismal science, recent economic studies of the finances of shanty dwellers are fascinating. To begin with, income tends to be sporadic. For any given period the average adult tends to owe money on a number of small loans from friends, family, loan sharks, and employers. But surprisingly, the average slum dweller is also likely to have money loaned out to others. This allows her to smooth out her cash flow over time. In fact, surveys suggest the third-world urban poor spend a lot of time and energy thinking about and managing money.[21,22] When Muhammad Yunus, now a Nobel Laureate, first studied the needs of poor Bangladeshi women in the early seventies, he discovered that their greatest need was for small increments of capital that could be put toward starting their own businesses. Out of his interviews the micro-credit movement arose.[23] Further studies suggest that micro-loans are often put toward providing more basic day-to-day needs,[24] thereby demoting micro-credit to a possibly necessary but usually insufficient condition for the alleviation of poverty. More important for our purposes, the home economics of the desperately poor still remain for even the experts a mystery.[25]

Chronic malnutrition challenges the empathic capacities of the well-fed. There is just so much about it that most of us find incomprehensible. We do know that protein deficiency results in lethargy and apathy and, if prolonged, stunts growth. Iron deficiency weakens the body and saps energy. Yet knowing their typical experiences of malnutrition tells us little about how protein or iron deficiency alters the shape of a life path. It is difficult if not impossible to disentangle the apathy that is a result of protein deficiency from the paralysis of will so often accompanying poverty. For emotional trauma also results in lethargy and apathy. And since personal dispositions are at least partially ingrained through the repetition of learned responses, malnutrition and trauma-induced behavioral patterns will tend to persist long after the source of these behaviors has passed. Nor can we tell how the nutritional deficiency affects self-image or the long-term shape of the family. To understand that, we must construct stories on very limited information. The globalization of mind is largely a process of humanity constructing countless stories in an effort to comprehend people they will never meet.

The origins of human motivation are obscure, a mysterious amalgam of biological, psychological, sociological, and economic factors. It is difficult to discern how deprivation in one area affects motivation in another. Cause and effect are here intimately bound together; social constraints can leave a person psychologically bounded and vice versa. Economic limitations diminish the ability to lead a healthy life; conversely, when one is riddled with disease, it is difficult to earn a living.[26,27] Without understanding motivation we can know little about the experience of a life path, how say, a young woman hopes and dreams and acts to achieve her ends. Yet, if we cannot understand how people relate to their own life paths, our empathy for them will remain embryonic and immature. And in our failure to understand, our global consciousness can distort as much as it reveals.

Even the people living in the slums can never really know one another fully. Few of us can say much about our own neighbors. We know little of their dreams and the secrets they hold close to their hearts. Their most intimate desires are rarely spoken, and their aversions tend to be shrouded in social convention. Even our own minds are a labyrinth of self-deceit. Emotions appear to us in the penumbra of shadows, outlines of a deeper, more comprehensive experience, in which past traumas, habitual tendencies, and future possibilities vie for the spotlight of consciousness. Meanwhile, our thoughts are a knot of inner contradictions, a tangled mass of misunderstandings and self-justifications. At the end of the day we are left wandering through a hall of mirrors, seeking in theories the nature of our neuroses, pondering through philosophy the structure of the mind. The problems are compounded when we seek to understand the experiences of the most downtrodden. Not only must we grapple with incomplete information, but also with our own reactions. Severe suffering transfixes attention; hence, portrayals of poverty tend either to be painted in the anodyne neutrality of statistics or else the darkened hues of observers' own reactions. The healthy development of global consciousness involves learning how to walk a middle path between fixating and looking askance.

Like archeologists struggling to construct a civilization from a few potshards and pieces of jewelry, we must somehow feel for people whose lives are shrouded in mystery. There are numerous means at our disposal. We can review financial, health, economic, and educational statistics, but statistics tend to illustrate averages in outline. We can access anthropological, sociological, and religious studies, but these tell little of the inner life. We can experience the lives of the desperately poor through literature, poetry, and film, but artistic productions are subject to distortion and an emphasis on the exceptional. Finally, we can engage with poor people first hand through service and travel, but even here we come up against our own projections, imagining in others our own fears and traumas. Of course, through a variety of sources we might piece together a more complete puzzle. But even the experts rarely have the time, let alone the empathic capacities. Moreover, it is important that we do not just accumulate but also integrate the things we learn, attaching proper weight to a study, a statistic, a memoir, or a film.

The problem with understanding the distant and exotic is that we seldom have the time to refine our understanding. One month we are spellbound by the plight of the urban poor, the next month it is climate change. But the point of global consciousness is to become aware of the world as a whole, in much the same way we would think about the national budget in relation to military or social expenditures and each of these in relation to a set of national values, with which we might struggle over the course of our lives. The danger is that we will merely map the world – a millimeter deep and one hundred thousand miles wide. Hence, in seeking to comprehend the lives and experiences of the desperately poor, we are once more thrown into the cartographer's dilemma. If we map everything, our map will need to be as large as the territory, so we will have to travel across it to know what is in that territory. The idea that we must immerse ourselves in the study of third-world slums in order to understand what people there feel is reminiscent of the environmentalist who is so mistrustful of the mind that he will only work on local issues with which he can become intimately acquainted.

One of the major arguments of this book is that global concerns like climate change, nuclear proliferation, and mass poverty challenge us to do the seemingly impossible: we must comprehend a world too vast to be mapped and then feel for everyone living in it. As we have seen, this is not so hard as it first appears. Information technologies now allow us to access more knowledge about distant peoples and places more quickly. Economic development allows us to invest more resources in learning about them. Both the increasing rate of global economic development and the emergence of a new global technological infrastructure are bringing about the cultural convergence of all peoples, which is decreasing the amount of diversity we are challenged to comprehend. And shared global concerns are leading us all to focus on the same global political challenges, thereby deepening our sense of commonality. As people the world over become more educated, and as the natural and social sciences develop, we are coming to know more about everything, including third world-poverty. Barring some major unforeseen global cataclysm, we can count on our knowledge of third-world poverty increasing. We can count on the emergence of an ever-growing body of literature on its causes. And we can count on the best literature, which makes understanding the problems we are exploring easier to grasp, to rise to the top. We can count on more expert consensus, better research methods, and more educated representatives to appear, who have grown up closer to these concerns. All of this will help us to better understand the poorest of the poor, and we can count on it happening if global development does not go disastrously wrong, the prevention of which is, of course, central to the theme of this book.

The globalization of mind also involves the normalization of radical diversity. As I write these words, I am sitting in the Harvard Coop, a legendary bookstore and coffee shop just across the street from Harvard Yard. Each day I see here my friend, Sunny Abakwue, a Nigerian survivor of the Biafran genocide, who is hard at work on his twenty-first novel. I see my friend Gerald, a pleasant and kind man, burdened by, a crooked spine, and always, a heavy load of books. I see Hektor, a distinguished, Columbian environmental consultant, who has saved six years of vacation time to come here to study English. Yesterday I spoke with Clyde, an African-American who spent years working in the Massachusetts state prison system and now runs a successful local access television show. I see flocks of East Asian parents, with their late teen children, scoping out the world's most elite university. I see tourists and I see the homeless seeking respite from the summer sun. The diversity is ethnic and socio-economic. After having spent over a decade in the far more homogeneous town of Boulder, Colorado, the whirl of diversity first left me a little alienated and drained. But it has quickly become the new normal. The major cities of the world are becoming increasingly diverse, and more and more people living in these cities are learning to flow with difference. Like any new skill, the ability to connect with people whose lives are very different from our own takes time at first but gets easier the more we do it. Urban people in the rich countries of the world are adapting to radical diversity, and this too will make it increasingly easy to connect with the third world poor.

Understanding radical differences seems to require something like wisdom. Wisdom is a fine wine that must be fermented for years. It involves the careful observation of patterns, in oneself and the world, and their oscillations over time: the stages of a human life, the cycles of a business, and the political swings of a nation. It involves lighting upon points of leverage, knowing when to act and when to be still and when to make an impact with the least effort necessary.

This is no mere academic exercise. It is not enough for wisdom to be multidisciplinary and accurate, not enough even for it to be empathic. Wisdom feels into the matter at hand, probing for meaning and searching for answers. Through such an endeavor we can construct a complete picture of a social milieu, the way the little girl becomes a woman and fits into her world, the way the small business becomes a corporation and transforms its world, the way the nation grows up and take its seat amongst the nations of the world, and how each thing fits together in ever widening circles. This is a tall order for the average man or woman. But it may be what the globalization of mind requires. If global consciousness is to be more than the domain of fuzzy visionaries, we need to bring to it everything at our disposal: our relationships, our technology, our institutions, our knowledge, and perhaps most importantly, our care. What the poverty-stricken can teach us is that even this will often not be enough for understanding. And it is here that wisdom is most valuable. For wisdom gives guidance if not in the domains of our expertise, then in our relationship to the unknown. Wisdom can perhaps provide us with the resources needed to live gracefully with some of the ambiguities that global consciousness implies. It might not teach us everything we need to know, but it can guide us through the unknowing.

SECTION 5

GLOBALIZATION OF ETHICS

One thing you lack," he said. "Go, sell everything you have
and give to the poor, and you will have treasure in Heaven.
Then come, follow me." At this, the man's face fell.
He went away sad because he had great wealth.

JESUS OF NAZARETH

SHALLOW PONDS

"If I am walking past a shallow pond and see a child drowning in it," notes ethical philosopher Peter Singer, "I ought to wade in and pull the child out. This will mean getting my clothes muddy, but this is insignificant, while the death of the child would presumably be a very bad thing." Singer used this seemingly banal scenario in a short article in 1971 to strike at the profound injustices implicit in local commitments. "If it is in our power to prevent something bad from happening, without thereby sacrificing anything of comparable moral importance," notes Singer in a simple formulation, "we ought, morally, to do it."[1] This seems to strike most of us as fairly obvious. But Singer used this formula to stretch the notion of moral commitment. For if you would save the child when the only expense involves ruining your clothes, why not save a child in Africa for even less? Other philosophers have played with the formula, accounting for the fact that it may cost more to really save a child in Africa than we had previously thought. Hence, Peter Unger proposes a scenario in which we are confronted by a drowning child while wearing an expensive new suit, which costs several hundred dollars, suggesting only the most callous would let that interfere with saving a life.[2]

With scores of established aid organizations, working in innumerable ways to prevent bad things from happening in the world, it has become relatively easy to save a life. If you are near a computer or a smart phone and you have a little money in your bank account, right this moment you can "prevent something bad from happening, without thereby sacrificing anything of comparable moral importance." You can contribute money to feed the hungry, to aid disaster victims, to house refugees, to distribute condoms, and to eradicate diseases. In fact, you can take this prompting as an opportunity to take out your credit card, open up your computer, and go to a site of some charity to which you have been meaning to contribute. If you do not take this opportunity to do so, you can notice how you justify your inaction and how those justifications impact your further reading. Whatever you do, before you donate you may want to read further.

Estimating what it means and how much it takes to save a life is probably far more difficult and more costly than aid agencies tend to suggest. Singer has more recently estimated that it takes about $750 to sustain, and not just save, the life of someone living in absolute poverty.[3] But by any measure, a hundred dollars could fund numerous vaccinations and rehydration kits.[4] A hundred dollars might not sustain a life, but it could certainly keep many from dying. But if it is so easy to save lives, and doing so means sacrificing "nothing of comparable moral importance," like the ability to feed yourself or your family, then every moment you stand by and do nothing, you are in effect watching children drown.[5] We do this day after day after day, and few of us feel the pangs of guilt.

All other things being equal, the drowning American is no more worthy of help than the drowning African. But most Americans would save the American child in the pond, while few contribute the money needed to save anonymous Africans, even though it is far easier to send money than to wade into a scummy pond. Part of this can be explained by the immediacy of the situation. The emergency of the drowning child calls forth action, while the bureaucracy of an aid organization calls forth intelligent reflection. Political and economic contingencies do not tend to drown children, but they do cause famines. And this makes contributing money to famine relief a bit more morally complex. The drowning child calls forth a well of emotions; the plea for money to aid hungry children calls forth skepticism about who gets the money, how it is distributed, and why there is a problem in the first place. Moreover, the drowning child is a one shot deal;

the need for aid, along with requests from Save the Children, can be never ending.[6] Hence, those of us who stand by day after day, spending our money on lattes, while millions die of easily preventable diseases, may not be such callous heels. At least some of our inaction can be attributed to confusion and some to legitimate skepticism. Yet given the ease with which we might help, it is clear that in our usual inaction something is morally amiss.

The principle of moral equality is like a sword that cuts to the heart of innumerable ethical conundrums. All people are equally worthy of care and consideration. We are equal before just laws, and we are equal in the eyes of impartial observers. No impartial observer would choose one healthy drowning child over another, for impartiality is precisely the ability to treat each claimant equally. The life of a rich man and that of a poor man, the life of a stranger and that of a friend, are each worthy of the same care and attention. Whatever the worldly implications of moral equality, there is something ennobling about this idea, that at least on some fundamental level, we are all equal.[7,8] Moral equality makes of all humanity a single family. It extends the sphere of ethical consideration to all human beings. And insofar as it challenges us to consider the needs of all people, it deepens global consciousness.

We can look at this through the eyes of an imagined God, who is impartial to human differences, loving all of humanity equally. Perhaps the effort to conceive of such a God accounts for much of the moral value of monotheism: to the extent that we can imagine a God that cares for all humans equally, we too will learn to view humanity without partiality to friends and family.[9] There is little reason to believe that in the eyes of such an impartial God even our own mothers or fathers, sisters or wives would matter more than any other person. On some fundamental level, every individual is of equal moral worth. But the absolute poor hardly seem to matter at all if we measure our concern in dollars donated or the amount with which concern ourselves with their well-being.[10] Confronted by a hungry and homeless office-mate, most of us would probably take up a collection or give her shelter. Many would do the same for a dog or cat. And yet, the malnourished mother, somewhere out in Africa, hardly pulls at our attention.[11] The problem is not simply that we know too little to make an impact; most of us do not care enough to find out. We do not care to discover what is going on with the desperately poor in distant places, because somewhere inside ourselves we do not consider them to be of equal moral concern. Whatever we might profess, we pick favorites in a vicious circle of inattention and unconcern. However hard we try, we cannot see the world through the eyes of an impartial God. On the contrary, even the Gods we imagine seldom take moral equality seriously.

All other things being equal, most of us would attach equal moral worth to every single person; but of course, all other things are not equal. While one man lies on his deathbed, another must support three children. If forced to choose who should live and who should die, few would pick the one who is already dying. Most would pick the man with three kids. It is similar with life boat ethics. If we are forced to choose who should be let onto a lifeboat, most of us would give more weight to say, the winner of a Nobel Peace Prize, or even a simple grade school teacher, over that of the hedge fund manager. For while all lives may be of equal moral worth, some are of greater benefit than others, and some, we believe, have more for which they might live.

Moreover, we live in a world of friends and family and countrymen, and there are obligations and responsibilities that accompany these relationships.[12] The willingness to favor a friend, a husband, a child, or a compatriot, over a random stranger, is essential to community.[13] Being there for a depressed companion, instead of volunteering with the Red Cross, sustains trust and deepens commitment. This is the foundation to any healthy relationship. It lends to our lives a sense of safety and security, and it lays down the conditions needed for love to flourish. The world would be a cold place indeed if we gave equal attention to everyone.

But we almost always go too far in our partiality to those who are near. We give not just a little extra but vastly greater attention to the New Yorker who dies in war, far more resources to the jobless Texan, than to the homeless migrant worker. We give as if the billion malnourished people scattered across the globe did not exist at all. We give as if the drowning child in front of us is the only child who will ever drown. Even if the dollar we give would be of vastly greater benefit when passed through UNICEF to the child in Somalia than it would be if given to our own children, who would need perhaps many hundreds of dollars for the gift to make any demonstrable impact on their well-being, most of us would still default in giving to our own kith and kin. This may not be a conscious choice. In fact, it may simply be the result of intellectual laziness. A dollar is vastly more valuable to the person who earns a dollar a day than it is for the person who earns fifty, and it is more valuable for him than it is for the man who earns a thousand. But even though we might make a vastly greater impact on the well-being of the person living in absolute poverty, even though we may find giving to them more rewarding, we tend to ignore the plight of the least well off. The jobless Kenyan is not a worry, nor the dismembered Iraqi a source of discomfort. Far from giving them unequal attention, we tend to give them little attention at all.

It is easier to empathize with people we know, who share the same language and live the same dreams. It is often even easier to empathize with a lost Beagle who is there before you in flesh and blood. The desperate eyes and wagging tale tend to stir up more compassion than that of an anonymous person barely surviving in some random battered nation. Few readers of a work like this know what it means to live in a hovel or to lose a child to inexplicable disease. Few have felt the ceaseless hunger and the chronic debilitation of malnutrition. Not only have we not experienced these things, we do not know, and may never even see, people living under these conditions. We have already seen how difficult it is to empathize with such individuals. Even when we struggle to understand, thinking and reading and worrying, we are left deficient, unable to comprehend experiences so distant from our own. This can have an insidious impact on our moral commitments.

Most suffering people, and even domesticated animals, possess some means to convey their plight. But the desperately poor tend to be different. They live on rural back roads and in shantytowns, in obscure nations, speaking exotic languages. They are often illiterate, innumerate, and numbed by their pain. They tend to lack the language skills, lack the technology, and lack the freedom that might allow them to reach out and tell us how they feel. We can occasionally hear their voices in the autobiographies of say, the Egyptian, Taha Hussein, or the Moroccan, Mohamed Choukri,[14,15] where we might learn of what it is like to grow up amidst a North African famine or in an Upper Nile village. But while such writings are often the national treasures of their home countries, to most of us they remain so much untouched exotica. We have to look hard and listen with care to penetrate the self-enclosing walls of absolute poverty.

There is a tendency to think of love like dollars, a limited quantity to be spent prudently. In this zero-sum game, expending love on one person means withdrawing it from another. Here it is best to spend where it will be of the most benefit. But in truth, love is less like a quantity than it is like a valve. Open the valve, and love flows freely; close it, and the love dries up. Love tends to replenish itself. But when we think of love in zero-sum terms we tend to close ourselves off to all but a limited circle. And when the people closing their hearts are the most privileged, it is the poor who have the most to lose.

There is also a tendency to think of the hungry, the diseased, and the displaced in the aggregate. Most of us first awaken to their plight through data: this many hungry, living on so much money a year, needing only that many dollars to get what they need. Hunger is in this way an abstraction, which we are challenged to confront in the aggregate - not this or that hungry person but rather all of those hungry people. It is easier to empathize with somebody than it is to empathize with a group, and it is easier to empathize with a group than it is with an aggregate.[16] The numbers tend to overwhelm us with the magnitude of suffering. Instead of dealing with a hungry person or some group of hungry people, we must cope with "world hunger." Aid agencies try to give the impression that aid goes to individual children so as to counter this way of framing the issue. But in reality, they tend to distribute aid like we distribute care: en masse. To do otherwise would waste contributions.[17]

World hunger is a systemic problem that must be confronted in the aggregate if it is to be eliminated. When farmers in Iowa grow corn for ethanol, instead of growing wheat and potatoes to be eaten, less food is produced globally, so the food that is produced is in higher demand, and thus the price of food rises. A similar dynamic occurs when people in developing countries like India and China start eating more meat as their incomes increase. Since it takes about 8 pounds of grain to produce a pound of beef, a global increase in meat eating decreases the total world food output, so the price of food rises here as well. Since the personal budgets of the absolute poor are already stretched tight, and since their dietary needs are inelastic, meaning they do not change much as the price of food rises and falls, small increases in global food prices can mean massive increases in world hunger.[18] It is difficult to confront such abstractions with the sense of immediacy we would bring to the pain of a loved one. But it is systemic concerns like the rise in global food prices that can quickly push the number of malnourished people in the world from eight hundred million to a billion. So to understand the causes of world hunger, we have to think of the problem systemically. But if we want to do anything about world hunger, we need to feel the pain of the hungry with the same intensity we would feel for a friend in need. Otherwise, there will be a strong temptation to ignore their concerns when considering domestic agricultural policy.

The problem of understanding and caring for people so desperate and different is only compounded by the half-truths and misapplied truths we use to explain away any sense of obligation. The battlements of privilege are stacked high with justifications. We lack the time, lack the money, and lack the knowledge needed to help.[19] We do not know where the money we send, to say, Oxfam or Save the Children, really goes: how much is eaten up by bureaucracy and how much is a mere band-aid. Some argue that Africans are so poor because their leaders tend to be so corrupt and their nations have weak institutions.[20,21] No amount of money can bring the needed changes in these domains; on the contrary, adding outside dollars to such an environment can often intensify corruption and institutional deficiencies. For the aid we give can entrench local elites[22] and distort markets.[23] Market systems, it is argued, will finally begin to function when we let them alone.

Personally, I find this line of reasoning an important component to bear in mind when trying to make sense of world hunger, but I am skeptical of its ultimate merit. To begin with, the tendency to justify doing nothing, and to relieve ourselves of any burden of responsibility, is so common that we may want to set a rather high bar for anyone who argues for inaction. It is not simply a drowning child that confronts us when we look to world hunger but our own lack of empathy, our ignorance, and our apathy. The idea that it is harmful to feed the victims of famine, shelter refugees, and build wells is, to say the least, counter-intuitive. Critics of aid usually focus on the ineffectiveness of USAID, using sophisticated economic models to demonstrate that it has been ineffective.[24,25] But most of this aid was given by the American government to other governments whose allegiance it sought during the Cold War. Israel received more of this aid than all of sub-Saharan Africa combined.[26] Egypt received the second most so as to assure they maintained their treaty obligations to Israel. Much of it went to Mobutu in the Congo, who was notorious for his corruption.[27] To put such monies in the same category as those earmarked for Oxfam or Save the Children is categorically absurd. Economists who fail to make such basic distinctions should be greeted with derision.

Yet elites in poor countries do tend to be severely corrupt and this does contribute to the poverty in their states. And whether or not these corrupt elites are taking aid money, they do tend to benefit from aid, insofar as it can allow them to get away with doing nothing about their countries' most pressing needs. But the most common reason for endemic corruption in poor states is the inability to pay civil servants adequately, and hence the tendency of petty government officials to take advantage of their positions.[28] That poverty causes corruption can be inferred from the fact that when most states grow wealthy, the corruption declines. The growing wealth will usually be put toward education, and an educated populace can more easily discern and expose corruption. The educated have a stake in the system and tend to be outraged when corruption interferes with their ability to participate in governance. Increasing levels of development makes it easier to collect taxes, thereby making it easier to pay adequate salaries to officers, bureaucrats, and justices. And this gives these officials the security needed to carry out the law impartially. Curbing corruption strengthens the rule of law and the efficiency of markets.[29] Contracts can be trusted, transactions clarified, currencies stabilized. The fact that poor elites tend to be severely corrupt isn't an argument for not giving. It is an argument for giving to activist organizations like Human Rights Watch, Freedom House, and Transparency International.[30] Protecting human rights makes it easier to expose corruption, encourage transparency, and facilitate market transactions. Rather than giving a man a fish or teaching him to fish, this sort of aid prevents the police from stealing the profits of fishermen. It provides a reason to fish, and it prevents the multinationals from depleting local fisheries.

While real aid has often failed to bring about economic development, it has been highly successful in furthering literacy and longevity, and in preventing famine and disease.[31] While aid to famine victims can sometimes appear a bottomless pit, it is important to note that it has been almost three decades since the Ethiopian famine of the eighties and that there have been no such famines since. Some of the responsibility for this lies in the increasing democratization of the developing world. The Nobel Laureate economist, Amartya Sen, likes to point out that no famine has ever been known to occur in a democracy.[32] But insofar as aid has furthered literacy, and increasing literacy tends to be correlated with increasing democratization, at least some portion of the famines that have been prevented because of increased democratization can also be attributed to the effectiveness of aid for education.

Yet even if aid could save millions of metaphorically drowning children, and giving aid were as simple as going on a website and punching a few buttons, many would still be wary. The ghost of Thomas Malthus tends to lurk beneath the surface of all too many discussions on global hunger. Malthus argued in the late nineteenth century that population tends to increase geometrically, while food production increases arithmetically; thus, a growing population will tend to outstrip food supplies if there is no check on its growth.[33] This concern often lies at the root of inaction, particularly amongst environmentalists, who tend to find the ecological nature of this argument intuitively appealing. The poor are hungry, they argue, because the world is overpopulated.[34,35] Neither food aid nor agricultural science will bring down the numbers. If we feed the poor today, they argue, we postpone the crisis for tomorrow. Moreover, increasing food production would devastate the marginal lands upon which food is grown, thereby adding environmental destruction to unsustainable population growth.

Such concerns arise from a sort of global consciousness, but this consciousness is embryonic. It is global insofar as it concerns itself with a systemic view of the world; but it is undeveloped insofar as its premises are inaccurate and its perspective so ungrounded in a concrete understanding of hunger in the real world. And in framing world hunger as part of a more systemic problem, of which feeding the poor will do little to change, Malthusian logic tends to close hearts, fortifying positions in the towers of privilege. Malthusian environmentalists are simply wrong about the effects of hunger on population growth. The world's fastest growing populations are not the well-fed Scandinavians or Germans but rather the Liberians and the Afghans.[36]

Poor populations grow so fast because poor couples want children who can help them work the land and take care of them into old age. Children are a form of social security in these places.[37] Population rates tend to decline when these societies emerge from poverty into the global middle class, for surplus wealth provides a sense of security, and this diminishes much of the motivation to have large families. Whether it is the state or the individual who does the investing, surplus wealth tends to be put toward education and retirement savings. The education provides opportunities, and the savings obviate the need for children to care for their parents into old age. By giving them the skills needed to work outside the home, education also provides opportunities to women. When women have options, they are less likely to want to devote themselves to the role of full-time parent. Instead, the role of parent becomes merely one amongst many possible life paths. As a result, women choose to conceive fewer children.[38] And thus, greater wealth makes it not only more secure but also more rewarding to have fewer children.

Much of what aid can accomplish is thoroughly non-controversial. Aid can jump-start economic development and the freedoms that accompany development. Aid can fund schools;[39] microcredit can provide opportunities to women.[40] Aid can fund the development of appropriate technologies.[41,42,43] And it can help build the infrastructure that facilitates trade. Critics of aid often exaggerate the differences between their own views and those of aid advocates. As Jeffrey Sachs, perhaps the most recognized and respected cheerleader for increasing aid, points out, he and the most recognized critic of aid, William Easterly, can both agree on the importance of getting back to the basics of providing bed nets and eradicating diseases.[44,45] Bed-nets and disease prevention tend to increase productivity by increasing the number of workdays per person, per year, and over the course of a life, thereby aiding in development.[46] And it is far from inconsequential that each of these measures happens to be itself a worthy end.[47,48,49] When we start to think of aid as a means to economic development, as opposed to economic development being a means to greater freedom and happiness, then we have begun to confuse means and ends.[50,51] Intelligent and responsible aid can support both democratic and economic development, freedom and happiness, in a virtuous circle of mutual support.[52]

The world is drowning in a shallow pond. There is nothing heroic about wading in and saving lives. In fact, nothing could be simpler than getting on a computer right now and sending one hundred dollars to Oxfam, or if you are wealthy sending a thousand. And it takes little theorizing to turn this kind of action into a duty: if we have a duty to wade into the shallow pond to save the drowning child, then we also have a duty to save the hungry child with a few clicks of the mouse. Recognizing such a duty, we could then proceed to set limits on when and how often we should act. This is the way ethicists usually convince us to do more good, and in so doing, they fortify our civility and deepen our humanity.

But there are problems with turning this impulse to act into a duty. Ethical injunctions like this rarely move people to act; even the moral philosophers seldom seem to act on the injunctions they hold so dear. More importantly, it is not enough simply to act: we must also understand. We must understand the lives of the desperately poor, and we must understand the forces that shape their lives. Without understanding, we will intervene in the wrong ways, at the wrong times, with the wrong attitudes, for the wrong reasons. Perhaps ethical injunctions were more powerful some time in the not-so-distant past, prior to the rise in global consciousness, when the call to action tended to be more limited in scope. Our worlds were smaller, and so were our commitments. But these days, moral injunctions seem to grow along with our own growing horizons. When we do give, we tend to expect that we are not opening a valve but rather a floodgate.

The twenty-dollar donation to Oxfam will surely be met with twenty more requests.

Ethical arguments can be powerful. They challenge us to think impartially and to apply our moral intuitions consistently. This tends to foster global consciousness by placing us, with all of humanity, in the same boat. Ethical arguments inspire us to extend our sense of who and what matters, and to act on our commitments. This also deepens global consciousness. Ethical injunctions transform us by bringing structure to the random planks of commitment we pick up along the path of life. By filling out our commitments, we extend our sense of community.[53] And we integrate our values and sentiments. But we don't just integrate our own values and sentiments, moral reasoning integrates us into wider associations of others whose well-being we must account for, and in so doing, it deepens global consciousness.

We all share the same world, breath the same air, and divide amongst ourselves the same limited food supplies. The reasons we cite for aiding a friend or co-worker can as often as not just as easily be applied to distant and exotic people. To refuse aid would be callous; providing it requires little sacrifice. If we were in their shoes, we would expect the same. Of course, the application of moral equality can take many forms. Each of us may attach a different weight to local, as opposed to global, commitments. We may arrive at differing conclusions regarding what the poorest portion of humanity actually needs and how to provide it. But as soon as we declare that all human life is of equal moral worth, we open ourselves to the possibility of a profound shift in consciousness. For through such a declaration, we become fully human members, not just of some limited community or nation but also of the species. Global consciousness brings to the detached reason of impartiality a sense of identification and feeling. When we can empathize with the other we are more likely to act in support of their well-being. When we can contextualize their lives, we are more likely to be effective in doing so.

SEAS OF SUFFERING

Dante's *Inferno* is a sanitarium of murderers immersed in rivers of boiling blood, flatterers sunk in excrement, heretics trapped in flaming tombs, suicides transmuted into thorn bushes, profligates hounded by voracious dogs, sodomites banished to a desert of burning sands, and politicians plunged in a lake of burning pitch.[1] The punishments seek to demonstrate the suffering that accompanies immorality. They are graphic, vivid, brutal, and boundless, unrestrained in their cruelty, and seemingly endless in extent. From the comfort of the twenty-first century, the punishments can appear unjust and even absurd. And given their extent, it is not unfair to wonder whether Dante and some of his readers indulge in a little vicarious sadism. Whatever the motives, Dante paints suffering in the sublime: splendid, stunning, arresting, and vast. He is transfixed, like Job before the wonders of God. But he is also touched, moved by the stories and feelings of those he encounters. The appeal seems to lie in this merging of the personal and impersonal, the vast sea of suffering and the individual drowning. The sufferer in is never just a number; on the contrary, he is an archetype and an immortal, and his story always matters.

The suffering Dante encounters in hell is not dissimilar from that encountered in our own world of the living. Consider a sampling of major world events. Half of the residents in Kinshasa, the largest city in the Democratic Republic of Congo, eat only a single meal a day, while another quarter eat only one meal every other day. Muslims and Christians in the Central African Republic have begun brutal killings, with reports of cannibalism, and many fearing a degeneration into genocidal reprisals. And as always, hundreds of millions of people suffer from malnutrition, many millions of which can be expected to die, as they do annually, of hunger and hunger related illnesses.

With a little artistic license, we could paint something akin to the Inferno with these colors of sorrow: drowning masses drifting from loved ones on an open sea; tortured demonstrators, mutilated, bleeding, humiliated, and terrified; starving children, whose distended intestines cannot hold fluid; genocide victims, stacked one atop the other, as if some inventory ready for dispatch; the diseased, displaced, worm infested, and traumatized, all lighting up the synapses of our brains like the endless stars of a clear night sky now falling. There is a lens through which our little sampling of news can appear a literary hell. But unlike Dante, we seldom capture the warmth of relations and the depth of feeling. Herein lies the difference between news and literature.

Of all available news items our list is but a small sampling. Like Dante, we could prolong the depictions of torment, but we could also paint a rosier picture of economic growth and technological development. Whatever the angle, most of the items will fall from center stage by springtime, only to be replaced by another set of events, which will themselves in time be replaced in an endless cycle of sensational events. While the news industry may dramatize and distort, few can countenance the boundlessness of human suffering. Thus, much of the most horrifying news is self-censored. We choose not to see, and they choose not to print, suffering more intense than some rarely mentioned but easily identifiable threshold. It is painful to stand by and watch others suffer. Just before the average viewer gives up in despair and changes the channel, the press grants reprieve. There is a strong temptation to point fingers at irresponsible reporters, but it is not as if their profession makes them somehow immune to the pain of vicarious suffering. While it is possible to fully comprehend the circumstances behind each news item, it is improbable that many will burden themselves with this excruciating and full-time job. Like Dante, we wander through the wastes, inquiring into the meaning of assorted torments, knowing that the primary difference between our subjects and ourselves lies in our ability to turn away when we have had enough. Our time is limited, our gaze all too often Olympian. But like the distant Gods of ancient Greece, our interest, sometimes capricious, sometimes contemplative, can bring change.

The global scene confronts us with a seemingly endless series of ethical dilemmas. We struggle with what to buy, how it is produced, where it is sold, and how much we use. We wrestle with where to give money, what to study, who to believe, and how to vote. And we fiddle with our freedoms, our luxuries, and our options, as if the beauty of our lives is compromised when stood next to death, disease, and destruction. When we move from the national to the global scene, it is not only the quantity of ethical dilemmas that changes but also the quality. Deciding to let one person die is not like letting ten thousand die. Nor is distributing money to one person the same as giving it to one hundred. The latter decisions involve calculating and planning, mobilizing and organizing. Since their impact is greater, more variables must be considered. And few solutions when carried out on such a scale ever achieve resolution. Mentoring a teenager or aiding an unemployed friend has a beginning, middle, and an end. But eradicating global poverty is the work of generations. This changes the way we think about global ethical commitments.

Ethical philosophers use scenarios to draw out and challenge moral intuitions, our gut feelings about right and wrong.[2] The child drowning in the shallow pond is a particularly poignant scenario; it makes the problem of world hunger, which usually seems distant and abstract, appear immediate and personal. But the child drowning in a shallow pond may obscure as much as it reveals, for the most salient feature of global ethical dilemmas is the very fact that they are not only distant and abstract but also vast and variegated. The analogy of the child drowning in the shallow pond suggests that solving world hunger is actually quite simple. But as we have seen, and as Singer well knows, it is extremely complex. Moreover, world hunger is only one of a number of global challenges we might wish to entertain. We could also work to end war, save rain forests, facilitate development, and promote human rights. Working to solve many of these issues can contribute to the alleviation of world hunger.[3] The issues are interrelated, but for most people working on any one of these issues, solving world hunger will not be their primary focus. Each of us brings to any given set of global issues our own set of values and concerns. While the issues may be entangled, our values and priorities vary.

We are less like the man on a walk through the park, glancing at a shallow pool of water, and a bit more like Dante on a rowboat through hell. We are dealing with masses of which the individuals are only instantiations. And like Dante, we are overwhelmed. There is no way to save the seemingly infinite number of beings to whose suffering we can only be but a witness. Right now people are destroying the habitats of billions of insects, millions of plants, hundreds of thousands of animals, and tens of thousands of people. Each of us is destroying forests and oceans and cultures and villages, sometimes through the things we buy and sometimes through the ways we vote. Each of us is party to a suffering that was happening before we were born and will continue long after we have passed from the stage. We are sojourners through a sea of suffering. While it may be too much to say we can do nothing to stop the misery, it would be equally foolhardy to suggest we can banish earthly suffering. The thought that we cannot end suffering can be unnerving, but ethical inquiry should make us uncomfortable.

Consider the case of the so-called Copenhagen Consensus and the $50 billion account. Assembled by the environmental skeptic Bjorn Lomborg, a group of prominent economists was asked to write papers for a 2004 conference detailing how they would spend $50 billion dollars to make the world a better place.[4] In many ways, this could be the start of an all night dialogue amongst bright and energetic college students, dreaming up ways to save the world. But from another perspective, the proposition is comparable to giving Dante a lifeboat and

asking him to choose whom he will save and whom he will abandon
to hell. With $50 billion you can only end so much disease, feed so
many hungry, save so much rainforest. It is a lifeboat with limited
seating. Needless to say, the Copenhagen Consensus was probably
named before the meeting: some favored fighting disease, others hunger, still others promoting trade. Environmental concerns placed low
on the agenda, but given the organizer of the event this was probably
to be expected. Whatever the case, the exercise made an important
point: even with $50 billion dollars, you have to triage, and that is
an idea anathema to many do-gooders. Some ideas are just not high
leverage enough to pursue. Sure we can extend the pie, take a little
money from the military and place it in foreign aid, take a little from
the cappuccino fund and give it to Amnesty International. But in the
final analysis, each of us must make choices about who lives and who
dies, for there are limited seats on the aid boat.

Quantitative changes are always qualitative. When the different
kinds of problems are so many as to stupefy, when the quantity of
resources required is so vast as to strain the imagination, when the
number of sufferers is so great as to admit of no definitive solution,
then the primary problem of ethics shifts from that of which principles we should adopt, or even how or to whom we give, to one of
how we are to cope with seemingly immeasurable suffering. Ethics
must orient our interest in such a way that it allows us to sustain our
inquiry and deepen our care. It is not enough to convince someone to
become a vegetarian if they are unable to stay a vegetarian. Ethical
inquiry must make us behave more ethically. Otherwise, it has little
use other than as an exercise in applied logic for ethics classes. We
might decide it is right to give more money to the hungry or that we
will dedicate our lives to ending climate change but next week find
ourselves blowing money on a new car. Intellectual decisions do not
always stick. The mind says yes; every fiber of our beings rebels.

Let us look once more at the drowning child in the shallow pond.
By contemplating the drowning child, we expand our hearts, deep-

en our allegiances, and discover new commitments. For we find that our everyday values demand much more from us than we ever could have imagined. If we are typical, we begin the exercise believing ourselves decent, willing to go out of the way to help a desperate person in need. But we end the exercise with the realization that what we believed to be decent was actually quite callous.[5] While saving a life could be as easy as turning on the computer and donating some negligible sum to Oxfam, somehow we always find something better to do. Our actions suggest the bare minimum of moral decency is actually quite extensive. The problem lies less in the act of giving, for this is quite easy, but rather in the immensity of global suffering. We are like Arjuna before the resplendent glow of Krishna's sublime immensity.[6] Global challenges are too many to reckon, too vast to comprehend, and too painful to face. So, the temptation is great to turn away. In such cases, it is neither our callousness nor our failure to think clearly that keeps us from giving to Oxfam. Rather, it is our confusion and pain, our guilt and fear. And while these are beyond the scope of typical ethical inquiries, they are often decisive in our moral decisions.

The Copenhagen approach to thinking through our commitments fairs no better, and a good bit worse, than that of Singer. To its benefit, the exercise reminds us of the constraints to setting global priorities rationally, for it forces us to choose what we would fund by providing a limited pie of funds. This has a way of focusing minds. If we imagine ourselves to have only limited resources to spend, we will arguably spend them more rationally. But the approach appears premised on a contraction of the heart. Setting limits based on the funding we can reasonably expect to be available for aid is not just a way of maximizing the good that can be achieved with those funds; it is also a way of bringing closure to the ethical challenge. Perhaps there are many who can keep their hearts open in triage, but the papers compiled by the Copenhagen Consensus, steeped in the cold rationality of academic detachment, suggest this quality is rare. This may have been predictable; once the limit to ethical obligations has been set, we need no longer work for its extension. If all we can feed is 500 million hungry people, then demanding we feed more will only make people feel aggravated. But of all people, economists should know that financial pies are not limited. In the same way that growing the economy can increase funding for social programs, expanding our hearts can increase aid. Activism appears to share far more in common with marketing than it does with accounting. When we contract our hearts, we close the coffers; hence, one of the primary jobs of the aid activist is to pull at our heartstrings. In their hardheaded realism, the Copenhagen Consensus ignores the greatest impediment to most aid work. When important aid projects fail to happen it is usually due to a lack of funds, and whether or not these funds are available is usually a question of how hard some people work to acquire the funding.

Insofar as we are like Dante, we must accept our limitations as we sail through a sea of suffering. But insofar as we are of the world of the living, we have the freedom to save lives. However, as in the case of the human attention span and the ability to process information, our capacity to impact suffering is limited. As individuals, most of us will have no more than hundreds or perhaps thousands of dollars to spare. Global consciousness forces us to grapple with who we can save and who we can't. The failure of globally conscious individuals to grapple with this question could be described as a moral failure. We know there are challenges like climate change, overpopulation, and the destruction of rain forests, and that our own actions probably impact these issues. But few of us have taken the time to figure out how and why and to what extent. Before we consider laying upon ourselves further duties to give or to act, most of us would do well to learn a little more about what lies at the heart of global suffering. Perhaps a new metaphor is apt.

Amidst my one and only Caribbean cruise, with the ship far out to sea, I spotted in the distance a small boat packed with people. Moments later, the ship slowed and the Captain announced we had

alighted upon a boatful of Cuban refugees. We would wait for the
Coast Guard to arrive and make sure they were all right before con-
tinuing on our way. It felt good to know this floating eatery, where
wealthy Americans roast in the sun, was nevertheless good for something. But as the Coast Guard arrived and the sunburnt Cubans tried
to start their broken down engine in a feckless attempt to outpace the
Coast Guard cutter, it fast became apparent that the Coast Guard were
no escorts for the oppressed. According to a law passed under President Clinton, Cubans attempting to flee to America are to be accepted only if they are discovered on dry land; those found in the water,
the "wet foots," are to be returned. Still, the imperceptive passengers
cheered the Coast Guard as if to welcome the Cubans, who in turn
probably misunderstood the applause as a typical case of American
bigotry. And perhaps at that moment, with the Coast Guard on their
tail and the cruise ship accolades echoing in the distance, they felt a
twinge of buyer's remorse. As a distant accomplice to this injustice,
my own good cheer was certainly sullied with that same sense of
regret. I felt embarrassment regarding my privileges, guilt regarding
my ignorance, outrage regarding the law, and disgust with the unwillingness of fellow passengers to engage the issue for more than
a fleeting moment. Perhaps this is an appropriate metaphor for how
each of us can feel in the face of global suffering.

We are sojourners on an ocean of suffering, grouped together on
the upper decks of a cruise ship. To contact the suffering below, we
must go to the lower decks; but our ship moves too fast for any kind
of real engagement. As soon as we understand what is happening, the
moment has passed, and there are a hundred distractions to make us
forget. Should we somehow manage to contact the sufferers below,
we can seldom question them, like Dante, nor aid them personally,
like Singer. Unlike the Copenhagen crowd, we do not have billions
of dollars to dispense at will. And our floating palaces are slow to
maneuver. The sufferers remain distant, mute in their suffering, like
the Cuban refugees desperately fleeing oppression, as we in turn, im-

possibly seek to contemplate their gaze and know them as something more than mere numbers. There is a sense in which we are helpless before global suffering. And this sense of helplessness radiates through a wide range of feelings.

While we cannot always pick up the most needy or deserving, we can save some limited mass of sufferers nonetheless. Each of us has the power to achieve a remarkable amount of good in our lifetimes. Through changes in diet, choice of travel, means of livelihood, and the act of giving, over the course of a life, we can lift from suffering a cruise ship of beings: hundreds of thousands of plants, tens of thousands of insects, thousands of animals, hundreds of humans. It is often in our opportunism that we can be most effective, seizing the moment here, following there the overflow of our hearts. But we will seldom seize the moment or feel for the afflicted if we are unable to absorb the endless vista of suffering. We don't need to be articulate on each and every aspect of the issues we engage, but we must be able to face the suffering en masse. Without this capacity, our efforts will be fleeting, our focus faltering. Insofar as global consciousness challenges us to take in the suffering of the world, it provides us with an emotional and intellectual foundation for action.

Each of the above approaches to suffering – that of Dante, of Singer, and the Copenhagen crew – has merit. We need to see and feel the suffering like Dante, push ourselves to do more like Singer, and choose how we use our resources carefully like the economists of Copenhagen. While we may criticize some aspect of each approach, they each deserve our salutations, for if we fail to reward the care that leads to these sorts of accounts, we lay up yet another barrier in the path of service. But none of them is enough. Dante is a mere passerby; the Copenhagen crowd is prone to detachment; and Singer is unduly dependent on the unreliable force of will. Neither do any of them exist in a vacuum. Each of us is informed by a multitude of approaches to suffering. Whether or not we have been exposed to Dante or Singer, their approaches are accessible to each and every one of us, in the air so to speak, and we pick and choose amongst them, just as we pick and choose amongst the issues, based on our personal proclivities and proximity to the challenges. While we may be able to direct our attention to this or that bit of news, direct our dollars to this or that organization, the nature of global suffering is such that we will always be passersby dealing in abstractions and opportunities. While we may develop some expertise that maximizes our effect, we will always be worker bees in the construction of a greater global collective hive. To craft a work of this magnitude and to sustain our care in a vast world of suffering, something more will be required of us than anything we have thus far explored.

THE OCEAN OF LOVE

Until he extends the circle of his compassion to all living beings,
man will not himself find peace.
ALBERT SCHWEITZER

The biosphere is comprised of a burgeoning diversity of species: pine trees and crocodiles, wolverines and algae, lotus flowers and blue whales. Humans may dominate the planet, possessing the power to terminate species and bring new ones into existence. But packed tightly together, the mass of humanity is so slight as to fit within a mere cube stretched a mile in every direction.[1] And yet, as long ago as 1846, Marx could write that there was no untouched nature left, "except perhaps on a few Australian coral islands of recent origin."[2] The warming of the atmosphere, caused by the human release of global warming pollution, has since that time altered every ecosystem on the planet further and will continue to do so into the foreseeable future.[3,4] We are voracious little shrews, transforming the land and ecology of every place we inhabit. We have brought into the world today about a billion sheep, a billion pigs, 1.4 billion cattle, and 19 billion chickens.[5] And we are responsible for their lives, for the lands they inhabit, the soils they degrade, and the pains they suffer. For it is to the satisfaction of our wants and needs that they owe their existence.

Thus far, our interest in global consciousness has focused mostly on humanity. The argument by now should be clear, but a recap may prove helpful. To meet the demands of global challenges, we must be able to think globally, for global consciousness helps us to understand and cooperate with people on the other side of the planet. We must be able to cooperate with people on the other side of the planet because so many of our greatest challenges are now global in scope and thereby require global responses. All of humanity is now packed quite closely together. Travel, trade, technology, and war tie us together spatially. And the depletion of oceans, destruction of rainforests, and most importantly, climate change, bind us together temporally. Concerns that once impacted only particular groups, at particular times, and in particular places, now extend outward to far-off settings and distant generations.

If we do not tend to our common connections, we will fail to redress our common concerns. In this sense, we are a global society. But we are fast becoming a society whose relations and institutions might persist across generations. Hence, we are not just a society but also a civilization, one great global civilization. Like the Chinese, the Romans, the Russians, or the Ottomans, what befalls one portion of this global civilization, at one point in time, befalls all other portions and deep into the future. If we fail to think of humanity as united across space and time, our relationship to one another will be one of mutually inflicted harm. It will be harmful because the relationship will be unconscious, and in our unconsciousness we will inevitably step on toes. Such a mutually harmful civilization is a state of anarchy that cannot subsist. Believing oneself to be part of a global civilization might not be a sufficient condition for sustaining this civilization, but it is probably necessary. It is quite possible, while not probable, that humanity has become so interconnected that if we fail to develop a sufficient degree of global consciousness, human civilization will itself ultimately fail. The stakes are high. But the argument thus far has left out something of vital importance.

It is not just humanity that is globally interconnected. The well-being of humanity is bound to the fates of billions upon billions of plants and animals. One massive study, carried out by ecological economists and published in the journal Nature in 1997 estimated the net value of the biosphere's ecosystem services and natural capital – the fish, trees, minerals, land, water, and natural services like water purification and fertilization – to be about $33 trillion annually.[6] Whether or not this is a good estimate of the net value of each of these resources and services alone, the total value of all of the biosphere's resources and services added together is inestimable. For without the biosphere there would be no one left to do the estimating. But the study is valuable in at least one sense: it demonstrates the economic value of things that are all too often taken for granted. Much of what we are talking about here is alive. Living beings hold not only economic but also intrinsic value, a value that only grows in the eyes of the beholder with the extent of his love. If we love the fish, the trees, and the land itself, their value can only grow in our estimation, for while they may carry some value that can be measured in dollars, they will also carry an intrinsic worth whose value is inestimable. And it may be the case that until we love all life, it may occupy too slight a portion of our minds to even think to assign it an economic value.

Just as it is necessary to cooperate with people on the other side of the planet to achieve global goals, and just as that cooperation is facilitated by empathy for all of humanity, our fellow feeling for non-human life can help us live more sustainably. For this sense of fellow feeling motivates us to concern ourselves with the fate of the life upon which we depend for our survival. The love for real sheep and cows, pandas and sea otters, redwoods and oak trees, brings to their protection an added sense of urgency. These are not just "resources" in the abstraction but also living beings. All of this is poignantly illustrated in the human relationship to livestock.

If humanity were to simply stop exploiting farm animals, we would save not only the animals themselves but also much of the land that is now required to sustain their lives. We can begin to get a sense of how much land would be freed up through a few statistics. Depending on how high the quality of protein and metabolizable energy content in their feed, it takes between 4 and 20 pounds of grain to produce a pound of live weight beef cattle.[7] Looked at another way, according to the U.S. Department of Agriculture, American livestock consume about 7 times more grain than the entire U.S. population combined.[8] All other things being equal, this grain might instead sustainably feed 840 million vegetarians.[9] Of course, all other things are not equal, and it is unlikely that much of this grain would find its way to some of the hungriest parts of sub-Saharan Africa, which now lacks reliable infrastructure and imports only a small portion of its food.[10] Still, we can expect this calculus to change as Africa develops, infrastructure improves, economic globalization intensifies, and population increases. Thus, caring more for non-human life, through eating less of it, can make it easier to feed people. Insofar as well-fed people are more likely to feel secure, they are less likely to feel a need to have large numbers of children. They are also less likely to open up rainforests for cultivation.

The land that is required to sustain a meat-based diet is simply stunning. Looking beyond the United States to the planet as a whole, about a third of all arable land is devoted to growing food for livestock. And these same livestock require an additional quarter or so of the earth's ice-free surface area for grazing.[11] This helps explain why the Brazilians are destroying their rainforests. According to the United Nations Framework Convention on Climate Change, subsistence farming is responsible for 48 percent, and commercial farming 32 percent, of deforestation respectively.[12] But while rainforests may often be cut down initially to provide land for agriculture, over 90 percent of the Amazonian lands that have been deforested since 1971 are now used for livestock pasture.[13,14] This deforestation has caused the extinction of tens of thousands of species, and according to the Intergovernmental Panel on Climate Change, it may be responsible for up to a third of the carbon dioxide emitted by human activity. Thus, the land being used here for the exploitation of one set of animals causes the extinction of others and threatens humanity.

But these are numbers in the abstract; somehow, we need to be made to feel, and not just for this or that local concern. It is not unusual for love to inspire care. Insofar as it drives mothers to protect their young, it steers the course of evolution. Insofar as it binds whole peoples together, it impacts the fate of nations. Consider the institution of marriage. Perhaps it is possible to forge a harmonious marriage that is loveless. We often hear of such marriages in pre-industrial societies. But even there the harmony of marriage does not tend to be loveless but rather based on a love that grows over time. If love is not there in the beginning, it emerges, not always, but often enough, as people who were once strangers come to experience themselves as intimately bound to a shared fate. Perhaps they could sustain a loveless marriage, but this would be meaningless. Love makes partners want to understand; it makes them want the marriage to work; it makes a working marriage a thing of beauty; and that sense of beauty lends meaning to partners' lives. Love makes marriage easier, and it makes it better. Trying to make a marriage work without love is like trying to make a life without purpose. One can do it, but why? Strong feeling can be a powerful motivator. Sometimes it is the only motivator that works. Often it is the only motivator that holds meaning.

Sustainable living is similar. We can live sustainably without loving all life, but since sustainable living is intimately tied to the respect and care for nature, loving all life is a more direct path to sustainability. We can treat the destruction of rain forests, the depletion of oceans, climate change, species loss, and desertification as unrelated problems, each calling for a dissimilar response, with each response calibrated to reduce harm to humanity. We can even treat the problems as interrelated, with the destruction of rain forests contributing to the loss of species and the loss of species contributing to desertification, and all of it contributing to and exacerbated by climate change, while all the while concerning ourselves only with humanity, and not an iota for nature. But if our only concern is with humanity, each environmental challenge will demand a different ethical injunction, calculated to handle a different problem. And as environmental impacts multiply, the number of injunctions will increase exponentially. We are told not to eat this, not to drive that, not to buy this kind of product, not to use that kind of bag. Since we impact the environment through almost everything we do, all of our actions come to be restricted, making of environmentalism a sort of postmodern Puritanism. In the end, we are left with a politically-correct laundry list. And perhaps there is no avoiding this list. Yet some ways of arriving at the list are better than others.

Loving all life is a thing of beauty that is itself meaningful. It needs no further end, and for that reason, it is not experienced as a burden. In this way it is like a marriage of love. Loving all life heightens sensitivity and frees us from petty cravings. It opens our hearts and connects us to every living thing. It constantly reminds us of what is truly important by opening our eyes to the inherent value of what otherwise appears mere background noise. In this way, loving all life develops our sensitivity to all things. It challenges us to be aware of more, to tend to more, and to increase our care. Through loving all life we come, paradoxically, to be more human, better able to empathize and to feel. And through being more human we become better people, better able to share, to care and to take responsibility.

Loving all life develops in us a disposition of sensitivity.[15] We come to recognize through our love that we are always and already inflicting harm: on the insects we trample, the food we eat, the animals we evict, the species we annihilate. If we are committed to loving this multitude, then our sensitivity will almost certainly grow. We will want to minimize harm. And in the process of minimizing harm, we will tend to reduce our ecological footprints: eat lower on the food chain, live in smaller spaces, use more renewable resources, and burn less fossil fuel.[16]

At least that is what we tend to do when we love all life. There are many who love all life and yet view the world through a mystical and cosmic lens. For them the universe itself is life, thus nothing within it can be created or destroyed. Having attained this realization, every tiny part of the universe is equally sacred. And from this viewpoint, it can appear as if there is little reason to protect the life of our planet.

To speak of loving all life is to invite this response. But there will be few who go to such extremes and fewer still who develop such a view and yet fail to develop for specific forms of life an increasing sense of care. The mystical response simply requires too much attention and discipline. And whatever some mystics may say about the consequences of their actions being unimportant, they nevertheless tend to live the most austere lives and inspire in others a corresponding simplicity. Others may develop a love for all life and yet fail to comprehend the impact of their actions. Environmental impacts tend to be subtle and their comprehension requires thought. Without giving thought to environmental problems, we will fail to develop solutions. Thus, loving all life does not eliminate the laundry list of environmental ethics; it simply integrates the profusion under one injunction.

Loving all life is an elegant solution to a complex set of ethical injunctions. It integrates multiple injunctions into one. It is easier to feel into a single injunction, discovering over time its deeper implications, achieving over time its highest fruits. Ours is an era replete with stresses, too much to know, too much to do, too much to feel, and much too much that calls for commitment. But love is something into which we can relax. It has a tendency to soothe the savage breast. It is a healing balm, it is a salve, and it eases our worried minds; thus, it tends to minimize stress. In this way, love is something to which we tend to be drawn. When it is a love that arises from within, and is not contingent on the feelings of another, love deepens our equanimity, our sense of contentment with anything that might arise. And it feeds on its own experience. Love inspires more love, in oneself and in others, and thus love tends to spread, leaving in its wake waves of influence. The leader with love in his heart, the Nelson Mandela or Vaclav Havel, draws the largest crowds. Love runs deeper and stronger than mere injunctions. And it forgives us our transgressions. An endless series of restrictions will tend to be endlessly broken, thereby invoking perpetual guilt. But love is a feeling to which we aspire. It is the roadhouse that is never empty.

There are deeper problems still with the attempt to follow a broad set of loveless strictures. When moral injunctions are many, we tend to seize on particulars. We focus on some single commandment or else fixate on a particular action. God ceases to be the God of love, becoming instead the one who hates gay people. Environmentalism ceases to be a global concern, becoming instead an ethic that culminates in the purchase of locally grown food. The human mind has a strong tendency to fixate. We zero-in on some particular concern, laud it above all others, perfect its practice, and ignore the rest. We make of our commitments fetishes, irrational objects of sexualized pursuit, channeling all of our drives into one, as if that one were the sine qua non. And in reaching too far we tend to lose balance. We forget to ask whether the whole world could now live on locally grown food; forget that when people lack food they tend to overpopulate, forget that the amount of fuel used in transporting and growing food is but a minuscule portion of all fuel consumed. We forget, in short, what is most essential. And we forget because we are overly focused, and we are overly focused because we lack an abiding principle. It is not love that makes us do the irrational but rather a lack thereof.

Loving all life will not remind us of these things. It will not dictate that we need to give money to help the hungry or minimize our consumption of meat so as to reduce the amount of global acreage devoted to agriculture and the suffering of farm animals. But loving all life will guide our thinking in this direction, challenging us to consider these moral concerns. Loving all life challenges us to place our commitments under one broad heading. It provides us a reference point whose arms are wide. A single principle can hold an inherent defense against haphazard fixation. It can continually remind us of what matters. And it can serve as a reminder to others of why we do the things we do. Thus, it is an inspiration in an often-brutal world. And it is just such an inspiration that might best deepen our global consciousness. The value of such a love does not negate the value of some of the solutions which have come before in the book. Rather it draws them together under one impulse that is easier to sustain. The love for all life is the compliment to and culmination of a wide array of solutions to the challenges we have thus far confronted. In the coming chapters we will explore this love within the context of organized religion, inquiring into the institutional forces that are further drawing us together into one world.

SECTION 6

GLOBALIZATION OF SPIRITUALITY

EVOLUTION OF GOD

Almost a millennium before Christ, and over the period of seven or eight hundred years, a score of religious and philosophical teachers rose up in the world's most advanced civilizations to lay down a new moral foundation for religious life. They appeared in Palestine, China, Greece, and India, and their names are still fresh: Lao Tzu, Confucius, Buddha, Socrates, Plato, Aristotle, Mahavira, Jesus, and Krishna. They were the descendants of the Greek Homer and Hesiod and Jewish prophets like Elijah, Isaiah, and Jeremiah. They were the predecessors to Jesus, who left his mark a couple hundred years after the last of them passed. Their teachings lie at the foundations of whole civilizations, and the orders they created persevere to this day.[1,2]

Historians call this the axial age.[3] It was a time of flux. For the Chinese, it was the period of warring states, an interval between empires in which scores of tiny kingdoms struggled for mastery, bringing ruin in their wake. For the Jews, it was a time of transition, in which the elite were exiled to Babylon and the civilization they built was marginalized on the world stage. Meanwhile, the Athenian empire was at its height, with cracks appearing in the foundation, as the Macedonians were growing in fortitude and the Romans steadily advanced across the Mediterranean.

The independent emergence of so many great spiritual traditions in such a short span of time is mysterious. Yet, they did not appear in a vacuum. The teachings of Jesus synthesized Judaic monotheism and Greek universalism.[4] The fluid Taoism of Lao Tzu was a response to the formalism of Confucius. And the Middle Way of Buddha both developed from and challenged the teachings of the Hindu

Upanishads.[5] Such cross-fertilizations only partially explain the auspicious appearance of so many teachers, with such similar messages, in so many disparate places simultaneously. A look at social conditions takes us closer to an explanation.

The chaos of the Axial Age preceded the emergence of several powerful empires: the Macedonian Greeks in the Near East and Central Asia, the Romans in the Mediterranean, the Han in China, and the Mauryans in South Asia. These vast empires provided the peace and stability needed for ideas to be disseminated. Variations of the Golden Rule were developed by almost all of the axial age spiritual teachers, and the Golden Rule would prove particularly useful for encouraging disparate ethnic and religious groups to live together harmoniously. This must have made Axial Age religions a convenient tool for emperors wishing to harmonize their domains. The need must have been particularly acute in the cities of these great civilizations where swelling numbers often threatened unrest. This was a time of great change, which strained social bonds.

In their universal appeal, Axial Age teachings resolved some of the glaring contradictions of the religions that preceded them. The infighting amongst Olympian Gods, the genocidal ethnocentrism of the Hebrew Yahweh, and the caste system of Hindu India were in many ways morally repulsive. The reasonable inquiry of Socrates, the love of Jesus, and the pragmatism of Buddha must have relieved some of the strain in these previous systems.[6] The written word was also growing in importance for educated elites at this time. Founding texts like the Torah, the Bhagavad-Gita, and the Republic served to anchor attention. Meanwhile, the texts facilitated the consolidation and spread of teachings. They could move from location to location without being altered. And once written, they could be expanded upon through subtexts and exegeses. Whatever the root reasons for the rise of Axial Age teachings, there were a multitude of forces that co-conspired in their spread. And as the Axial Age teachings circulated, they evolved along with the idea of God.[7]

Were the ancient God of the Hebrews a world leader in the twenty-first century, the International Criminal Court would indict him for genocide. But the God of the Torah, who commanded his foot soldiers to kill every, man, woman, child, and living thing in town after town, grew up over the centuries. He began His career egocentric, ethnocentric, and murderous, like some Latin American revolutionary, making enemies of those in the way and punishing followers for their lack of allegiance. Since the Torah drew upon many sources, to say that God was transformed is really to say that those writing about Him changed – or at least they compiled a different set of writings about God.[8] As ancient Israel grew into a great civilization, with kings and priests, merchants and scribes, it grew more populous, more sophisticated, more educated, and more diverse. Trade and conflict brought the Hebrews into contact with countless other peoples: the Phoenicians, Samaritans, Greeks, Persians, Abyssinians, and Romans. And this exposure challenged them to tell their stories to new audiences in new ways, for they had to think of how their stories might be seen through the eyes of others. Yet, the Jews were a small fish, and the larger Roman shark swallowed them up. The faith that at first sustained a tiny band of vulnerable nomads was then thrust into a wider world. Amidst the splendor of Rome and the philosophy of the Greeks, the egocentric and ethnocentric God of the Hebrews, and the religion He commanded, began for many to feel cramped and arbitrary.[9]

Religions tend to be unusually good at bringing people together. A shared religion can unite people through rituals, beliefs, and spiritual experiences. Shared music and dance synchronize behaviors, bringing groups of people into alignment with one another.[10] Shared rituals bring people together around pivotal life transitions. Shared beliefs orient people around fundamental assumptions concerning the nature and purpose of human existence. And shared spiritual experiences tie them together through a sense of interconnectedness. Spiritual experiences tend to open hearts, and they can feel very good. So when a group of people share these experiences, they tend to connect deeply and come away satisfied. A religion must be able to unite vast numbers of people, but it must also be able to bind them together across space and time. While an exclusivist God might best sustain a small tribe living in a tough neighborhood, a more inclusive God can forge a civilization. This requires tolerance and inclusion. As religions compete for followers, the more inclusive religions will tend to gain more followers, if for no other reason than the fact that they will have a larger pool of potential followers from which to draw. So when we speak of the evolution of God, we are not just speaking of a fundamental religious concept but also of a social organizing mechanism.[11]

The God of the Hebrews opened His heart and opened His mind, so to speak. Through Jesus, God gave to the poor and the marginalized. And while the actual Jesus may not have spoken much about universal love, Christianity grew from a small band into a great movement, and the Jesus that is passed down to us in the scriptures became the God of love. After Jesus, Paul laid the foundations for a universal church, open to Jew and Gentile alike. The Church eventually built upon the decaying spasms of Roman greatness. As the western portion of the Roman Empire fell, the Catholic Church remained, eventually taking on much the same structure as Imperial Rome. Meanwhile, in the east, the Church became integral to the Byzantine Empire, where citizens continued to call themselves Romans for the next thousand years.

God continued to grow more substanceless and universal with the advent of Islam. The God of the Qur'an is like some force of nature, too vast and elusive to comprehend, too powerful for any relationship than one of complete surrender. Allah is characterized through ninety-nine names: the Creator, the Merciful, the Almighty, the Grateful, the Sublime, the Watchful, the Vast, the Wise, etc. The names go on, an array of contradictions, paradoxes, and imponderables. This was not just the God of the prophets and the mystics, but of ordinary Muslims. The God of Islam can be wrathful and he can be forgiving; this variety of faces allowed early Muslims to use God to justify Holy

Wars and to build a multi-faith empire. Perhaps most importantly, the God of Islam commanded Muslims to respect people of other religious faiths, at least most of them, most of the time.[12] While Muhammad claimed to be the final prophet of God, and Islam the last of the great Abrahamic faiths, God nevertheless continued to evolve over the centuries.

By the late Middle-Ages, mystics like Meister Eckhart, St. John of the Cross, Rumi, and Hafiz saw in God the beautiful and harmonious face of the infinite. For Catholic mystics, Muslim Sufis, and Jewish Kabbalists alike, God is vast and imponderable, yet somehow tender and personal – and not just in some abstract sense. We can feel the presence of this God in their love poetry and in the descriptions of their realizations. The God of the mystics is sometimes lover, sometimes friend, sometimes father, and sometimes son. This intimacy with God was in some ways a response to the aridity of medieval theologians and philosophers, the Islamic Averroes and Avicenna, the Christian Aquinas and Abelard, and the Jewish Maimonides. These thinkers sought to explicate God's nature – omniscient, omnipotent, omnibenevolent – and in the process, God ceased to feel an omnipresent part of everyday life.[13] Some of the shift to mysticism can probably be attributed to the growth of Catholic monastic orders like the Dominicans and Franciscans. Whatever the reasons, God continued to evolve. It was as if through the whole medieval period, God was struggling to somehow encompass more, and yet coming up short, either too abstract or too intimate.

With the dawn of the Enlightenment, God became the universe itself. For Deists like Thomas Jefferson, God merely laid down the laws or conditions according to which the universe operated, like some well-oiled machine. For Spinoza, God was pantheistic, natural, immanent in all things, and yet also transcendant.[14] For Hegel, God was the world itself, evolving in self-awareness through humanity.[15,16] Each advance in human knowledge seemed to bring an advance in God's self-knowledge. God eventually became like some great eye rising up from out of the world to look down upon Itself. For Teilard de Chardin, and in our own time Thomas Berry, this view became scientific and ecological.[17,18] God here is a concrete, well-studied, and evolving universe.

God's evolution from one monotheistic faith to the next is debatable. It is always easy to impose a developmental frame where none exists. The God of the prophets was certainly less ethnocentric than the one that led Moses out of Egypt. And the God of Jesus was more loving and abstract than the God of the prophets.[19,20,21] But whether or not God continued to develop, in the sense of becoming more inclusive, is an open question. Was the awe-inspiring and incomprehensible God of Mohammed an improvement over Jesus' God of love? Or was this a development in complexity with no qualitative increase in goodness? And how about the immanent God of Spinoza, so subject to rational explication and yet so lacking in inspiration? With each "advance" something seems to be lost, as if God is testing random mutations. What is clear is that the meaning of God was transformed, and each change made God in some way more universal than the last instantiation. It is also clear that this more universal God became more and more accessible over time, first to the prophets and later to all believers, first to the mystic few and then to the educated in general. Finally, God seemed to be transformed in each instance to something more appropriate to the times.

As new teachers and prophets and mystics appeared, they reinterpreted the meaning of ancient scriptures, addressing counter-arguments, integrating criticisms. We find this in the Catholic Church where a body of scriptural interpretations is built up from St. Augustine to St. Thomas Aquinas to the recently deceased Pope Benedict XVI. Here each interpretation builds on the others like some universal body of law.[22] In Islam, Sharia Law, is developed over one and a half millennia. Each reinterpretation subsumes those that came before, so that multiple meanings are built into an ever-evolving dogma, often rigid, often limiting, but also inclusive of previous interpretations.[23,24] We find something similar in Judaism, where scriptural exegesis grows into commentaries on commentaries, with each interpretation deepening the nuances and the meanings of some original passage in the Torah. But in the case of Judaism, none of the meanings is conclusive. Instead, there is a wide embrace of paradox. This sense of paradox may imbue the Jewish sense of humor with irony, the Jewish quest for learning with passion, and the Jewish sense of self with complexity. There are many reasons for God's perpetual conversion. The God of the ancient Hebrews was a God of contradictions, sometimes loving, sometimes genocidal, vast and incomprehensible, yet bigoted and egocentric. The teachings of the Old Testament were not self-evident. They required interpretation and reasoned consideration. And to understand them, it was best that they be read. Over the centuries, this made Judaism a progressive faith of thinkers and debaters. The arguments amongst Jewish thinkers led to multiple interpretations and schools of thought.[25] And the debate continued through Christianity, Islam, and more recently Mormonism.

As humanity develops, our sense of ultimate causes also evolve.[26] From agricultural to industrial to information age culture, civilization grows more complex. There are more occupations, more organizations, more words, more artifacts, more information, and more independent centers of power today than at any time in history.[27] More individuals, more cultures, and more economies are knit ever more tightly together. In this way, the complexity of the world is integrated and its pieces are tied tighter together in wider webs of interconnection. If our ideas of God have anything to do with our experience of the world, if those ideas are in any way based on the ability to think abstractly, if those ideas have anything to do with what we know of the way the world functions, then our ideas of God must evolve with our civilization. And as our civilization becomes vastly more complex than that of the early Hebrews, Christians, or Muslims, God too must be transformed.[28]

The God of a globally conscious world must be universal, able to transcend and include the great conflicts of the new millennium, to account for the well-established postulates of modern science, to inspire in humanity a greater sense of harmony and union, to account for our increasingly intimate impact on future generations, and to offer hope to an increasingly globalized humanity. Perhaps the new God will be immanent, from the Latin "to remain within," inside ourselves and inside the earth. Or maybe God will come cloaked in more ethereal garb, transcending our differences through the heightened abstractions of a Plotinus, Aquinas, Philo, or Maimonides. And maybe we will experience the reemergence of the same God who appeared in ancient times, only this time through new prophets, with widening circles of ethical concern and with new practices through which to achieve the good life. That our ideas of God are growing and changing with the scope of our conceptions of the world may be debatable. One can always counter with this or that fundamentalist sect. The mandate for change is less debatable. While the ethnocentrism of an atavistic and ancient God may still speak to some, if religion is to be relevant, it must become more universal.

THE GREAT RECONFIGURATION

Our century is probably more religious than any other.
How could it fail to be, with such problems to be solved?
The only problem is it has not yet found a God it can adore.
PIERRE TEILARD DE CHARDIN, THEOLOGIAN

After the western half of the Roman Empire fell to barbarian invaders, the Catholic Church slowly began to take on the pretenses of Rome. Ranks within the Church hierarchy were modeled off of the Roman military. And while Rome would remain the center of power in Europe, it was the Rome of the Church, not that of the Empire. Of course, some of this pretense was simply using the name of the Roman Empire in the same way oil companies flout the word "sustainable." The Church was not the only group to trade on the good name of Rome. Thus, Voltaire could quip much later in the eighteenth century that the loose assemblage of territories originally brought together under Charlemagne in 800 C.E., and assembled under the moniker of the Holy Roman Empire, was neither Holy, nor Roman, nor an Empire. But the Roman Catholic Church carried the mantel of Roman authority because it did so much to sustain what was previously known as Roman civilization. Christianity lent to Europe a common culture of rituals and beliefs, the common language of Latin, and a source of authority that might mediate disputes amongst rival powers. It preserved Roman civilization through learned monks and the integration of classical philosophy into Christian theology. And it was able to do this through the binding power of religion.

When states fall, their core religious institutions will often remain viable, thus binding their citizens to wider civilizations.[1] As barbarian invaders entered China from the steppes of Asia, they repeatedly found themselves governing a great civilization, a task for which they were seldom prepared. But the Confucian bureaucracy, with its finely reasoned system of ethics, its meritocratic exams, and its well-trained officials, was ready at hand. Even as Confucian officials resisted alien rule, sometimes militantly, they sustained Chinese civilization through their maintenance of state institutions and norms. Confucianism thus sustained Chinese civilization as barbarian dynasties rose and fell.[2,3] And so it goes with each of the world's great religions, whether we look to Islam, Buddhism, Christianity, or Judaism. Each has held together a people as the states of which those people were a part came and went.

Religions seem to shape our identities more than do states because they are able to affect us so much more deeply. This was touched upon briefly in the preceding chapter. Spiritual experiences, embodied in ritualized life transitions, bind us together through their power and symbolism. In the most powerful spiritual experiences, the world of discreet objects, along with one's sense of self, tends to melt, and inside and outside, self and other, are experienced as one great whirling ocean. Returning from this experience to everyday consciousness, there tends to be a greater sense of connection and purpose.[4] But less powerful experiences can also be transformational. To surrender into union with others in music or prayer, or to contemplate the deeper purpose animating our lives, can put wind in our sails and make our lives more full. The people with whom we share these momentous occasions come to appear the people who matter most in our lives. Religious rituals also indoctrinate us into a shared set of values and beliefs. They organize communities through shared services and community activities.

But on a deeper level, religion integrates non-conventional consciousness. Peter Berger draws a distinction in his now classic *Sacred Canopy* between the sort of everyday waking experience through which we conduct our day-to-day affairs and the more extraordinary experiences of birth and death, dreaming and social displacement. He points out that these abnormal experiences are quite common; they are the joints around which self and society may be unhinged if they are not somehow integrated. According to Berger, these states are a problem for which religion is the solution.[5] Religion integrates our personal lives into the wider social body by weaving our most unconventional experiences back into a shared system of values and meaning.

Perhaps it is for this reason that whenever peoples have been thrown together, through war, migration, travel, or trade, religions have tended to arise, or else reassert themselves, to provide a shared sense of identity and meaning.[6] This process tends to be conditioned from above, for state authorities can govern more easily when the people they seek to govern share a common identity. But it is also often stimulated from below, since people who are alienated from themselves and from one another tend to crave the binding force of shared religious ritual and experience.[7] We can see the process at work in the rise of the mega-churches in the more homogeneous suburbs of America. As the suburbs grew in size, and neighborhood churches could no longer meet the needs and interests of a rising generation, the members of which often came from distant cities and states, mega-churches grew up, providing a safe place for singles to meet and for families to share in a sense of community.[8] The binding power of religion need not be dramatic.

Religion has laid the grooves for many a civilization, providing a basis for peace and social harmony. It casts wide the net of group identity to include rival polities and societies, deepening the bonds of empathy, and strengthening cooperative institutions.[9] And like little else, religion orients the gaze toward the totality of all things, apportioning attention and shaping worldviews, so that out of shared worship a common civilization might emerge. But as civilization itself grows more globally interconnected, the great religions of the world must increasingly speak to a world civilization.[10] And since shared religious traditions have often laid at the foundations of great civilizations, the world's great religions have come less to pull people together and more and more to push people apart. The civilizations Samuel Huntington wrote of in his now classic *Clash of Civilizations* were almost always knit together by a shared religious tradition.[11] But the problem with knitting together civilizations with religion is that it is a recipe for just such a clash of civilizations. The world's great religions now, all too often, divide an increasingly cosmopolitan humanity.[12]

Ours is a time of great change. Human population has grown from less than two billion a hundred years ago to over seven billion today. This massive population growth has made of us an increasingly urbanized species. As we are cramped ever-more tightly together, we are simultaneously confronted by an array of global challenges. We are now more than ever caught up in the lives of people living in distant places. Hence, we tend to feel more and more as if we are all in it together. Humanity feels closer to us both physically and causally. Perhaps people felt something similar in the Axial Age, as population grew and new empires rose in power. Insofar as cities have been hubs of trade, they have always brought together a wide array of peoples. But the urbanization of today is different. Cheap air travel brings people together from farther afield, while increased trade is leading to the emergence of a shared set of global norms. It is not so unusual to relate to someone from halfway across the world on casual and familiar terms in a way that would have been virtually unheard of a century ago. While such interactions have been rare throughout history, today they are a commonplace. All of this is merely a reminder of several now well trodden themes of the book. But the major religions have ceased to bind people together in such a way as to spur the kind of cooperation that matters most.[13],[14] All too often they do just the opposite.

The ground is moving under our feet. While we may cling to some religious foundation that once lay at the basis of our shared identities, the foundations seem to be cracking apart.[15] One of the great achievements of the twentieth century was the fostering of universal literacy in the developed world. And literacy rates continue to increase, not just in the developed, or even the developing world, but also in failed and failing states.[16] A higher proportion of humanity than ever before is literate and college educated. This learning makes it easier to scrutinize the values, norms, rules, and creeds into which we have been conditioned. Not only knowledge but literacy itself is power. Education has a way of turning power structures upside down, for it shows us that things might be otherwise, and that is a difference that makes all the difference.

As we have seen in previous chapters, the growth in what we know springs not just from literary but also from technological sources. Through the Internet we are exposed to groups about whose existence we would otherwise be unaware. The barriers to entering new groups are lowered along with the barriers to leaving our own: easy in, easy out. Meanwhile, the groups with whom we are closest are now more often exposed for their transgressions. Just yesterday, the Mormons appeared to be the rising religious faith in America. But as devout Mormons check the claims of church elders against information they find on the web, they are discovering their founder to be a polygamist and likely charlatan. And for many, their faith is slipping away. Something similar is happening in mainline Protestant sects. As their ministers and parishioners both are exposed to more of the non-canonical Christian texts, along with the history of early Christian movements, their whole conception of Christianity is being shaken to the core. But while many mainline Protestants are losing their faith, at least as many seem to be broadening their notions of what it means to be a Christian.[17,18,19] Such revelations could be multiplied across sects the world over.[20] And while they make it ever more difficult to establish religious authorities that are immune to question, there is little uniformity in the response to this challenge.

Science also continues to gain ground in its several hundred year battle with religion that began with the dawn of modernity and is still not complete. The long march of modernity has, in the words of Max Weber, been a deepening process of disenchantment. The Medieval world was an enchanted place, in which fairies inhabited the forests, long dead ancestors appeared present to the living, the human social order appeared consecrated by God, and every thing had its place in a self-referencing system of spiritual correspondences.[21] Since that time, science has stripped the world of one illusion after another, and in the process dissociated mind from body, humans from nature, nature from culture, and self from other.[22] The process can be said to have began with the recognition that the earth does not lay at the center of the universe, it grew with the recognition that humanity evolved from the lower orders of life,[23] and it continues as we learn increasingly more about the biological roots of human behavior. Neuroscience, genetics, primatology, and evolutionary psychology are converging on a set of shared beliefs concerning human nature. As more and more of human behavior can be explained biologically, even humanistic theologians and spiritual thinkers are being sidelined in favor of an increasingly biological story of humankind. The founder of evolutionary psychology, E.O. Wilson, believes the interlocking system of mutually re-affirmed truth that has long been characteristic of the natural sciences is gradually spreading through the social sciences and humanities as more and more of human behavior is being explained biologically.[24] Hence, according to Wilson, we may find the social sciences and humanities arguing less over perennial truths in future years and instead using biological research to advance a more certain knowledge of humanity. Whether or not such an advance of science is for the better remains to be seen.

Religion used to provide a gateway to the good, the true, and the beautiful. But over the course of the modern era, science came to dominate discussions of what is true, secular art came to address the human need for beauty, and religion was left with the rump of morality.[25] Now religious thinkers and philosophers alike are challenged to integrate a wealth of new research on the biological origins of ethics. While a biological account of morality may give no guidance on the great moral questions of the day, it can nevertheless go far in setting the parameters of moral discussion.[26] But as some reject a religiosity that fails to provide believable answers to the great questions of life, others seek solid ground in whatever fundamentalism is most ready at hand. Islamic radicals and Christian fundamentalist are in many ways two sides of the same coin. Both groups tend to be anti-liberal, both tend to interpret scripture literally, both are prone to violence, and both are wholly postmodern phenomena.[27] Christian apocalypticism and Islamic terrorism also share with Friedrich Nietzsche and many post-modernists a nihilistic disdain for the modern societies of which they are a part.[28] And both Christian fundamentalists and Islamic radicals alike share with the new atheists a tendency to place belief at the core of religion.[29] Prior to the modern era, religious thinkers tended to em-phasize the ways in which God is unknowable. The emphasis on liter-al interpretation so characteristic of fundamentalism today is in many ways a response to science's demand for black and white answers.[30]

The meaning of all of the trends is certainly difficult to descry. But we seem to be witnessing something like the long and drawn out end of a great war in which both sides try to grab as much territory as pos-sible just as the peace talks move toward closure. While the secular-ists may be beating back the fundamentalists this decade, last decade the fundamentalists seemed to be winning, and it is difficult to tell where it will end. But the ground that is being fought over appears increasingly sterile and denuded of life. Whether Islamic radicals, Christian fundamentalists, or the new atheists win more converts, none of them seems able to provide an answer to either the postmod-ern predicament or the great questions of life. Even as Christian and Islamic evangelism intensifies, the bottom is falling out from these and other religions. And even as science gains ground on religion, scientific writings are becoming increasingly imbued with religious implications as scientists speculate on the meaning of the universe, the origins of human consciousness, and the nature of morality.[31]

But the reason the bottom is falling out is precisely the same rea-son many are gravitating back to a new spirituality. Postmodernity has overturned most traditional sources of authority and this has left us seeking some deeper source of grounding.[32] When times are tough, even the tough minded seem to get religion. At the same time the rug is being pulled out from under religious authorities many of us are yearning for some sort of spiritual connection. Our lives have been upended and we are thus seeking a deeper foundation upon which to ground our lives. And it just so happens the yawning chasm into which the great religions of the world seem to be slipping is the same void from which religious realization arises.[33] This is a subtle point that could easily be washed over and is somewhat difficult to express.

The religious urge could be said to lie in the gaze into the dark unknowing void from which all questions and all meanings arise. We tend to seek religion, in other words, when we stare life in the face and realize we do not have the answers. God is in this sense not so much something we might attach characteristics to but rather the source from which all characteristics come into being.[34,35] Out of the void of our confusion, we come to see the universe and everything in it –our nations, our families, the value of justice, the importance of pleasure, the beauty of a sunset, everything we might see and feel and think, in short – in a new light. Hence, when our lives and worlds are shaken by the great earthquakes of the day, and the foundations upon which our lives are premised seem to tumble into some great void, we tend to turn toward religion. And in an era in which everything is up for question, and thus seems repeatedly to cast us into this void, it is not so much that we need to travel to it; rather everything seems to drag us down into it - whether we like it or not. Meanwhile, the same forces that have spread the knowledge that has done so much to smash the foundations of religiosity are also generating new religious memes and repackaging old practices.[36] What we are witnessing seems to be not the death of God but a great reconfiguration. If religion is being beaten, it is not being beaten to death. Rather it is being broken into its several components, beliefs and rituals, practices and experiences. What we are left with is a set of religious modules that many have come to mix and match.

Meanwhile, we long for and increasingly need something to unite all of humanity, not just the members of this or that sect. We need to unite humanity because we have practical global tasks that need to be accomplished like forging a global climate deal and stopping the spread of nuclear weapons. But we also need to unite humanity for our own personal sense of rootedness and security. The failure to attain global consciousness in a globalized world can leave us feeling misplaced and out of sorts. As we have seen, religion has often served as an antidote to this sort of experience. But the religion many of us are returning to is often not even recognized as such. What seems to be emerging is something far more pliable and universal. Like so many other aspects of order, a religious order that has been shattered is re-emerging at a higher level of integrated complexity, and that level is increasingly global in scope. And like so many other aspects of the emerging global order, it is difficult to discern the shape it might ultimately take.

THE SPIRITUAL RENAISSANCE

My religion is Kindness.
THE DALAI LAMA

I believe in God, not in a Catholic God.
There is no Catholic God, there is God...
POPE FRANCIS

We can get a sense of where the globalization of spirituality is heading if we imagine the process accelerated through some outside force. So here is a thought experiment that while extremely unlikely might nevertheless make vivid some of the issues that arise when religiosity is globalized. Let us say the heads of the world's great religions decide to join together to stave off an immanent world war that is years away but ever looming. They hold a conference where they agree to create a series of interfaith spiritual centers to promote mutual understanding and respect amongst the world's great faiths. After seeing some extraordinary initial results, the Clinton Initiative, the Gates Foundation, Mark Zuckerberg, and Carlos Slim all decide to dedicate a substantial portion of their fortunes to the project, thus inundating the venture with hundreds of billions of dollars. Following this influx of cash, the religious leaders agree to make the spiritual centers monuments to global civilization. For they are convinced that without some statement of the unity of humanity, the world risks nuclear holocaust.

Money then begins to pour in from billionaires and non-combatant states like Norway, Sweden, Venezuela, and Qatar, and the project soon accumulates over a trillion dollars. Each religion seeks to benefit from the fund, but they operate under a charter specifying interfaith action. So the leaders choose 100 global cities in which they will create not just interfaith monuments to global civilization, but centers of worship for each of the faiths. Each center would have the resources to rival the Vatican in splendor, but each would also bring all of the world's religions together in the same location. World leaders agree because of a groundswell of public support for the project. And still, the venture has hundreds of billions of dollars left to spend on an interfaith fund to end world hunger. Let us postulate one more condition of this thought experiment: let us assume the project is a success and that it is not sabotaged. Remember this is a thought experiment and not a prognostication.

Now let us flip forward in time to 2100 and imagine what might have changed about each of these faiths. The most obvious development is that so many major centers of worship are now all in extremely close proximity. Each faith is thus much more aware of what the others are doing. Liberal members of each faith are empowered with greater resources through which to carry out shared projects with the members of other faiths. It is now also easier to engage in joint social and political action, which we might therefore expect to happen more often. Since the number of supporters matters a great deal in the success of such projects, many projects that might otherwise flop now succeed by organizing across religions. Further, the adherents of these faiths have grown a little more tolerant, both because they are so exposed to one another but also because they see their leaders working more closely together. Further, some people have begun referring to the other faiths as something equivalent to denominations. They have begun to treat each other a little more like rival sects within the same faith, much as we are beginning to see amongst Protestants, Catholics, and Jews in America. Some new converts, along with the curious and more ecumenical, begin to occasionally sample other faiths. Formless spiritual practices like meditation and various devotional visualizations begin to be shared across traditions. More universal faiths like the Unitarian Universalists and Baha'is rise in prominence due to the salience of their message of world unity. Traditional faiths begin to downplay the more ethnocentric aspects of their traditions, which might lose them members, while playing up the more inclusive portions, which might gain adherents. And new faiths, whose message is tailored to the great global challenges of the day, begin to make an appearance.

Let us call this the "religious food court" in honor of my friend Avinash Raman to whom we owe thanks for this thought experiment. The idea is that globalization will eventually bring the world's great religions closer together. Members of each faith will thus be more exposed to members of other faiths, more likely to work together in joint projects for the common good, more likely to draw from a common pool of teachings and practices, and more likely to tolerate one another's differences. And when they are set side by side, we will begin to pick and choose amongst practices and faiths, making of religion a modularized smorgasbord of options, a global food court so to speak. Much of this is already occurring, and for all of the reasons cited above.

Fast forward half a millennium and it is quite possible that some sort of intermingling of all faiths will have occurred, something like the fusion of Hindu cults, each worshipping a different God or Goddess, in its own unique way, with its own special practices, as part of a commonly shared set of religious symbols and institutions. It is no accident an Indian inspired our thought experiment. Indians regularly choose amongst a variety of cults, constituting a smorgasbord of options. Numerous Indian religious founders have also built syncretic traditions, from the ruler Akbar the Great to Guru Nanak, founder of the Sikhs; from Swami Vivekananda, who brought yoga to the west to Gandhi, the Maharishi, and scores of other teachers.

But the thought experiment was not reality, and it set aside the very real impediments to a fusion of faiths. And it is with the intractable religious core of civilizations that we now must reckon. As we have seen, religions bind people together through harmonizing their most intimate experiences. Religions do this through answering the great questions of life, through propagating mutually referential myths and symbols, through ritualizing key passages in life, and through crafting codes of conduct.[1] Through a religion we gain access to the inner life of a community, and this binds people together socially. In so doing, religions help sustain societies over time; hence, their position at the foundation of civilizations.

The secularization process involves throwing off the burdens of membership in these religious communities. It frees people from the myths, the codes, the threats, and the rituals. Hence, Voltaire's rallying cry of the Enlightenment, "remember the cruelties." Religion has often been a cruel straightjacket from which secularization has brought liberation. This process of secularization, which can be traced at least as far back as the Renaissance, allowed individuals to work out their lives for themselves and to find their own answers to the meaning of existence. For this reason, secularization is often perceived as a threat to inter-communal existence, for as the individual is freed from the community, the community itself tends to become fragmented.[2] The community building and the social services once performed by communities of faith get taken up by civil society and government.[3] And the arts and sciences begin to answer the great questions of life. Thus, the great religious traditions, which were once so deeply involved in defining the purpose of humanity, are themselves left struggling to redefine their own purpose. They are turned in on themselves, not in contemplation of God, but rather of their own mortality.

Religion has not tended to go gently into that good night but has often raged, kicking and screaming, against the dying of the light. A common response has been to circle the wagons so to speak, to draw the boundaries between the sacred and the profane ever more tightly, and to reify religious dogma. Theologies and beliefs that were once held loosely have been brought center stage, while the notion of a God that is inscrutable has been largely abandoned in favor of more definite notions of divinity.[4] Strict interpretations of scriptures have increased the world over. Whether we look to the Taliban in Afghanistan and Pakistan, the American religious right, or the Hindu, Bharatiya Janata Party, this rearguard action has become imbued with a fighting spirit. But its enemies are many, and in a globalizing world in which the only hope for peace and the continued development of civilization seems to lie in more expansive notions of human identity, its days appear numbered.[5] The very fact that we can refer to this profusion of fundamentalisms as a single phenomenon is in fact indicative of the power of globalization. These local creeds must inevitably be swept up in the great tidal movement, which is forcing a reconfiguration of religions, creeds, and identities.

As some seek to hold back the tides, others are riding the waves with religious innovations. One of the more interesting responses to the global environmental crisis has been the rise of "dark green religions." More an array of inchoate tendencies than organized sects, dark green religions seek to bring back to religion a reverence for the earth and all of its life. This can involve anything from the adoption of neo-Pagan rituals to the worship of Gaia. Most such efforts involve the embrace of some sort of environmental ethic. And many of the practices and ethics taken up by the adherents of dark green religions are also being adopted by more liberal sects of the world's great religions. While the movement is small, it is growing. And the forces that have brought it into existence can only be expected to grow stronger with each passing decade. Today's experiments in dark green religion will almost certainly influence the shape of faith in the coming era.[6,7]

Universal faiths emphasize the unity of all religions and the principles that bind them together. And these are also on the rise. Insofar as they address the nature and meaning of life, all religions are in a sense universal. But some religions do a better job than others of addressing their own contingency and of respecting other creeds. The Baha'is are a quintessential example. The religion grew from the teachings of Baha'u'llah in Persia in the mid-nineteenth century, and it focuses on the multiple pathways to God. Originally a Muslim heresy with cultish tendencies, the religion has spread throughout the world. Baha'ism emphasizes world peace, gender equality, and a respect for all faiths. Though there are only about 5 million Baha'is, the religion is in fact the second most widespread in the world.[8] The Unitarian Universalists are similar to the Baha'is in both their respect for all faiths and in their global orientation. While the numbers involved in these sects may be minuscule, their impact may be quite significant, for they have raised the bar for every other religion. Every time a fundamentalist preacher declares his own creed the only legitimate one, the public tends to dimly weigh his words against the tenets of these more universalistic teachers and traditions.

Both dark green religions and universal faiths tend to lack what I have come to call a religion trap. Any hunter who lays his traps only for the fastest, the strongest, and the most capable will tend to go hungry. For the best laid traps are easy to enter and difficult to leave - like the Hotel California or Facebook. Christianity and Islam are similar. They require little work to enter, a simple ceremony and the repetition of a few phrases respectively. But if you leave Christianity, in theory at least, you go to hell. And while the Middle East abounds with non-practicing and unbelieving Muslims, according to some interpretations of the Qur'an apostate faces the threat of death. The result is a set of traps, which have resulted in the world's two largest religions. Few will choose the abstruse worship of Gaia, with its vast panoply of implied ecological commitments and little hold over the believer's soul, over the hypnotic magnetism of an old time religion trap. Survival is seldom easy for new sects of any variety. Most religions tend to grow over the course of hundreds of years, attracting their followers through the pull of political power and by drawing supporters from similar, declining creeds. But the fledgling sect must build institutions without the support of followers and somehow attract followers with little institutional support. Building institutional support takes financial resources, which newer creeds tend to lack. So they must inspire their followers to give more money than those of other more established sects if they are to gain a foothold. Yet, this emphasis on money can be highly corruptive, so new sects must not only raise more money, they must also preserve their purity as they become institutionalized. In short, there are many institutional impediments to the establishment of a religion and it can take some time before the beliefs that seem most suitable to the times become widely adopted.

But once one recognizes the merit of all religions, it is but a short step to the mixing and matching of spiritual doctrines and practices. Religion today is far more a hodge-podge of practices than we tend to think. It is not unusual for even an evangelical Christian, let alone a more open-minded Methodist, to practice a little yoga, read a little Rumi, and occasionally meditate to get to sleep. Hindus, Jews, and Western Buddhists, in particular, can be quite promiscuous with their practices, disregarding the boundaries between religions altogether. By seeking out the most effective spiritual practices, most suited to their own peculiar needs and tastes, and by studying the most moving teachings, legions of spiritual seekers are now redefining religion. A man attends a non-denominational Christian Church, practices yoga, and reads the Dalai Lama; a woman celebrates Jewish holidays with family, revels in popular science accounts of the creation, and firmly believes the earth to be a living being and all its creatures worthy of reverence. The combinations are endless and personal. While few go to extremes in their syncretism, there is a general trend toward mixing and matching religious practices.[9] That the causes of this trend will only grow with time can be comfortably forecast. As more of us are exposed to more practices and beliefs, whether we believe it right or wrong, good or ill, we are adopting those we like and discarding the rest. Unknowingly, and on the most intimate level, we are becoming religious cosmopolitans.

With a smorgasbord to choose from, and little to impede the sampling, people tend to taste test, trying a bit of this and a bit of that until something strikes their fancy. But most minds lack focus. Even for the diligent and focused, meditation is more often than not an exercise in patient daydreaming. Attempts to fuse practices tend to result in confusion. The mind tacks back and forth between one injunction and the next, resting briefly in tranquil concentration, only to spring to action once again with the thought that perhaps a visualization or a prayer would be better. In this way, the toolkit of practices can bewilder and confuse. Hence, many teachers are beginning to systematize the range of techniques, refining and classifying the menu.[10] The spontaneous testing of spiritual and therapeutic techniques, amongst individuals and within communities, has yielded, over the decades, a treasure trove of wisdom regarding the optimal application of therapeutic practices. While the test subjects have been individuals and groups in their natural settings, subject to all the placebo effects of religious hypnosis, there is nonetheless something scientific about the way they have gathered information. Through personal experimentation, word of mouth reports, popular writings, and scholarly analysis, the techniques have been cleansed of much of their dogma, stripped down to their bare essentials, and made accessible across cultures and creeds. One can easily discern at work here a sort of natural selection – or perhaps we should say in this case a supernatural selection.

There is a spiritual renaissance at work in all of this experimentation and it has been a long time in the making. The twentieth century witnessed the development and spread of a virtual arsenal of spiritual and therapeutic techniques. Mental therapies like psychoanalysis, psychiatry, hypnotherapy, and coaching; somatic therapies like Rolfing, Feldenkrais, and Chiropractic; energetic therapies like Reiki and Acupuncture: each grew to be everyday items in the standard lexicon of developed countries. Scores of contemplative practices, plucked from the mystical traditions of the world's great religions – endless variations on the themes of meditation, yoga, prayer, and chanting, as well as more exotic practices like pranayama and feng-shui – were planted in fertile new terrains where, like invasive species' with no natural predators, they grew and thrived. Each had its peculiar aim.

And all of them pointed the way to freedom from worldly inhibitions and attachments. Few Westerners had even heard of the vast majority of these practices at the beginning of the twentieth-century. Many of the practices were, in fact, still unborn at this time. But by the dawn of the twenty-first century, large swathes of the population were adepts and teachers.

Spiritual practices can involve meditation, prayer, chanting, and mantra. Most involve some systematic opening to inner experience. They deepen moment-to-moment awareness, broadening the scope of concern, clarifying intentions, and deepening compassion. When the mind settles, it is easier to maintain a comprehensive perspective. We tend to see further in space and time, and we are able to consider a wider array of concerns. Spiritual practice frees us from many of the anxious worries and nagging cravings occupying limited mental space. Released from the attachment to worldly conditions, the mind has far less with which to be concerned. A mind so unburdened can become placid and serene. The eyes literally see more; the ears hear more. Such a mind can become both piercing and global, and it is capable of discovering remarkably holistic patterns and solutions. After spiritual practice, as the mind refocuses, it tends to gravitate to deeper, more meaningful concerns. And a deep and wide field of concerns tends to shine a spotlight on the interstices between groups, the no man's land between conflicting armies and the society of nations that still has no name. It is for these reason that spiritual practitioners tend to be global thinkers.

It is now quite common for a person, over a lifetime of spiritual seeking, to acquire a toolbox of spiritual and therapeutic techniques that can be mixed and matched at will and activated by a wide array of doctrines. These techniques are often studied and explored in great depth, in a religious marketplace conducive to both niche specialization and the exploration of the unknown. The result is that spiritual practice is disembedded from religion in an unprecedented manner, and religion is personalized. Since this arsenal of techniques can be mixed and matched according to the needs and interests of the individual, the toolkit is easy to share with others. Like information on the Internet, spiritual practices now have a way of leaking into our lives. We are exposed to them through friends and movies, books and trainings. This rapid spread of spiritual memes increasingly lends to religious traditions a porousness that would have been unthinkable but a few short generations ago.

The process of mixing and matching spiritual and therapeutic techniques could be said to constitute the heart of the new secular religion of the Information Age. To some this will strain the definition of religion. But religion has long been notoriously difficult to define. The structure of religious institutions differs immensely across space and time. Confucianism and Stoicism were more worldly wise philosophies than religions, but they met the need for that special something the Abrahamic faiths met in other contexts. Polytheistic religions like Roman Paganism and Hinduism are in many ways just an array of cults, each with their own unique rituals, dedicated to their own peculiar Gods. To those participating in these cults, the notion of some wider religion of which their sect is an offshoot often makes little sense. But each of these traditions helped to bind people together in their concern for ultimate causes. In short, there are many new guises religion might assume in this new mode of production and the development of science only deepens the radical disruption of traditional religious pursuits.

Science has split the world open and placed it on display, and it has become like some great museum through which we might come to see and understand the inner workings of all that lies therein. We can now gaze into the vast night firmament and trace the arc of the universe, how it exploded into existence and continues to expand. We can depict what an ant feels as it searches for food and responds to pain. And we can give a reasonably accurate depiction of the inner working of the human brain: why we think in such convoluted patterns, feel such irrational passions, and band together in such devastating combinations. It is quite possible we will soon know why we have even come to be aware of a world at all, why this panoply of colors and sounds and sensations animates our awareness. As science has laid open the world for our viewing pleasure, the human mind has struggled to keep pace. The advance of the natural and social sciences has stretched the mind spatially to take in the whole of the world, temporally to include events stretching back to the beginning of time, and categorically to account for the inner lives of beings whose existence we were all but unaware of just a few short centuries ago. And as science has taken over many of the functions of myth, the universe has come to appear both more comprehensible and ever more astonishing.

Perhaps the most interesting religious development in our own time has been the emergence of a new story of the universe. Just a few decades ago, one could find histories of consciousness, of humanity, of human prehistory, of the evolution of species, of the geological formations of planet, and of the universe itself, but little about how it all fit together. But over the course of the last couple of decades, and increasingly with each passing year, these stories have begun to converge into one common tale of the origins of human consciousness. The story includes the origin of the universe, the formation of the earth, the emergence of life, the appearance of a biosphere, the evolution of life, and the tale of human history, all the way into the present. This narrative shows up in geology,[11,12] paleoclimatology,[13] paleontology,[14] biological anthropology,[15] evolutionary psychology,[16] big history,[17,18] philosophy,[19] and secular spirituality.[20] And it is remarkably similar from one discipline to the next. It is as if we have finally answered enough of the questions concerning human origins and the nature of the universe that we can finally relax and look at the big picture. And what has emerged is a new story of origins, which seems to assert itself from whichever direction we look.

What we are witnessing is more than just a great reconfiguration. Humanity is on the brink of a spiritual renaissance. New doctrines, new practices, and new religious communities are arising, piecemeal. While their ultimate shape may still yet remain indeterminate, we are nevertheless laying the foundations for a new religiosity. And that religiosity is more global in scope than ever before. It draws on practices from all over the world, from a universal secular story of humanity, and from a shared concern for shared global challenges. This religiosity pulls in adherents from each of the world's great faiths. And it is increasingly supported by the world's great religious leaders. This spiritual renaissance appears to be laying the inner foundations of a new global civilization.

SECTION 7

GLOBALIZATION OF CIVILIZATION

NEW WORLD LEADERS

Global leaders increasingly speak an interfaith language of basic morality. The Dalai Lama, Desmond Tutu, and Pope Francis each speak this common tongue. They have little choice. Global audiences are wide and almost always consist of a profusion of faiths. These audiences share a diversity of cultural norms, economic circumstances, and educational capacities. This places religious leaders in the same position as politicians in democracies, struggling to hold together broad coalitions of followers through consensual values and agreeable language. To do so, they must ground their appeals in universally recognizable terms, and this usually means getting back to the basics of morality.

Moral basics are reassuring in a complex and confusing world. They serve as simple heuristics, rules of thumb that can be called on for guidance, when we lack the ability to give attention to all of the options. The Golden Rule is one such principle: do unto others as you would have them do unto you. Kant's categorical imperative is another: to act as if the maxim of your action were to become a universal law.[1] Without such directives we might lose ourselves in a sea of possible courses of action, and we might forget the essential in the quest for the expedient. But we need more than just reminders. Moral principles will mean little if there is little will to carry them out. Leaders need to inspire goodness in their followers, and for this they must themselves possess goodwill.

Without some foundation of moral principles that is beyond reproach and that can provide a compass to guide us through the ocean of worldly engagements, we can easily lapse into moral relativism and withdrawal. It is for this reason the Dalai Lama or Pope Francis can so easily move the world weary and sophisticated with a simple message of kindness.[2,3] Such a message shines a light through the fog of information that permeates our social milieu. Leaders like these can ease tensions, open hearts, give hope, and foster reconciliation. Most importantly, like Muhammad, Buddha, or Confucius, they possess the power to unite people. But the unification we need today is not the establishment of ethnic and national identities, rather it is the consummation of a common humanity and the harmonization of global concord.

This return to moral basics is vital to the resolution of global conflicts. Religious leaders acting the part of peacemaker are challenged to make ethical appeals recognizable by the several parties to a conflict. To do otherwise would be to forfeit their position of spiritual authority, for in an international conflict, the authority of religious leaders rests precisely on their ability to remain above the fray. Religious leaders who can cut through the haze of moral confusion, speaking in universal terms, about concerns basic to each and every human being, are increasingly called on to lead. They are sought out by the media and the spiritually hungry alike for personal and political guidance. And they are sought not because they can tell us things we do not know, but rather because they can remind us of the most basic truths we are so prone to forget.

Consider the Israeli-Palestinian conflict. The Jewish Trotskyite, Isaac Deutscher, once compared the conflict between Israelis and Palestinians to the case of a man jumping from a burning building and landing on another. The Palestinians did not deserve to have the Jews land on their heads; but neither did the Jews deserve the Holocaust; and when the great bulk of them came to Palestine, they did so out of desperation.[4] This sort of sympathy for both parties to a conflict muddies the waters of moral lucidity, for the problem then becomes a case of right against right, and such cases are often the thorniest. But there are not just two sides to this conflict. The Israeli Labor and

Likud parties are not in agreement as to the nature of the problem and neither are the Palestinian parties of Hamas and Fatah. Nor is there agreement amongst Christian Arabs or Israeli Muslims, Lebanese Palestinians or West Bank Jews.[5,6,7] The parties to the conflict are multiple, and each of their views is a constantly shifting bulwark against the others. Moreover, the conflict itself is trans-generational, involving the legacy of imperialism, the centuries long decline of Muslim power, the birth of the Palestinian people, and the millennia long quest for a Jewish homeland.

This multiplication of viewpoints is symptomatic of any border zone. At the hinge of three continents, and often situated on the margins of empire, the eastern shoreline of the Mediterranean is a profusion of peoples. At one and the same time this region is home to the vanguard and the refuse of empires past: impoverished Christians who never made it home from the crusades, Arab subjects of the former Ottoman Empire, Jewish refugees from Europe, displaced Bedouins, stateless Palestinians.[8,9] The sheer multitude of displaced persons, disputed borders, and past conflicts complicates any resolution that might be based on principle alone.[10] Of course, there are a great number of principles that can be asserted with some measure of objectivity. Regardless of the conflict, and according to virtually every reputable ethical system the world over, intentionally killing civilians en masse constitutes an atrocity that is an indisputable moral wrong. The colonization of another people's internationally recognized and well-populated homeland is a form of national theft and is likewise wrong. So also is it wrong to confiscate a farm so as to imprison a family or village in an unviable territory, or to hate a person for their ethnic heritage. Such claims would be obvious to any disinterested party. But they regularly fail to penetrate the psychological armor of trans-generational trauma. Rather, the complexity and intensity of the problem has a tendency to transmutate principle into propaganda.

The complexity leaves us prone to moral paralysis. A human being cannot function like a bee, with its five eyes. When we see the world through too many vantage points, confusion abounds and we lose our bearings. This is a classic problem of the highly educated and the cosmopolitan alike, stretching back at least to the time of Socrates.[11] As the number of perspectives from which any problem might be viewed increases, moral reasoning is strained, for tiny shifts in perception generate ever-increasing moral imperatives. These exhaust attention and paralyze the moral musculature. We cannot act because we know not which way to turn; or rather we are challenged to move stridently in multiple competing directions simultaneously. The danger is that, in the face of increasing moral complexity, we trade our ethical commitment for pragmatic expedience, abandoning decency to the manipulations of power. Then not principles but rather Israeli soldiers and Iranian nukes come to determine the momentum of history. This danger is characteristic of ever more conflicts in the world today, for the clash of civilizations that is at least one face of globalization produces a profusion of lenses through which any given conflict might be viewed. The global increase in educational attainments compounds the complexity. Not only do we see more but we also see more deeply and with greater sophistication. It is no wonder so many people seek succor in the simple instructions of global spiritual leaders.

As the demand for moral guidance has increased, religious teachers have sprung up to fill the void. As mentioned previously, whereas religion once claimed authority over truth, goodness, and beauty, only the rump of that empire remains. The natural and social sciences have rightly claimed authority over truth, while the nature of beauty is now explicated through the arts. The borders are arbitrated through a broad social consensus, violated only by the occasional creationist takeover of some provincial school board. Questions of truth are entrusted to the academics; questions of beauty to the esthetes; and an ever-diminishing number questions of goodness are left to religion.[12] Fundamentalists even respect the borders, seldom attempting to formulate a new physics, a new school of literature, or a new theory of social organization. The resources are lacking, to be sure, but so is the will. Even the most volatile religious groups, like sophisticated corporations, focus on their strengths of morality and goodness, leaving the rest to academia and the entertainment industry.

The religious domain has been unraveling for centuries. Once it stretched across the mountains of learning – rhetoric and logic, physics and biology, politics and ethics – as well as the still waters of music and art and drama. But at the end of the day, religion has been left with the unthankful task of informing us of the nature of our moral obligations.[13] Toward that end, hordes of teachers and sects vie for attention amidst political advocates and moral philosophers. The better teachers simplify their message, adding to the wounds of the body politic not the heat of greater pressure but a cooling balm and a helping hand. By kindly reminding us of our moral commitments, religious teachers nudge us toward civility. Few of us possess the learning and social sophistication to truly comprehend the complexity of the Israeli-Palestinian conflict, and those who respond with principle alone, whether for right or wrong, all too often end up merely adding more fuel to the fire. But each of us is capable of responding to a plea for patience, kindness, and understanding.[14] And far from fueling conflicts, such feelings can give us pause and a chance to turn to the better half of our natures. Basic civility and personal sanity open a window of opportunity to many an international conflict.

Civility can no longer be practiced within one group to the exclusion of all others, for we are all now too interconnected. Such an exclusive civility would inevitably slight outside ethnic, national, and religious groups, who everywhere we look seem to be just around the corner. Hence, the kind of in-group civility that many of us grew up with now all too often appears uncivil. For a cultural practice to be courteous and polite today it must be multicultural and global, accounting for the wide spectrum of human need and interests that we find in the world today. But few of us have a sense of the needs of such a diversity of peoples, and it takes time to learn which behaviors are insulting and which respectful. What we need is a new set of global norms, but this is still in the making, and the rudimentary first steps toward such a construction will probably continue to appear shabbily tacked together for some time to come.

Yet global leaders, who are better travelled and thus often more cosmopolitan in outlook, might set the tone. Every time a group of priests, rabbis, and imams together condemn some act of terrorism or imperial overreach, they affirm not only our common morality but also our common humanity. Their statements marginalize religious fundamentalists and all of the conflict they are so prone to inspire. They also establish ground rules for decency. Whatever their intentions, when religious leaders speak in unison and appeal to our common humanity, they aid in the establishment of a global ethic. Since they are often more effective than political leaders in establishing ethical norms, their common voice has the spillover effect of promoting spiritual over secular authority. We listen to what they have to say because we believe that they see things which remain veiled to the rest of humanity. And the attention we pay such leaders concentrates our minds on the moral dimension of global concerns.

This moral dimension is often critical to the resolution of sticky global challenges like climate change, terrorism, and nuclear proliferation. Climate change cannot be stopped without a moral commitment. Since the primary contributors to climate change are not the nations most threatened by rising atmospheric temperatures, and the ones most threatened by warmer and more erratic weather patterns are not the greatest contributors, a solution that maximizes well being amongst nations will have to involve moral sacrifice on the part of those who emit the most CO_2.[15,16,17] Without that sacrifice, the nations most responsible for climate change will be the slowest to act, for they will be the least likely to suffer its impact.

But of course, it is not only nations for whom a moral commitment to reversing climate change is necessary. Nations do not live in McMansions, dine on beef, and drive SUVs. If such personal behaviors cannot be reversed, then neither can we slow the release of global warming pollution. The problem is that these habits do not just vanish when we recognize their harm and disincentivize their continuation, for habits like these are integral to our lives.[18] They are imbedded in our nervous systems and implicit in our visions of the good life. Reversing them calls for moral sacrifice. Switching to clean energy can minimize the sacrifice, but making the switch requires commitments, both personal and political. And these commitments in turn involve sacrifices of time and energy.[19]

We cannot wiggle our way out of sacrifice. This should be obvious. While we may continue to develop ever more energy efficient technologies and change the set of incentives and disincentives that encourage excessive consumption, doing so will take hard work. It will involve building businesses and changing laws. Thus, it is surprising how seldom the need for moral sacrifice is mentioned in discussions of climate change. When sacrifice is mentioned, it usually comes coupled with complaints about "hair-shirt" environmentalists. But if the environmentalists arguing for moral sacrifice have not done a very good job, it probably has something to do with the fact that they are scientists, activists, and economists, not professional moralists. Somehow representatives of the humanities have been sidelined in the climate debate,[20] and this has turned the discussion into one about numbers instead of morals.[21] It is one thing for your environmentalist son or your biology professor to ask you to minimize your driving and quite another to hear it from your preacher.

Religious leaders specialize in making practical moral arguments, and they have been granted the authority to do so by virtue of their positions. Whenever a preacher argues for a single moral sacrifice, she must contextualize her argument within a framework of all other moral sacrifices. While she might prejudice her pet cause, say the rights of fetuses or the importance of nonviolence, it is rare for a religious leader to ignore all other causes. Moreover, religious arguments for moral sacrifice tend to be framed in the interest of the listener. It is in the best interest of individuals to make moral sacrifices because those sacrifices are part and parcel of the good life. They are necessary to the maintenance of work and family life, and without them we could not live in harmony with our fellow humans. The unwillingness to sacrifice thrusts a man into the wilderness of social isolation and subjects his mind to the bark and bite of ceaseless cravings. Conversely, through sacrifice we learn to surrender and share our joy with others. And we free ourselves from the desires and aversions that block the way to peace of mind.

When preachers and imams make such arguments, they often integrate them into the foundational tenets of religious traditions stretching back centuries, if not millennia. The sustainability of traditions like Catholicism and Sunni Islam is indicative of reliability and functionality. Following their instructions is unlikely to leave a man financially destitute and social unfit. And this is easy to surmise, because any doctrine that regularly resulted in such anomie would quickly lose adherents and fade away. Participation in such lasting traditions grants preachers and rabbis permission to instruct. Once granted the authority to make moral pronouncements, religious teachers are free to advise changes of habits and the adoption of lifestyles, and unlike scientists and economists, this is part of their job.

Religious teachers are authorized to encourage virtues like empathy and tolerance, compassion and care, fairness and equity, giving and sharing, harmony and cooperation. One need say little about these qualities. We all know what it means to share and care, and when the reminder is applied to earthquake victims in Haiti or rape victims in the Congo, understanding can be immediately translated into action. Simple reminders regarding the virtues of harmony and cooperation can transform the debate on climate change and the Middle East peace. Simple reminders of goodness can transform the debate because they reorder our values. Upon hearing the voice of moral equanimity, petty stresses roll away, and we are reminded of the things that matter most. In such moments we lay ourselves open to a transformation of values. And it is just such a transformation that will be needed to mitigate the ever-growing list of global perils.

But simple moral teachings do something far more pivotal for global consciousness: they lay down the ethical prerequisites of a global civilization. While our access to others in distant places might be facilitated through developments in telecommunications; while they might be deepened through trade, simplified through empathy, and made intelligible through the development of a comprehensive viewpoint; while we might attain empathy through greater understanding and more spiritual practice, and while we might attain greater solidarity through more comprehensive ethical commitments; it is the guidance of great teachers, addressing our everyday needs, and the most basic wants of all peoples, that might lead us to the day to day work of building a global civilization. Global moral leadership cannot be neglected if we are to build a global civilization that works.

THE GLOBAL CONTRACT

The point of view of eternity is not a perspective from
a certain place beyond the world, nor the point of view
of a transcendent being: rather it is a certain form of thought
and feeling that rational persons can adopt within the world.
And having done so, they can... bring together into one scheme
all individual perspectives... Purity of heart, if one could attain it,
would be to see clearly and to act with grace and
self-command from this point of view.

JOHN RAWLS

Imagine yourself party to a gathering which takes place prior to your own birth. Identities here are cloaked in a "veil of ignorance." You do not know whether you will be born rich or poor, black or white, able bodied or disabled. Nor do you know anything about the features of the society into which you will be born: the system of governance, the nature of property, or the conditions of the least well off. From this carefully crafted position of ignorance, you are enjoined to determine the sort of society in which any reasonable person would want to live. So begins a thought experiment of the political philosopher John Rawls in his now classic *Theory of Justice.*[1] The experiment posits a sort of constitutional convention. Those who gather are to agree on the basic principles upon which the society they are born into will be based.

By masking our identities, Rawls distances us from our own interests. Since we do not know whether or not we will be born into a socially marginalized group, we have a strong incentive to make the society fair and just. But since prosperity benefits everyone, parties to the gathering also have an incentive to craft principles of justice compatible with the generation of wealth. It is an ingenious device. Whereas political philosophers, in crafting an ideal, usually struggle with their personal interests, prejudices, and predispositions, the idea of this "original position" provides a heuristic of genuine impartiality: not knowing who they will become, everyone is equally impartial. Written in 1973, Rawls spent the greater part of his magnum opus arguing that reasonable people, gathering in the original position, would craft a sort of late twentieth century welfare state. The marginalized would be protected, the poor supported, freedoms secured, property respected. After all, if you do not know which social position you will occupy, you will want to assure to each social stratum a minimal level of well-being, while assuring to the whole of society maximum prosperity.[2]

Rawls laid out a framework and set off a debate. Over the course of the next few decades, virtually every school of Anglo-American political philosophy gave its own answer to the original position. The liberals,[3] libertarians,[4] socialists,[5,6] feminists,[7] and communitarians[8,9] each produced their own theories of justice. But whether supporters or critics, almost all of the parties to the debate assumed the existence of a wealthy state; they assumed it would have the financial means to sustain a bureaucracy, maintain courts, pay police, administer elections, educate citizens, and support the needy. But globally and historically, such prosperous and functional states are anomalous. Were parties to the original position to possess an adequate appreciation of the social constraints imposed by debilitating poverty, it is arguable they would choose not liberalism or libertarianism, feminism or socialism, but rather to live in a state prosperous enough to function. This points to a still deeper problem.

Peter Singer argues that the most serious problems of justice in the world today do not exist within but rather between states. Given the choice between living in a poorly functioning wealthy state or a well-functioning poor state, few would choose the poor state. With about a billion malnourished people living on less than a dollar a day and about two billion more living on less than two dollars a day, the chances of being born poor are very high. And the difference in happiness between wealthy and poor nations tends to be extreme. Unless you knew beforehand you were going to be born into a wealthy state, you would probably want to extend to the people of poor nations some sort of social safety net when setting up a constitution in the original position. Furthermore, you would be careful to explicate principles of global justice that limit the ability of the rich states to exploit poor states.[10]

The question should not be what sort of society you would want to live in but what sort of world. Wealthy states routinely exploit the people of poor states. In pre-modern times, this might have involved the expropriation of land, debilitating taxes, and enslavement. The footprint of imperialism is often easy to discern in weak states, which have porous borders and a legacy of trauma. Imperialism devastated the Congo and the Ganges delta in the nineteenth century. And the slave trade destroyed inter-tribal trust in West Africa, the Sudan, and the Balkans. When, following WWII, the European powers and Japan relinquished their empires, they often left behind administrative units riven with tribal friction. The border conflicts of India and Pakistan, Israel and Palestine, and North and South Korea all grew out of post-colonial power vacuums and border disputes. While outright colonialism is rare today, bar a few outposts like the West Bank and Tibet, international exploitation continues apace, in new guises, with new objectives, through ever more refined institutions. The exploitation of today is only subtler.

Wealthy states shape international agreements to their favor, and when they can get away with it, bend the rules. They occupy a disproportionate share of seats on the G-8, the G-22, and the U.N. Security Council. And they hold disproportionate power over international economic institutions like the International Monetary Fund, the World Bank, and the World Trade Organization. While the poor may fair better in a world of rules than in one of interstate anarchy, it does not follow that the laws crafted by rich nations are fair. Far from it. Few parties to the original position would choose to live in a global order of unrepresentative institutions, whose purpose is to serve the powerful and wealthy unless they knew beforehand that they would be born rich. Nor would they be likely to tolerate our current system of global trade. The current international order is difficult to justify objectively.

The trade agenda of wealthy nations has often been equated with that of a man who, having climbed a ladder and reached the top, kicks away the supports, so no one can follow in his footsteps.[11] When they first set off on the path of economic development, America, Germany, and most other developed nations, protected their infant industries. Taiwan, Japan, France, and Singapore all cut taxes, gave subsidies to favored industries, built infrastructure, and shut out competition, so that their own native industries might grow to maturity. Only then did they cut the subsidies, remove the tariffs, and embrace the incentives of global competition. While South Korea and England were able to shelter their own shipping and textile industries in the early years of industrialization, they now demand that poor nations, in a much more volatile climate of global competition, let the markets decide. If poor nations are to participate in global trade agreements, or receive loans from international banks, rich countries demand that they lower tariffs, cut subsidies, and open their arms to foreign competition. Before they have the chance to stand on their own two feet, infant industries in poor states must bear the burden of global competition. The playing field is uneven. Competitive systems tend to favor the healthiest, nimblest, richest, and strongest. The most powerful nations are positioned to succeed, and with their power, they further stack the deck in their favor.[12,13]

Rich nations have only removed tariffs in the industries in which it is safe to do so. Agricultural subsidies have largely been ignored, since removing these subsidies would be devastating to agriculture in the wealthiest countries. While Japanese and European farmers are supported with tax breaks and the buying of surplus production, poor farmers in Nigeria and Nicaragua cannot compete. Instead of buying food produced just down the road, city dwellers in the world's poorest states instead buy food from heavily subsidized rich world farmers. The food may be cheaper, but the price is high; through their purchases, they destroy the prospects of their own countrymen and agricultural economies. By making farming in the third world unprofitable, stacked trade agreements burden poor nations with one more impediment to development.[14] Once again, the rich nations have kicked away the developmental ladder just as they reached the top.

Wealthy nations manipulate trade agreements because they can. It is not just the trade deck that is stacked in their favor. The whole international order is prone to their disproportionate influence. Rich nations dominate the U.N. Security Council. They comprise the bulk of the North Atlantic Treaty Organization and the World Trade Organization. Rich nations run the most important global institutions because it is usually they who started these institutions. What's more, it is their presence that makes these institutions noteworthy. The African Union is neither lacking in participants nor in activity; neither is the Arab League. What they lack is power, the ability to enforce their positions with military might and financial largess. If the current world order lacks the capacity to give them this clout, it is largely because they played no part in its creation.

The current world order emerged piecemeal, each institution a specific response to specific crises for the benefit of specific actors. Instead of global government, we have global governance: a range of official and semi-official, overlapping institutions, each with its own functions, its own mandate, and its own representative structure.[15] The IMF, WTO, G-8, G-22, NATO, and the World Bank each govern, but not even the U.N. constitutes a government. A global bureaucracy of treaties and agreements accompanies these powerful bodies: the Universal Postal Union, the International Bureau of Weights and Measures, the Law of the Sea Treaty, the Montreal Protocol, and the

International Criminal Court. The list of international organizations goes on, a typical set of government agencies, each with its own domain, its own functions, and its own professional networks. Practical agreements, quietly made, regulate the activities of an emerging global order.[16] And through these agreements and the behaviors they incentivize, we are further conditioned into global consciousness.

The current world order did not spring from the brain of a Zeus; it is the result of no revolution, and world leaders did not conspire in its creation. There is no moral justification for the current global order: no justification for why some are born into poverty, while others are born into privilege. Few with the capacity to make the world over would construct such an international order. It neither benefits the least well off, nor is it particularly effective in promoting prosperity, given the debilitating effects of severe poverty that are allowed to persist under its governance. The current order is a modus operandi; it provides a means through which the world might function but little more. But to paraphrase Galileo, upon being forced to recant his theory of helio-centrism, somehow it moves. Somehow we muddle through global challenges, making piecemeal agreements to settle global concerns. The current world order may not be just, and it may not last, but for now, it functions - just. Through our muddling about with global governance, we are learning the meaning of global cooperation. All of humanity is familiarizing itself with the issues, the concerns, and a workable balance of powers. And we are deepening the experience of global consciousness.

Over the course of the next century, we are likely to see several challenges to the current world order. As global temperatures continue to rise, world leaders will come under increasing pressure to forge a climate deal. While recent climate conferences have tended to yield little fruit, and may continue to be relatively unproductive for some decades to come, rising temperatures will sooner or later make world leaders feel the heat. Since a serious global climate deal would be likely to introduce some sort of tax on carbon, the prospect of such a deal presents a significant opportunity to strengthen global institutions and end poverty. The tax could provide a reliable stream of funding that would help the U.N. fight hunger, eradicate disease, mitigate famine, develop agriculture, prosecute war criminals, protect rainforests, prevent wars, and regulate weapons of mass destruction. While few people oppose these objectives, many are concerned about the growth of international institutions and the threat they might pose to national sovereignty. So, we should expect a climate deal that also seeks to fund global institutions or redistribute wealth to meet with significant resistance. But we live in a time of great change and should expect unimaginable international alignments to come and go before century's end.

Rising powers will also exert pressure on the current international order. Should they continue to grow as expected, emerging states like China, India, Turkey, Indonesia, South Africa, Mexico, and Brazil will want a seat at the table. They will almost certainly demand more voting rights in the International Monetary Fund and the World Bank, whose leaders have been chosen traditionally by the European Union and United States respectively. And many of these countries can be expected to campaign for permanent seats on the U.N. Security Council. Currently, the U.S., UK, Russia, France, and China can each now veto decisions, effectively paralyzing most major international actions. Should several more permanent members be added to the Security Council, thereby making for a larger and more representative body, there will be many who seek to do away with the veto. Should China continue to grow and the U.S. to decline in relative strength, the U.S. may want several more democratic allies on the Security Council to bolster its strength; meanwhile, China may want more emerging powers to strengthen its position. General Assembly members may also favor a more representative Security Council.

A more representative Security Council can make for a more stable international order, and may also present opportunities for a global climate deal. Believing people will not simply go from identifying with their own nations to the whole of the world but will instead first begin to think of themselves as members of the larger civilizations of which they are a part, Samuel Huntington Jr. proposed that each major civilization should have a representative on the Security Council, with the Organization of American States, the African Union, the Association of Southeast Asian Nations, the European Union, the Arab Union, China, Russia, Great Britain, India, and Japan each receiving a permanent seat. Walter Russell Mead proposed that permanent seats be awarded to some number of emerging democracies like India, Mexico, Japan, Turkey, Indonesia, South Africa, and Brazil. The former Foreign Minister of Singapore, Kishore Mahbubani, has proposed an even more extensive reshuffling of the Security Council, whose complexity puts it beyond the scope of this chapter. Each of these thinkers is respected as somewhat conservative in their approach to international relations. But if this is what we are hearing from more conservative thinkers, we should expect the pressure to reform the Security Council to only grow with each passing decade.

The world is spinning in widening circles of integration. History is moving along a trajectory of ever-greater interconnection. Economies are more interlinked, politics more co-determinate, cultures more bound together than ever before. We now know more about the far away places of the world than we have at any period of human history. And a multitude of aid organizations and international institutions have grown to scale over the past several decades. These comprise the institutional foundations of an emerging global order. With their presence has come an ethical obligation to construct the legal and political architecture of a just world order. If we do not know the form it will take, we are well familiar with the concerns it must address. Humanity cries out for some set of principles upon which it might base its global governance.

The earth is one and all of humanity is intimately bound together. And while such words as these may have rung true through the pen of an Emerson and the ethics of Gandhi, they are now truer than ever before. Humanity is tied together through telephone networks and airways, fiber optics and cloud computing. Through the patterns of trade and through social networks, we are woven together in a single garment. We are all of a piece. Together we will flourish, and together we may perish. Over the course of the next several decades, it is arguable, though impossible to prove, that the greatest threat to well being lies not in deficits or political corruption, but rather in overpopulation and nuclear devastation, climate change and pandemic disease. The world cries out not for local but rather for global solutions.

THE NEXT GREAT CIVILIZATION

The future always comes too fast and in the wrong order.
ALVIN TOFFLER, FUTURIST

If the United Nations does not attempt to chart a course for the world's people, in the first decades of the new millennium, who will?
KOFI ANNAN, FORMER SECRETARY GENERAL OF THE U.N.

The Aeneid is a Roman epic that tells the tale of one civilization giving way to another. The story begins at twilight, lit by the hues of a city aflame, and the agony of death rising on the breeze; the soldiers of Greece stream through the gates of Troy, as Aeneas, the hero, slips away, with his intimate circle, along a secret passage leading to the sea. Aeneas will momentarily embark on an exile that culminates in the founding of Rome - out of the ashes of one civilization the next shall be born - but as a lifetime of memories now vanishes, and the commotion of battle erodes the defenses of Troy, he is afflicted with tenderness for the fallen and a vision for the future. The chaos may mark the closing scene of one drama, but for Virgil, this will later be seen as the first in a far greater epic. Greek civilization is yielding to Rome. It is a moment much like that of today.[1]

It has become commonplace to speculate on American decline. Measured in military might, cultural influence, and the power of wealth, America is indisputably the most powerful nation on earth today. But that sense of power is elusive. Like many great civilizations – the Spanish, the Ottomans, the British, and French - America has become burdened with debt and military commitments.[2] The American empire is a complex of bases spread across some 120 nations.[3] Removing the bases will create power vacuums throughout the world, which will most likely be fought over and filled by other rising powers. As the most powerful nation in the world, every war impacts American interests and is therefore an American responsibility. And as the most powerful nation, Americans tend also to feel some sense of responsibility for those over whom they wield power. Thus, the greatness of American power is a sort of burden, an albatross that cannot be flung off without consequence. It is not only a military but also an economic and moral burden. Meanwhile, America is probably the most complex civilization ever to appear on the face of the earth. One can find here the highest number of artifacts, of occupations, and of techniques. More than in perhaps any other nation, Americans must learn more, tend to more, and keep up with more simply to function. The challenge of keeping up with so much has, amongst other things, prolonged adolescence and lent to the culture adolescent propensities.[4] Like adolescents, there is a tendency for Americans to feel their lives to be in perpetual flux, to believe they have never arrived, to experience themselves as somehow incomplete. This experience of life and the world is unsettling and results in a tendency to seek the path of least resistance. But given their complexity, preserving American institutions demands of Americans a marked degree of maturity, for it takes maturity to patiently sort through complexity.

Managing the complexity requires a labyrinth of governmental bureaus, the purposes of which are to most Americans a mystery. Government bureaus regulate commerce and cleanliness, building codes and traffic safety, air pollution and product quality, yet few Americans really understand what all these agencies are up to. The bureaucracy has even taken on functions of the family and community, which have ceased to carry out many of their traditional functions. Government bureaus seek to prevent childhood obesity, regulate visitation rights, assure inoculations, and generally guarantee a safe home environment. The bureaucracy also serves to bind together an immensely complex social experiment for which there is really no historical precedent. It is not nearly enough to simply wish away the so-called nanny state as many libertarians and conservatives do or to actively work to tear it down. For it carries out a multitude of vital functions that cannot be easily replaced. It is because citizens cannot understand the bureaucracy that they tend to condemn it as excessive. Yet as soon as one constituency speaks of cutting a program, another rises to defend its purpose. Not only does this result in government bloating, with all its attendant debt, it lends to the social system the appearance of a clumsy old dinosaur. Higher taxes would settle the problem once and for all by bringing debt relief and the sense of security that comes with knowing there is a social safety net through which one is unlikely to slip. But too few Americans respect the system to give more for its maintenance. To paraphrase Nathan Glazer, a social democrat often pigeonholed as neo-conservative, one longs for the clean slate of the New Deal days, when it was possible not just to preserve decent programs but to create the right ones.[5]

America is locked into a social and bureaucratic complexity from which there appears no exit. Lock-in is common for successful civilizations.[6] China experienced a long slow lock-in over the course of several millennia through the development of extensive dikes used to control the muddy Yellow River. With each passing generation more silt accumulated, and as the dikes grew taller, the threat of flooding and the costs of control only rose with the waters.[7] Until quite recently, the system of dikes was an impediment to economic growth. The Ottoman Empire was similarly locked into its own internal logic. An empire of lesser regional powers and diverse ethnic and religious groups, the Ottomans for centuries encouraged extensive local autonomy. But to compete with the emerging nation-states of Europe, they needed to homogenize their legal system and build an army of citizens, and this required subjects to identify with the state. Without a vigorous program of modernization that state would fail. But instead of lending allegiance to the Empire, Egyptian and Tunisian and Saudi subjects used the breakdown of the state as an occasion to call for their own.[8,9]

America is locked into its own system of bureaucratic complexity. The system lacks adherents, because few can comprehend its labyrinth of departments and functions. Yet, without supporters, leaders lack the political capital needed to carry out the reforms that might allow for renewal. Meanwhile, the budget is strained by increasing wants, few of which citizens appear willing to forego. Americans of all stripes have grown literally and figuratively fat. The military, the debt, the bureaucracy, and the rhetoric are all bloated. It is a classic fin de siècle, the decadent close of a passing era, accompanied by simultaneous outbursts of apocalypticism and creativity.[10] We are educated enough to expect the fall of Humpty Dumpty; we even possess the tools needed to set his injuries; but we often seem to lack the will and the sense of purpose needed to join together to put him back together again. It is little wonder Americans are consumed with an increasing sense of vertigo.

But as one era closes, another beckons to take its place. American civilization is far from spent. Perhaps America will fall gently, an institution here, another there, becoming in the end a decadent and incoherent facsimile of its once great self, an old warrior looking back on better days, but not fully broken and still able to function – a bit like the British and French of today. Perhaps she will be superseded by other rising powers, becoming one amongst many in a multi-polar world, with slower growth, a weaker military, and a humbler leadership role, but still an undisputed great power.[11] Yet perhaps, like an aging leader, handing off the baton, to a younger and better-adapted protégé, America will yield to an emerging global civilization, in the same way the British handed their empire to the Americans.[12]

America has been central to laying the groundwork for a global civilization. It was the Wilson administration that first envisioned the League of Nations and that of F.D.R. that conceived of the U.N.. The World Bank and the International Monetary Fund were brought to life in the U.S.; Americans built the Internet, and they have played a pivotal role in virtually every major global gathering of the late twentieth and twenty-first centuries. Regularly the most highly ranked, American universities have spawned the world's leading thinkers. And the American environmental and spiritual movements of the late twentieth century pioneered the consciousness that is the subject of this book. As these global institutions and modes of thoughts grow stronger nation-states will continue to weaken. It is an unlikely moment for any nation to rise to global predominance, let alone an inward looking giant like China, which we can expect to become increasingly consumed by its own profound socio-economic transformations.

There is in America a sizable market for global consciousness. American culture is a trans-generational fusion of immigrants, a unique blend of peoples, in some ways a virtual microcosm of the U.N.. The descendants of African slaves and Anglo settlers, Native Americans and East European Jews, Italians and Germans, Chinese and Mexicans, Arabs and Indians: there is a lobby in the States for virtually every major ethnic and religious group. This lends to internal debates an unusual cosmopolitanism. And it trains Americans to adapt to diversity. Looking outward toward the wider world, American power forces American leaders of all varieties to think globally. Because their sphere of influence is wider, so must be their range of concerns. Global consciousness is in the air Americans breathe. And there are many environmentalists and spiritualist aspirants for whom global consciousness determines the only civic commitments they know. One need not believe Americans alone possess this perspective. But its ethnic composition and great power status make the American position unique. As America declines, something must take its place. And if the recent history of declining empires is any predictor of the future, it is arguable that the next great civilization will be both global and largely influenced by the power it replaces.

If we are to meet the global challenges of the twenty-first century, we must develop global consciousness, and that consciousness must facilitate the development of global institutions. We are fast becoming a global civilization, and civilization without governing institutions is anarchy. But to construct global governing institutions we must first be able to conceive of the world as a whole. We must discern how its several parts combine and comprehend the significance and the meaning of their relations. We must do so in the abstract, through facts and figures and miscellaneous accounts, piecing together the puzzle of a world beyond the grasp of our immediate senses. The world is vast; it cannot be understood like a city, with all of its palpable sights and sounds. But whoever can make sense of this vast and variegated forest, mapping the trees in outline, grasping the dimensions, glimpsing the horizons, sits at the leading edge of change.

Prior to modernity, it was only religious and political leaders who had to make sense of so much, conceiving through scattered reports images of the lands they ruled. The social sciences barely existed. Few sought to understand the workings of anything larger than what today would make up a small nation-state.[13] But modernization molded ever greater numbers of people into one through mass education, and it extended what we understand through the accumulated knowledge of the natural and social sciences.[14] Humanity has only just begun to attempt to understand the world as a whole, for it is a far wider terrain, with a greater diversity of natural and human systems that must be taken into account. And while we possess the capacity, it involves sorting and handling a far wider array of concerns than all but a few of us now take into consideration. Either ordinary people must develop the minds of former great leaders or we must find new ways to integrate information that are elegantly simple. This book has laid out the problem in outline, giving hints and pointers, but venturing few solutions.

There is a danger that because it is so difficult to conceive of the world as a whole, we will leave the task to a new global elite of corporate executives, U.N. administrators, and global leaders. Already, there is a growing divide between the masses of the world and an emerging global elite.[15] As their organizations grow in size to address the concerns of an increasingly interconnected world, more and more of us will be indoctrinated into the viewpoints of this global elite. We will increasingly follow their directives, track their exploits, cheer their successes, and admonish their failures. For in a globalized world, it will be the actions of global leaders that determine whether we remain threatened or secure, whether we develop concrete agreements to limit climate change, whether we protect the oceans, regulate nuclear weapons, and feed the hungry. As global leaders rise in power, national leaders will increasingly come to appear like the new county officials. But whereas national leaders are usually held to account, global leaders seldom answer to any definite constituency. If we are to preserve our say in government, we must not only develop global consciousness but global norms and participatory institutions.

Our identities must also be transformed. At any given moment there are numerous sources of identification. We identify with our accomplishments, our status, and our work roles. We identify with the places where we live, the creeds we hold, and the lands of our birth. At any given moment, these several sources of identity are attached varying levels of priority: at Church a Lutheran, at the family reunion a Smith, at the voting booth an American, at the international conference a cosmopolitan, at the bar a drinker; the categories are constantly eliding and shifting.[16] With the dawn of the nation-state, Neapolitans, Sicilians, and Venetians became Italians; German, Polish, and Iraqi Jews became Israelis; New Yorkers, Virginians, and Georgians became Americans; and Maronites, Druze, and Shiites became Lebanese.[17,18,19] As global consciousness develops, rather than disappearing, the importance of these identities will once more shift, losing salience as we identify more and more with universal roles. These may be the familiar roles of environmentalist, free trader, Christian, or humanist. But should the process of globalization continue unimpeded, more and more will come to consider themselves global citizens. The identity shifts now arising may in the end prove tectonic.

National and international institutions are presently engaged in a seldom noticed but still epic contest. National governments are increasingly constrained by global standards and global opinions. The International Monetary Fund demands changes in economic policy to qualify for loan, the International Criminal Court requires the arrest of former officials to achieve legitimacy, and the European Union calls for improvements in human rights to attain entry. For smaller nations, the pressures can become ubiquitous. Leaders must mask their intentions before entering office, devise rigged elections to attain loans and legitimacy, cook the books, and sweep abuses under the rug, all to throw off the scent of the international bloodhounds. While Americans may look upon international institutions as a sort of chorus of eunuchs, to weaker states those eunuchs hold the keys to the dream palace of international recognition. Without that recognition, their trade will shrink, their strength falter, and their security recede. But even for America, international laws and opinions increasingly shape domestic debates over war, pollution, and economic policy. A balance of power is emerging between national and international institutions. But even as the shots ring round the world, most of us appear deaf to this debate, failing to inquire into the ideal balance.

The dominance of global institutions is obscured partly because we do not tend to think of them as belonging to one class. It seems strange to place Greenpeace activists, IMF officials, Al Qaeda terrorists, American Secretaries of State, and British Petroleum executives in the same category. Yet the several players increasingly engage in the same game of international politics, and the actions of any one of them determines the resources devoted to the projects of the others. They struggle over the same issues, use the same terms, seek legitimacy from the same institutions, and wield a similar set of powers. What ties them together and separates them from the rest of us is the global nature of their concerns. They cannot help but be globally conscious. Their success or failure, in a game of ultimate stakes, hinges on their ability to grasp the hinge points upon which global events inevitably turn.

The dialogue in which they engage brings these actors increasingly into the same conversations. And we are increasingly absorbed by their arguments. We are drawn in because the issues they deal with are important and impact our lives. As the human environmental footprint grows, global issues have taken on increasing levels of importance. Each of us is living, so to speak, on the same tiny island, with events in one place impacting all others. National issues are increasingly framed by global arguments, shaped by international policies, and altered by world opinion. Even when a state's chief concern is national sovereignty, there is a tendency to pay more and more attention to the international debate. For it is the international debate that increasingly shapes the terms of national sovereignty. Moreover, the path to political success, particularly in poorer and smaller countries, increasingly leads upward into global leadership. Environmentalists like to say that we are frogs in hot water, slowly being cooked. What they neglect to mention is that one of the ingredients in the stew is global consciousness. We are slowly being conditioned, one degree at a time, to a global perspective. Whether humanity or our consciousness will be the first to be cooked is an open question.

A global culture is emerging through a thousand secret springs: trade, travel, immigration, and telecommunications; it is emerging through world music and sporting events, global networks and conferences, international news and institutions. Each rising generation will become increasingly absorbed into the global conversation. And as generation follows generation, one after the other, national identities will increasingly dissipate. There is no need to speak of the end of national sovereignty or the withering away of the state. Sovereignty has always been more of an ideal, possessed by only the strongest of states, while the weakest have been hemmed in at every turn by interstate agreements and the manipulation of imperialists. Whether in the end it is relatively weak or strong, the state will remain for the foreseeable future. But the state today is surely waning. It is corroded from within by foreign influences and pressures and by a tectonic shift in identity. Like the country boys who made their way to the city in the days of industrialization, the best and the brightest are leaving home for the world. Meanwhile, the state is now constrained from without by a web of global influences. And there is little reason to expect these trends to be reversed.

Of course, nothing on earth is inevitable. The world may suffer a catastrophic war or economic collapse. We may shrink back into more local identities as we are overwhelmed by complexity and deluged by resource wars. Along with travelers and traders, plagues may spread across the pathways of human interconnectivity, radically dwindling the human population as we struggle to maintain local networks and national economies. And technological development may unleash another atom bomb, an unforeseen Frankenstein that this time destroys all of human civilization. There are many threats that hang above our heads by but a strand, like the Sword of Damocles. But these are precisely the type of events we tend to call apocalyptic. And the antidote to each is the same.

Either we must develop global consciousness so that we can work with others across the world to mitigate these sorts of threats or else we will be forced to develop that same consciousness to clean up after the cataclysm. Either we will develop global consciousness organically and responsibly, as we are bound ever more tightly together in strands of interconnectivity or else we will develop global consciousness as a desperate measure amidst the horrors of cataclysmic threat to human civilization. Whether or not American power persists, whether or not we solve global warming or put the nuclear genie back in the box, whether we form a global government or contract ever more deeply into an obsolete system of tightly demarcated states, in the end we have little choice and a thousand pressing reasons to develop global consciousness.

PERSONAL POSTSCRIPT

Specialization has reached moronic vehemence.
Learned lives are expended on reiterative minutiae.
Academic rewards go to the narrow scholiast, to the blinkered.
Men and women in the learned professions proclaim
themselves experts on one author, in one brief historical
period, in one aesthetic medium.
GEORGE STEINER, LITERARY PHILOSOPHER

When a subject becomes totally obsolete
we make it a required course.
PETER F. DRUCKER

For now we see but through a glass darkly,
but then face to face; now I know in part, but then
I will know fully just as I also have been fully known.
ST. PAUL OF TARSUS

MAKING SENSE OF THE WORLD

In Douglas Adams' science fiction classic, *Life, the Universe, and Everything*, a supercomputer is constructed with the goal of discovering the answer to life, the universe, and everything. Needless to say, it takes some time to construct such a machine. But once built, the computer sets to work framing the issue and crunching the numbers. Then, after a mere 7 million years or so of computation, it finally spits out its conclusion. The answer to life, the universe, and everything is 42. Of course, no one understands what this means, and after all those generations of waiting, such an insensible answer is a letdown. So they ask the computer to explain what this means. The problem, explains the supercomputer, Deep Thought, is that the Ultimate Question itself is unknown. And while the supercomputer goes on to construct an ever more powerful computer to provide the Ultimate Question, that computer is destroyed along with the earth just a few minutes before giving the answer.[1] Sometimes life can be like that.

There is a sense in which we all begin our efforts to make sense of the world and our lives in such a muddle. Either we mix all of the questions together into one big one and then bemoan the inability to get an answer that makes any sense, or else we sharpen the search too quickly and spend decades searching in the wrong direction. "You set out to find God," writes the Persian poet Rumi of a similar quest, "but then keep stopping for long periods at mean spirited road houses."[2] Sometimes we get caught up in the mission, sometimes the politics, and sometimes the labyrinthine hierarchies of psycho-social achievement. It is easy to lose oneself in the quest, particularly when the question that motivates that quest is so difficult to express.

To make sense of the world, we must make sense of our own place within it. Little in our lives will make sense if we cannot comprehend our place on the planet. But understanding the world isn't just about me and you and our own minuscule corners of the universe. The world that now confronts us is vast, and it may not function very well if we fail to make sense of it. For if we cannot make sense of the world, our responses to global events will forever remain in discord. Understanding anything requires more than just the knowledge of the sum of its parts. For instance, understanding global food security requires that we understand population dynamics, the nature of development, global warming, agricultural science, economic globalization, and human nutrition. If we merely grasp one piece of the puzzle, we can get the whole thing wrong. The same goes for deforestation, global warming, and global terrorism. These are complex problems that must be viewed systemically.

To conceive of the world as an integrated whole is no easy matter. All sorts of troubles inevitably arise. To begin with, the world is a rather sizable location, animated by a menagerie of beings and a profusion of events, so many things that, for the average person, most will forever remain a mystery. Making sense of the world requires a deep and sustained inquiry into how all things fit together. It involves comprehending our own standpoint and the meaning of our lives. In short, it requires global consciousness. Without global consciousness it is difficult to live meaningful lives and craft functioning institutions in a globalized world, for without it, we are left grasping at the winds of a world beyond our comprehension.

The problem is similar to that of the computer, Deep Thought. We cannot understand our answers without a better comprehension of the question. What does it really mean to make sense of the world? This is the sort of question that college freshman tie themselves up in knots over just prior to declaring a major. But we should not be too quick to dismiss it as merely a symptom of late adolescent angst. After all, the intensity of this quest to understand the world as a whole is usually dampened not through finding an answer but rather by declaring a major or choosing a career. All too often, we escape from the perplexity of contemplating a world too vast to comprehend by getting caught up in it. In other words, we escape the necessity of understanding through the imperative to act. Anthropologists, economists, philosophers, and physicists tend to know perfectly well how to approach understanding the world as a whole. Their research rests on mountains of studies. And their reach is dictated by the professional standards of a community of peers. This can all feel quite serious and substantial from within these communities. But from the outside, it can look like a hall of mirrors – self-referential distortions of some distant and more real world.

Academics do generate highly accurate and important studies that allow outsiders to their professions to better comprehend the world. This is important. In fact, without specialized academic studies, the world we seek to comprehend would be denuded of color, a pale simulacrum of a vast and multifarious reality. Imagine a forest without ecology, a city without sociology, an economy without economics. The real world is almost always far more rich and textured than we believe. And through the study of academic research we can gradually rid ourselves of our pallid delusions. Then the world can come alive. The problem is that if we really want to make sense of the world, we do not usually need groundbreaking research. For while groundbreaking research can be stimulating and important, it also tends to be far from essential.

Academics and professionals rarely choose their fields simply because they are the best means through which to seek understanding. Few would claim such purity of purpose. And that's fair enough. Comprehensive understanding is only one amongst multiple competing ends in life. The problem lies not in the intentions of academics but rather in their results, for it is primarily through their work that the rest of us seek to make sense of the world. They generate the studies of its capital, its peoples, its environments, and its history. They frame the debates on politics and business, geography and meteorology. And while useful, the information they generate can also be a distraction. Understanding everything there is to know about financial flows is not really what freshman get so knotted up over, after all. Rather, what makes the world so terrifying is contextualizing these flows within the context of everything else, and moreover finding some sort of meaning in this flux of information.

The quest for understanding is mediated by markets. Markets provide jobs and allocate research funding. And that research determines what each of us knows. It determines which nations, which tribes, and which corporations, are studied. It tells us what techniques, what patterns, and what distinctions are crucial. Yet, while the research may be useful, the market mechanism is a poor means of framing discussion. Because new information tends to be the most interesting, and the newest information is usually the most specific, we are often deluged with trivialities. News sources provide poll numbers when what we really need is a deeper analysis of how we might make our lives better. Sociologists study subgroups when what we really need is a meditation on the nature of civilization. But there is little market for this sort of information. These richer and more meaningful studies have usually already been undertaken, often repeatedly, over the course of centuries, by the great intellectuals of the modern era. The result is that there is often no market or funding for the most useful types of information. Academics and news sources, just like the politicians on whom they report, tend to follow the money. Otherwise, they cannot sustain their work.

Of course, this is not just an academic matter. The recent disruptions to the daily news and bookstore industries demonstrates how a particular mode of knowing the world might vanish altogether if it has no means of funding. Conversely, the rise of film industries in places like India and Nigeria demonstrates how other modes of knowing the world might arise if they can be made profitable. Our views of the world, whether abstract or empathic, atemporal or timely, are all affected by the market mechanism. For markets channel which information is available. And while that mechanism may set in motion a process that ultimately provides more, perhaps even better, cumulative information about the world, it does nothing to prioritize and integrate that information.

Any information we acquire about the world must be integrated if it is to mean much. That is, our knowledge of the world must fit together in a sensible and coherent fashion. And all of this information must be integrated with what we have learned through simply living in the world. Making sense of the world often means making sense of what we know of it. But there is only so much we can know. Having failed in our youth to stop the world from turning so that we might better examine it, we might learn some things from simply living a life. And at some point, if we are so bold, we may ask how we are to make sense of all that we have lived. But this may not be as easy as we think.

Consider what we might call Rumsfeld's Muddle. The former Secretary of Defense under George W. Bush, Donald Rumsfeld, once declared "there are things we know that we know... things that we now know we don't know. But there are also unknown unknowns... things we do not know we don't know." Sadly for Rumsfeld, there were many things he didn't know that he didn't know about being Secretary of Defense – in spite of having already held the job once before. And perhaps he would have done better had he considered a fifth category of information: things we say we know that we know are not so. Sometimes the greatest weapon of mass destruction is our own minds. All of us distort the information at our disposal. To economize on time and attention, we edit out portions of experience. We choose not to learn certain things so as to focus on others. And we often forget the lessons we once learned. Sometimes we avoid learning about the world because we are afraid to know, sometimes because we simply lack the time. Sometimes we lack the focus and sometimes we haven't the interest. Whatever the reasons, if we are to make sense of what we do know about the world, we have to grapple as well with what we do not know.

If we cannot understand the world as a whole, we will not know how to contextualize its several pieces. We can reconstruct the intimate milieus and timelines of history, but this does not mean we will know how history informs the present. We can measure the flows of exchange and the rise and fall of economic sectors, but this does not mean we will recognize when economics determines history. There is no guarantee, in short, that the things we have learned over the course of a life will prove at all useful or meaningful. For those who have spent some time here on earth, this can be a rather unwelcome realization.

If we cannot make sense of the world as a whole, we will be unable to discern its most salient forces. Without a full survey of the world, improvements in health, education, sustainability, and growth lack meaning. Growth and sustainability may be at odds. Improvements in education may draw from the health budget. Social improvements may lead to cultural fragmentation. If we are to comprehend the significance of any given public good, it must be situated within the context of all other public goods, which are sometimes complimentary and sometimes competing. Single-issue advocates all too often ignore this wider view: the components of the good life are meaningless when taken out of context. But as the social context grows to encompass the whole of the world, we will be increasingly challenged to speak of these sorts of trade-offs, just as we do in national budget talks. To make sense of the world itself, we must contextualize its several parts.

If we fail to understand the world in a meaningful way, wisdom will remain elusive. We will not know how to organize our lives and the systems of which we are a part, for whole spheres of unrecognized influences will sabotage our futures. Perhaps human civilization will fall prey to climate change or overpopulation, pandemic disease or thermo-nuclear war. But if we cannot contextualize these threats, we will forever oscillate between minimizing and exaggerating their significance. They will blow at our lives like random gusts in an incomprehensible storm. At our worst, we will fail to recognize significance altogether, for there will be too little consciousness of the ground from which significance arises. We will fail to discern the moral good, for the consequences of our actions will always ripple beyond the horizon of consciousness.

The postmodern world presents us with a Faustian temptation of omniscience. The forces impacting our lives are vast. We must know ever more simply to function. And those who know the most have increasing access to powers with which they might improve their lives and influence the course if events. Hence, we might feel compelled to know everything, betting our futures on an unreachable horizon of omniscience. This would be a tragic misunderstanding of a simple task. We do not need to know everything. Rather what we need is a balanced view that is meaningful. All too often we fall prey to the opposite temptation, shutting down the mind and seeking retreat in some infinite present. We are terrified by the sublimity, overwhelmed by the vastness, of a world too big to grasp. So we retreat into ourselves and into the moment. But just as we cannot ever know the world in its entirety, neither can we somehow shut it out. The world leaks into our lives, through the will to survive, the curiosity to understand, the desire to contribute, and the need to be human. To be human is to grapple with the world through the mind, which is not some alien imposition, but rather an outgrowth of the world. We use our minds to situate our lives within a wider circle of life and to project ourselves into the future, planning and adapting to ever-changing contingencies. This may not require that we know everything. But in a global civilization, doing this well will tend to mean knowing a lot.

There is a sense in which those who have sought understanding through the mastery of some subfield, at the expense of all others, are flying blind. They lose their center when they stray from their strengths. Of course, expertise can deepen intelligence, and intelligence can be applied to a wide array of concerns. A well-trained expert seeking to make sense of the world can bring to the task an eye for differences that make a difference, crucial distinctions that literally mean the world. But experts tend to exaggerate the salience of their own tiny sub-disciplines. The plight of some lost tribe becomes to the anthropologist emblematic of humanity. And with limited time and mental capacities, we lack the patience to evaluate their claims. Suddenly, the tiny tribe, the odd microbe, the latest gene, will grow to the undiscerning reader to take on immense proportion. While it would have been far more meaningful to track the advance of climate change or the patient growth in human numbers, instead we lose ourselves in trivia.

Understanding the world as a whole is integral to the development of wisdom. Without wisdom we lose a sense of context. And lacking context, meaning becomes ever more elusive. But we need more than wisdom; we also need equanimity, empathy, balance, and more. In short, understanding the world demands that we further develop our full capacities as human beings. So while it may not be a sufficient condition, understanding the world appears to be a necessary condition for the development of wisdom. This is what philosophers have so often sought and sometimes grasped: a comprehensive framework that might shine a light on the significance and meaning of all things. And like soldiers from out of the trenches, they have continually thrown themselves before the guns of a hostile world so as to advance the line of reason a few feet here, a few feet there. But the field of philosophy has of late been nibbled thin by psychologists, sociologists, political scientists, cognitive scientists, and an assembly of academic forces, each patiently and persistently expanding their own ever widening domains. Yet the world cries out for thinkers and leaders that might make sense of the world and help us rediscover how we shall live together.

Making sense of the world is a meaningful endeavor. But more importantly, it is vital to making global civilization work. To make global civilization work we need to construct for ourselves more inclusive maps. But to do this, we must first become conscious of the world in all its infinite and imponderable complexity. Like crafting a life, the task itself is impossible. Lives are comprised of a mysterious mixture of intention and contingency. But they emerge, over time, piece by piece, until the child becomes an adult and the adult makes for herself, out of the flotsam and jetsam of the world into which she has been thrown, a life that might keep her afloat. Global consciousness is a bit like this: strewn together out of scattered pieces of information, jerry-rigged over the course of a life. We can influence the development of global consciousness, but like a life, it is less the result of careful planning and more that of emergent opportunism.

The work of philosophers has now fallen to the people. Global consciousness thrusts each of us into the dizzying waves of a wide and wondrous world. Our historical position is comparable to that of a Columbus, peering out from the Middle Ages into the vast expanse of Modernity, hungry to launch himself into the great unknown, arrogant in his ambition, and yet somehow oblivious to his true significance. His ambitions appear from a distance of centuries those of a narcissistic child. Christopher Columbus was no hero – far from it. He was ignorant and oppressive and wrong about his discoveries. And yet his actions helped push humanity, on the hinges of the Renaissance and the Reformation, forward into Modernity by helping tie together all of humanity. Ours is the work of generations, and while heroism will help, accomplishing the great tasks before us may simply require that we confront the world into which we have been thrown.

Great historical winds now blow at our sails. Whichever way we turn, whether we raise our sails or brace our oars in resistance, we are nevertheless pushed forward into widening circles of global comprehension. We contribute to the birth of a global civilization every time we read a clothing label, complain about immigrants, worry about terrorists, ponder whether it is right to drive, concern ourselves with foreign policy, send e-mails, bemoan overpopulation, and cry for a drowning polar bear. As each of us struggles to wrap our heads and hands around an ever turning world, we are building a global civilization, more often than not unknowingly, but laying down a foundation and constructing a framework for a new worldview nonetheless. This is far from unusual. A society is built out of the lives of its members, each one simply living, with but a few perhaps tending to the whole. And yet, out of their scattered actions emerges a whole that is greater than the sum of its parts. We should expect no different of a global civilization. It will emerge from the minds that conceive its emergence and grow from the institutions that regulate its growth.

If we cannot think globally we will find ourselves unable to solve the great challenges of the twenty-first century. And many of the great challenges of the twenty-first century, like climate change, overpopulation, nuclear proliferation, species loss, and desertification, challenge the very capacity of humanity to live on this earth in peace and security. If we cannot make sense of the world, the deeper meaning of this vast historical transformation will remain elusive. The great forces impinging on our lives and determining our fates will remain obscured. And we will stutter and babble through our own lead roles in the immense human drama that is now unfolding.

But there is an inevitability at work in global consciousness. Global consciousness will grow out of the victory celebrations of every international agreement, as cross border networks deepen, advocacy groups grow in power, states yield more to international law, and each of us shares in a sense of greater common security. Global consciousness will also grow out of the detritus of every failed international agreement, as citizens across states ask what went wrong, reporters criticize politicians' failure to act, advocates organize for the next round of negotiations, and each of us share in a lack of security. We may debate the need for a carbon tax or the benefits of free trade, but whatever the results of such debates, the debate itself strengthens global consciousness. For in debating across borders, we strengthen global civil society. Every cross border conflict and every affront to human rights also strengthens global consciousness, for it brings global challenges to mind and thus challenges us to better understand the world. Of course, it will be easy to imagine some set of circumstances that halts the rise in global consciousness. Some new bug could kill the Internet, nuclear holocaust could collapse human civilization. But what is most extraordinary and all too often overlooked is the way almost every thing we expect to happen over the course of the next several decades plays some part in deepening global consciousness.

BIBLIOGRAPHY

Acemoglu, Daren and Robinson, James. *Why Nations Fail: The Origins of Power, Prosperity, and Poverty.* Crown Business. 2012.

Adams, Douglas. *Life, the Universe, and Everything.* Del Ray. 2005.

Alighieri, Dante and Musa, Mark, trans. *The Divine Comedy: Volume 1: The Inferno.* Penguin Classics. 2002.

Amar, Akhil Reed. *America's Constitution: A Biography.* Random House. 2006.

Anderson, Benedict. *Imagined Communities: Reflections on the Origin and Spread of Nationalism.* Verso. 1983.

Ansary, Tamim. *Destiny Disrupted: A History of the World Through Islamic Eyes.* Public Affairs. 2010.

Appiah, Kwame Anthony. *Cosmopolitanism: Ethics in a World of Strangers.* W.W. Norton and Company. 2007.

Aristotle. *Aristotle's Poetics.* Hill and Wang. 1961.

Armstrong, Karen. *History of God: the 4,000-Year Quest of Judaism, Christianity, and Islam.* Ballantine Books. 1994.

Armstrong, Karen. *Jerusalem: One City, Three Faiths.* Alfred A. Knopf. 1996.

Armstrong, Karen. *The Battle for God.* Ballantine Books. 2001.

Armstrong, Karen. *The Great Transformation: the Beginning of Our Religious Traditions.* Anchor Books. 2007.

Armstrong, Karen. *The Case for God.* Anchor Books. 2010.

Arthur, Brian. *The Nature of Technology: What It Is and How It Evolves.* Free Press. 2009.

Aslan, Reza. *Beyond Fundamentalism: Confronting Religious Extremism in the Age of Globalization.* Random House Trade Paperbacks. 2009.

Aurelius, Marcus. The Meditations. Penguin Classics. 2006.

Axelrod, Robert. The Evolution of Cooperation. Basic Books. 1984.

Banerjee, Abhijit and Duflo, Esther. Poor Economics: A Radical Rethinking of the Way to Fight Global Poverty. Public Affairs. 2012.

Baron-Cohen, Simon. The Science of Evil: On Empathy and the Origins of Cruelty. Basic Books. 2012.

Barzun, Jacques. From Dawn to Decadence: 500 Years of Western Cultural Life, 1500 to the Present. Harper Perennial. 2001.

Bateson, Gregory. Steps to an Ecology of Mind: Collected Essays in Anthropology, Psychiatry, Evolution, and Epistemology. University of Chicago Press. 2000.

Beck, Don and Cowan, Christopher. Spiral Dynamics: Mastering Values, Leadership, and Change. Wiley-Blackwell. 2005.

Bell, Daniel. The Coming of Post-Industrial Society: A Venture in Social Forecasting. Basic Books. 1976.

Bellah, Robert N. Religion in Human Evolution: From the Paleolithic to the Axial Age. Belknap Press of Harvard University Press. 2011.

Benhabib, Seyla. Another Cosmopolitanism. Oxford University Press. 2008.

Benkler, Yokai. The Wealth of Networks: How Social Production Transforms Markets and Freedoms. Yale University Press. 2007.

Benkler, Yokai. The Penguin and the Leviathan: How Cooperation Triumphs Over Self-Interest. Crown Business. 2011.

Berger, Peter L., & Luckman, Thomas. The Social Construction of Reality: A Treatise in the Sociology of Knowledge. Anchor Books. 1966.

Berger, Peter. The Sacred Canopy: Elements of a Sociological Theory of Religion. Anchor Books. 1967.

Berman, Morris. The Reenchantment of the World. Cornell University Press. 1981.

Berners-Lee, Time. Weaving the Web: The Original Design and Ultimate Destiny of the World Wide Web. Harper Collins. 1999.

Bernstein, William J. A Splendid Exchange: How Trade Shaped the World. Grove Press. 2009.

Berry, Thomas. The Dream of the Earth. Sierra Club Books. 2006.

Bhagwati, Jagdish and Panagariya, Arvind. Why Growth Matters: How Economic Growth in India Reduced Poverty and the Lessons for Other Developing Countries. Public Affairs. 2013.

Bookchin, Murray. The Ecology of Freedom: the Emergence and Dissolution of Hierarchy. AK Press. 2005.

Boorstin, Daniel. The Americans: the Colonial Experience. Vintage. 1964.

Boorstin, Daniel. The Americans: the National Experience. Vintage. 1967.

Boorstin, Daniel. The Discoverers. Vintage. 1985.

Borg, Marcus J. Meeting Jesus Again for the First Time: the Historical Jesus and the Heart of Contemporary Faith. Harper Collins Publishers. 1994

Brand, Stewart. Whole Earth Discipline: Why Dense Cities, Nuclear Power, Transgenic Crops, Restored Wildlands, and Geoengineering are Necessary. Penguin Books. 2010.

Braudel, Fernand and Reynolds, Sian, trans. Identity of France: People and Production. Perennial. 1992.

Brooks, David. The Social Animal: the Hidden Sources of Love, Character, and Achievement. Random House. 2012.

Broome, John. Climate Matter: Ethics in a Warming World. W.W. Norton and Company. 2012.

Brown, Donald E. Human Universals. Temple University Press. 1991.

Brown, Michael E. Lynn-Jones, Sean M. and Miller, Steven. Debating the Democratic Peace. The MIT Press. 1996.

Buchanan, Allen E. Marx and Justice: The Radical Critique of Liberalism. Rowman and Littlefield Publishing Inc. 1984.

Carr, Nicholas. The Shallows: What the Internet is Doing to Our Brains. W.W. Norton and Company. 2011.

Carter, Jimmy. Palestine, Peace Not Apartheid. Simon and Schuster. 2006.

Castells, Manuel. The Rise of the Network Society: The Information Age: Economy, Society, and Culture Volume I. Wiley-Blackwell. 2009.

Catholic Church. Catechism of the Catholic Church. Image. 2005.

Chambers, Robert. Narayan, Deepa. Shah, Meera and Petesch, Patt. Voices of the Poor: Crying Out for Change. World Bank Publications. 2001.

Chang, Ha-Joon. Kicking Away the Ladder: Development Strategy in Historical Perspective. Anthem Press. 2002.

Chang, Ha-Joon. Bad Samaritans: The Myth of Free Trade and the Secret History of Capitalism. Bloomsbury Press. 2008.

Chang, Leslie T. Factory Girls: From Village to City in a Changing China. Spiegel and Grau. 2009.

Chomsky, Noam. Aspects of the Theory of Syntax. MIT Press. 1965.

Chomsky, Noam and Herman, Edward. The Washington Connection and Third World Fascism. South End Press. 1999.

Choukri, Mohamed and Bowles, Paul, trans. For Bread Alone. Telegram Books. 2007.

Christian, David. Maps of Time: An Introduction to Big History. University of California Press. 2004.

Churchland, Patricia S. Braintrust: What Neuroscience Tells Us About Morality. Princeton University Press. 2011.

Clements, Jeffrey D. Corporations Are Not People: Why They Have More Rights Than You Do and What You Can Do About It. Berrett Koehler Publishers. 2012.

Cohen, G.A. Marx's Theory of History. Princeton University Press. 2000.

Cohen, G.A. Rescuing Justice and Equality. Harvard University Press. 2008.

Collier, Paul. The Bottom Billion. Why the Poorest Countries are Failing and What Can Be Done About It. Oxford University Press. 2008.

Collins, Daryl. Morduch, Jonathan. Rutherford, Stuart and Ruthven, Orlanda. Portfolios of the Poor: How the World's Poor Live on $2 a Day. Princeton University Press. 2010.

Conrad, Joseph. Heart of Darkness. Tribeca Books. 2011.

Coogan, Michael, Brettler, Mark Z, Newsom, Carol A., Perkins, Pheme. The New Oxford Annotated Bible with Apocrypha: New Revised Standard Version. Oxford University Press. 2010.

Cook, Michael. A Brief History of the Human Race. W.W. Norton and Company. 2005.

Costanza, Robert et al. The Value of World's Ecosystem Services and Natural Capital. Nature 387. 1997.

Cox, Harvey. The Future of Faith. Harper Collins Publishers. 2009.

Cronon, William. Uncommon Ground: Rethinking the Human Place in Nature. W.W. Norton and Co. 1996.

Dalai Lama, H.H. Ethics for a New Millennium. Riverhead Trade. 1999.

Dalai Lama, H.H. Beyond Religion: Ethics for a Whole World. Mariner Books. 2012.

Dawkins, Richard. The Selfish Gene. Oxford University Press. 1976.

de Chardin,, Teilard. The Phenomenon of Man. Harper Perennial Modern Classics. 2008.

de Soto, Hernando. The Mystery of Capital: Why Capitalism Triumphs in the West and Fails Everywhere Else. Basic Books. 2003.

de Spinoza, Benedict and Curley, Edwin, trans. Ethics. Penguin Classics. 2005.

de Tocqueville, Alexis and Gilbert, Stuart, ed. The Old Regime and the French Revolution. Anchor Books. 1955.

de Tocqueville, Alexis. Democracy in America. Penguin Classics. 2003.

de Waal, Frans. *The Age of Empathy: Nature's Lessons for a Kinder Society.* Broadway. 2010.

Deacon, Terrence W. *Incomplete Nature: How Mind Emerged From Matter.* W.W. Norton of Company. 2012

Des Forges, Alison. *Leave None to Tell the Story. Genocide in Rwanda.* Human Rights Watch. 1997.

Deutscher, Isaac. *The Non-Jewish Jew. The Merlin Press Ltd. 1981.*

Devall, Bill and Sessions, George. *Deep Ecology: Living as if Nature Mattered. Gibbs Smith. 2001*

Dewey, John. *Human Nature and Conduct. Henry Holt and Co. 1922.*

Diamond, Jared. *Guns, Germs, and Steel: The Fates of Human Societies.* W.W. Norton and Company. 2005.

Diamond, Jared. *Collapse: How Societies Choose to Fail or Succeed.* Penguin Books, Revised edition. 2011.

Dillard, Annie. *Pilgrim at Tinker Creek. Harper Perennial Modern Classics.* 2007.

Dimont, Max. *Jews, God, and History. Mentor. 1964.*

Doyle, Michael. *Liberal Peace: Selected Essays. Routledge. 2011.*

Dreze, Jean and Sen, Amartya. *Hunger and Public Action. Oxford University Press. 1990.*

Drezé, Jean and Sen, Amartya. *An Uncertain Glory: India and Its Contradictions. Princeton University Press. 2013.*

Drucker, Peter F. *The Age of Discontinuity: Guidelines to Our Changing Society. Harper and Row. 1969.*

Drucker, Peter F. *Post-Capitalist Society. Harper Business. 1994.*

Drucker, Peter F. *Management Challenges for the Twenty-First Century.* Harper Business. 2001.

Drucker, Peter F. *Managing the Non-Profit Organization. Harper Paperbacks. 2006.*

Drucker, Peter F. The Discipline of Innovation. Harvard Business Review. 2009.

Dunbar, Robin. Grooming, Gossip, and the Evolution of Language. Harvard University Press. 1998.

Dunbar, Robin. How Many Friends Does One Person Need? Dunbar's Number and Other Evolutionary Quirks. Harvard University Press. 2010.

Durkheim, Emile. The Division of Labor in Society. Macmillan. 1933.

Dworkin, Ronald. Taking Rights Seriously. Harvard University Press. 1978.

Easterly, William. The White Man's Burden: Why the West's Efforts to Aid the Rest Have Done So Much Ill and So Little Good. Penguin Books. 2007.

Edwards, Paul N. A Vast Machine: Computer Models, Climate Data, and the Politics of Global Warming. MIT Press. 2013.

Ehrlich, Paul. The Population Bomb. Sierra Books. 1969.

Ehrlich, Paul R. Human Nature: Genes, Cultures, and the Human Prospect. Penguin Books. 2001.

Ehrlich, Paul R., & Ehrlich, Anne H. The Dominant Animal: Human Evolution and the Environment. Island Press. 2008.

Ehrlich, Paul R., & Ornstein, Robert E. Humanity on a Tightrope: Thoughts on Empathy, Family, and Big Changes for a Viable Future. Rowan and Littlefield Publishers. 2010.

Elvin, Mark. The Retreat of the Elephants: An Environmental History of China. Yale University Press. 2006.

Fagan, Brian. The Little Ice Age: How Climate Made History 1300-1850. Basic Books. 2001.

Fagan, Brian. The Long Summer: How Climate Changed Civilization. Basic Books. 2004.

Fairbank, John King and Goldman, Merle. China: A New History. Belknap Press of Harvard University Press. 2006.

Fischer, David Hackett. Albion's Seed: Four British Folkways in America. Oxford University Press. 1989.

Fischer, David Hackett. The Great Wave: Price Revolutions and the Rhythm of History. Oxford University Press. 1999.

Fischman, Ted C. China, Inc: How the Rise of the Next Superpower Challenges America and the World. Scribner. 2006.

Flannery, Tim. Here On Earth: A Natural History of the Planet. Atlantic Monthly Press. 2011.

Florida, Richard. The Rise of the Creative Class: And How It's Transforming Work, Leisure, Community, and Everyday Life. Basic Books. 2003.

Fogel, Robert William. The Fourth Great Awakening and the Future of Egalitarianism. University of Chicago Press. 2002.

Food and Agriculture Organization. FAOSTAT. Food and Agriculture Organization of the United Nations. 2011.

Fox, Warwick. Toward a Transpersonal Ecology: Developing New Foundation for Environmentalism. State University of New York Press. 1995.

Frank, Thomas. What's the Matter With Kansas? How Conservatives Won the Heart of America. Holt Paperbacks. 2005.

Franklin, Benjamin. Autobiography and Other Writings. Oxford University Press. 2009.

Frederick Jackson Turner. The Frontier in American History. CreateSpace. 2011.

Freedom House. Freedom in the World 2010: The Annual Survey of Political Rights and Civil Liberties. Rowman and Littlefield. 2010.

Friedman, Benjamin M. The Moral Consequences of Economic Growth. Knopf. 2005.

Friedman, Thomas. From Beirut to Jerusalem. Harper Collins Ltd. 1989.

Fromm, Erich. The Sane Society. Fawcett Book, Reprint edition. 1965.

Fromm, Erich. To Have or To Be? Bloomsbury Academic, Revised edition. 2005.

Fukuyama, Francis. The End of History and the Last Man. Free Press. 2006.

Gaddis, John Lewis. Cold War. Penguin. 2006.

Gardiner, Stephen M. A Perfect Moral Storm: the Ethical Tragedy of Climate Change. Oxford University Press. 2011.

Gellner, Ernst. Nations and Nationalism. Cornell University Press. 1983.

Ghemawat, Pankaj. World 3.0: Global Prosperity and How to Achieve It. Harvard Business Review Press. 2011.

Gore, Al. An Inconvenient Truth: The Planetary Emergency of Global Warming and What We Can Do About It. Rodale Books. 2006.

Gore, Al. Our Choice: A Plan to Solve the Climate Crisis. Rodale Books. 2009.

Gorenberg, Gershon. The Unmaking of Israel. Harper Perennial. 2012.

Halberstam, David. The Fifties. Ballantine Books. 1994.

Hamilton, W.D. Narrow Roads of Geneland: Evolution and Social Behavior. Oxford University Press. 1998.

Hansen, James. Storms of My Grandchildren: The Truth About the Climate Change Catastrophe and Our Last Chance to Save Humanity. Bloomsbury. 2010.

Hanson, Valerie. The Open Empire: A History of China to 1600. W.W. Norton and Company. 2000.

Harrison, Lawrence E. and Huntington, Samuel P. Culture Matters: How Values Shape Human Progress. Basic Books. 2001.

Hawken, Paul. Blessed Unrest: How the Largest Social Movement in History is Restoring Grace, Justice, and Beauty to the World. Penguin Books. 2008.

Hazen, Robert M. The Story of Earth: The First 4.5 Billion Years, From Stardust to Living Planet. Penguin Books. 2013

Hegel, G.W.F., & Miller, A.V. trans. The Phenomenology of Spirit. Oxford University Press. 1976.

Hegel, George Wilhelm, & Nisbet, Hugh Barr. trans. Lectures on the Philosophy of World History. Cambridge University Press. 1981.

Hegel, George Wilhelm. *Introduction to the Philosophy of History.* CreateSpace 2011.

Held, David. *Democracy and Global Order: From the Modern State to Cosmopolitan Governance.* Stanford University Press. 1995.

Held, David. *Cosmopolitanism: Ideals and Realities.* Polity. 2010.

Henson, Robert. *The Rough Guide to Climate Change, 3rd ed.* Rough Guides. 2011.

Herodotus. *The Histories, Revised.* Penguin Classics. 2007.

Herring, George C. *From Colony to Superpower: US Foreign Relations Since 1776.* Oxford University Press. 2011.

Hesiod. *Theogeny and Works and Days.* Oxford University Press. 2009.

Hitchens, Christopher. *God Is Not Great: How Religion Poisons Everything.* Hachette Book Group Inc. 2007.

Hobsbawm, Eric. *Nations and Nationalism Since 1780: Programme, Myth, Reality.* Cambridge University Press. 1992.

Homer. *The Odyssey.* Penguin Classics. 1997.

Hourani, Albert. *A History of the Arab Peoples.* Warner Books. 1991.

Hulme, Mike. *Why We Disagree About Climate Change: Understanding Controversy, Inaction, and Opportunity.* Cambridge University Press. 2009.

Hume, David an Steinberg, Eric, ed. *An Inquiry Concerning Human Understanding.* Hackett Pub. Co. 1993.

Huntington, Samuel P. *The Clash of Civilizations and the Remaking of World Order.* Simon and Schuster Inc. 1996.

Hussein, Taha. *The Days: His Autobiography in Three Parts.* The American University of Cairo University Press, 2nd ed. 2010.

Iacoboni, Marco. *Mirroring People: The Science of Empathy and How We Connect With Others.* Picador. 2009.

Illich, Ivan. *Deschooling Society.* Marion Boyars Publishers Ltd. 2000.

Inglehart, Ronald and Weltzel, Christian. Modernization, Cultural Change, and Democracy: the Human Development Sequence. Cambridge University Press. 2005.

James, William. The Principles of Psychology Vols. 1-2. Harvard University Press. 1981.

James, William. Varieties of Religious Experience. Penguin Books. 2007.

Jaspers, Karl. The Origin and Goal of History. Routledge and Kegan Paul Ltd. 1953.

Johnson, Chalmers. The Sorrows of Empire: Militarism, Secrecy, and the End of the Republic. Metropolitan Books. 2004.

Johnson, Luke Timothy. Among the Gentiles: Greco-Roman Religion and Christianity. Yale University Press. 2009.

Judis, John B. and Teixeira, Ruy. The Emerging Democratic Majority. Scrubber. 2004.

Judt, Tony. Postwar: A History of Europe Since 1945. Penguin. 2006.

Kahneman, Daniel. Thinking, Fast and Slow. Farrar, Straus, and Giroux. 2011.

Kant, Immanuel. Grounding for the Metaphysic of Morals. Hackett Publishing Company. 1981.

Kant, Immanuel. Perpetual Peace and Other Essays on Politics, History, and Morals. Hackett Pub. Co. 1983.

Kant, Immanuel. Critique of Judgment. Cambridge University Press. 2001.

Kant, Immanuel and Eaglet, Marcus, trans. and Muller, Max, trans. Critique of Pure Reason. Penguin Classics. 2008.

Kateb, George. Human Dignity. Belknap Press of Harvard University Press. 2011.

Kenny, Charles. Getting Better: Why Global Development Is Succeeding - and How We Can Improve the World Even More. Basic Books. 2012.

Keynes, John Maynard. The General Theory of Employment, Interest, and Money. Kessinger Publishing LLC. 1936.

King Jr., Martin Luther and Carson, Clayborne. ed. *Autobiography of Martin Luther King Jr.* Warner Books. 2001.

Kinzer, Stephen. *Overthrow: America's Century of Regime Change from Hawaii to Iraq.* Times Books. 2007.

Kinzer, Stephen. *A Thousand Hills: Rwanda's Rebirth and the Man Who Dreamed It.* Wiley. 2008.

Kissinger, Henry. *Diplomacy.* Simon and Schuster. 1995.

Kissinger, Henry. *On China.* Penguin Books. 2012.

Korten, David C. *The Post-Corporate World: Life After Capitalism.* Berrett-Koehler Publishers. 2010.

Krishnamurti, J. *The Awakening of Intelligence.* Harper and Row. 1987.

Kurzweil, Ray. *The Singularity is Near: When Humans Transcend Biology.* Penguin. 2006.

Kymlicka, Will. *Multicultural Citizenship: A Liberal Theory of Minority Rights.* Oxford University Press. 1998.

Lakoff, George and Johnson, Mark. *Metaphors We Live By.* University of Chicago Press, 2nd edition. 2003.

Lakoff, George. *The Political Mind: A Cognitive Scientist's Guide to Your Brain and Its Politics.* Penguin Books. 2009.

Langmuir, Charles H. and Broecker, Wally. *How to Build a Habitable Planet: The Story of Earth from Big Bang to Humankind.* Princeton University Press. 2012.

Lappe, Frances Moore. *Eco-Mind: Changing the Way We Think, to Create the World We Want.* Nation Books. 2011.

Lasch, Christopher. *The Culture of Narcissism: American Life in an Age of Diminishing Expectations.* W.W. Norton and Co. 1979.

Leopold, Aldo. *A Sand County Almanac.* Ballantine Books. 1986.

Lerner, Michael. *Embracing Israel/Palestine: A Strategy to Heal and Transform the Middle East.* North Atlantic Books. 2011.

Lessig, Lawrence. *Free Culture: The Nature and Future of Creativity.* Penguin. 2005.

Lessig, Lawrence. *Code: And Other Laws of Cyberspace, Version 2.0.* Basic Books. 2006.

Lessig, Lawrence. *Republic Lost: How Money Corrupts Politics - and a Plan to Stop It.* Twelve. 2012.

Lifton, Robert Jay. *The Protean Self: Human Resilience in an Age of Fragmentation.* University of Chicago Press. 1999.

Lind, Michael. *Up from Conservatism.* Free Press. 1997.

List, Friederich. *National System of Political Economy.* J.B. Lippincott and Co. 1856.

Lovelock, James. *The Vanishing Face of Gaia: a Final Warning.* Basic Books. 2009.

Lumborg, Bjorn. (Ed.) *How to Spend $50 Billion to Make the World a Better Place.* Cambridge University Press. 2006.

MacIntyre, Alasdair. *After Virtue: A Study in Moral Theory.* University of Notre Dame Press, 3rd ed. 2007.

Mackay, David J.C. *Sustainable Energy – Without the Hot Air.* UIT Cambridge. 2009.

Maharshi, Ramana. *The Spiritual Teachings of Ramana Maharshi.* Shambhala. 2004

Malthus, Thomas. *An Essay on the Principle of Population.* Oxford University Press. 1991.

Mann, Michael E., & Kump, Lee R. *Dire Predictions: Understanding Global Warming.* DK Publishing. 2008.

March, James G. *A Primer on Decision Making: How Decisions Happen.* Free Press. 2009.

Marcuse, Herbert. *One Dimensional Man: Studies in the Ideology of Advanced Industrial Society.* Beacon Press, 5th edition. 1991.

Margulis, Sergio. *Causes of Deforestation of the Brazilian Rainforest.* World

Bank. 2004.

Martin, James. *The Meaning of the 21st Century: A Vital Blueprint for Ensuring Our Future.* Riverhead Trade. 2007.

Marx, Karl. *Capital: Volume 1: A Critique of Political Economy.* Penguin Classics. 1992.

Marx, Karl and Nicolaus, Martin, trans. *The Grundrisse: Foundations of the Critique of Political Economy.* Penguin Classics. 1993.

Marx, Karl and Engels, Friedrich. *The German Ideology, including Theses on Feuerbach.* Prometheus Books. 1998.

Marx, Karl and Engels, Friedrich. *The Communist Manifesto. A Modern Edition.* Verso. 2012.

McKibben, Bill. *The End of Nature.* Random House Trade Paperback. 1989.

McNeill, William H. *Keeping Together in Time: Dance and Drill in Human History.* ACLS Humanities. 1995.

Mead, Walter Russell. *Power, Terror, Peace, and War: America's Grand Strategy in a World at Risk.* Vintage Books. 2005.

Meadows, Donella H. Meadows, Dennis L. Randers, Jorgen and Behrens, III, William W. *The Limits to Growth: A Report for the Club of Rome's Project on the Predicament of Mankind.* Universe Books. 1974.

Micklethwait, John. *The Company. A Short History of Revolutionary Idea.* Modern Library. 2005.

Milanovic, Branko. *Worlds Apart: Measuring International and Global Inequality.* Princeton University Press. 2007.

Mill, John Stuart. *On Liberty and the Subjection of Women.* Penguin Classics. 2007.

Mitchell, Stephen. *The Bhagavad-Gita: A New Translation.* Three Rivers Press. 2002.

Momen, Moojan. *The Baha'i Faith.* One World Publications. 2007.

Moorehead, Alan. *The White Nile.* Harper and Row. 1960.

Moorehead, Alan. The Blue Nile. Harper and Row. 1962.

Morris, John G. Martin Behaim: The German Astronomer of the Times of Columbus. Kessinger Publishing LLC. 2007.

Moyo, Dambisa. Dead Aid: Why Aid Is Not Working and How There Is a Better Way for Africa. Farrar. Straus, and Giroux. 2010.

Muir, John. My First Summer in the Sierra. Dover Publication. 2004.

Muller, Richard A. Energy for Future Presidents: The Science Behind the Headlines. W.W. Norton and Company. 2012.

Murchie, Guy. The Seven Mysteries of Life. Mariner Books. 1999.

Naess, Arne. Ecology, Community, and Lifestyle: Outline of an Ecosophy. Cambridge University Press. 1993.

Naess, Arne. The Ecology of Wisdom. Counterpoint. 2010.

Nagel, Thomas. The View From Nowhere. Oxford University Press. 1986.

Narayan, Deepa. Voices of the Poor: Crying Out for a Change. Oxford University Press. 2000.

Narayan, Deepa, & Petesch, Patti (Ed.). Voices of the Poor: From Many Lands. Oxford University Press. 2002.

Nasr, Seyyed Hossein. Islam: Religion, History, and Civilization. Harper One. 2002.

Nasr, Vali. The Shia Revival. How Conflicts Within Islam Will Shape the Future. W.W. Norton and Co. 2007.

National Research Council. Nutritional Requirements of Beef Cattle. National Academy Press. 2000.

Niebuhr, Reinhold and Bacevich, Andrew J. intro. The Irony of American History. University of Chicago. 2008.

Nordhaus, Ted, & Shellenberger, Michael. Breakthrough: From the Death of Environmentalism to the

Politics of Possibility. Houghton Mifflin Co. First Edition. 2007.

Novak, Robert. *No One Sees God: the Dark Night of Atheists and Believers.* Doubleday. 2008.

Nozick, Robert. *Anarchy, State, and Utopia. Basic Books. 1977.*

Nussbaum, Martha C. *Frontiers of Justice: Disability, Nationality, Species Membership. Belknap Press of Harvard University Press. 2007.*

Nussbaum, Martha C. *Creating Capabilities: The Human Development Approach. Belknap Press of Harvard University Press. 2011.*

Okin, Susan Moller. *Justice, Gender, and the Family. Basic Books. 1991.*

Ostrum, Elinor. *Governing the Commons: the Evolution of Institutions for Collective Action. Cambridge University Press. 1990.*

Paarlberg, Robert. *Starved for Science: How Biotechnology is Being Kept Out of Africa. Harvard University Press. 2009.*

Paarlberg, Robert. *Food Politics: What Everyone Needs to Know. Oxford University Press. 2010.*

Pernick, Ron. *The Clean Tech Revolution: The Next Big Growth and Investment Opportunity. Collins Business. 2007.*

Phelps, Edmund S. *Mass Flourishing: How Grassroots Innovation Created Jobs, Challenge, and Change. Princeton University Press. 2013.*

Phillips, Kevin. *American Theocracy: the Peril and Politics of Radical Religion, Oil, and Borrowed Money, in the 21st Century. Viking Penguin. 2006.*

Piaget, Jean. *The Psychology of Development. Routledge and Kegan Paul, 1950.*

Pimentel, David. *Sustainability of Meat-Based and Plant-Based Diets and Sustainability. The American Journal of Clinical Nutrition. 2003.*

Pinker, Steven. *The Blank Slate: The Modern Denial of Human Nature. Penguin Books. 2003.*

Pinker, Steven. *The Better Angels of Our Nature: Why Violence Has Declined. Penguin Books. 2011.*

Plato and Bloom, Allen, trans. The Republic of Plato. Basic Books. 1968.

Plato. The Republic. Simon & Brown. 2011.

Pogge, Thomas W. World Poverty and Human Rights. Polity. 2008.

Polak, Paul. Out of Poverty: What Works When Traditional Approaches Fail. Berrett Koehler Publishers. 2009.

Polanyi, Karl. The Great Transformation: The Political and Economic Origins of Our Time. Beacon Press. 2001.

Population Reference Bureau. World Population Data Sheet. Population Bulletin. 2007.

Posner, Eric A. and Weisbach, David. Climate Change Justice. Princeton University Press. 2010.

Prahalad, C.K. The Fortune at the Bottom of the Pyramid: Eradicating Poverty Through Profits. Wharton School Publishing. 2009.

Prunier, Gerard. The Rwanda Crisis: History of a Genocide. Columbia University Press. 1997.

Purdy, Jedediah. For Common Things: Irony, Trust, and Commitment in America Today. Vintage. 2000.

Putnam, Robert D. Bowling Alone: The Collapse and Revival of American Community. Touchstone Books. 2001.

Putnam, Robert D. and Campbell, David E. American Grace: How Religion Divides and Unites Us. Simon and Schuster. 2012.

Rakove, Jack N. Original Meanings: Politics and Ideas in the Making if the Constitution. Vintage. 1997.

Rawls, John. The Law of Peoples, with "The Idea of Public Reason Revisited." Harvard University Press. 2001.

Rawls, John. Political Liberalism. Columbia University Press 2nd edition. 2005.

Rawls, John. A Theory of Justice. Belknap Press of Harvard University Press. 1999.

Regan, Tom. *The Case for Animal Rights. University of California Press.* 2004.

Rifkin, Jeremy. *The Empathic Civilization: The Race to Global Consciousness in a World in Crisis. Tarcher. 2009*

Riis, Jacob. *How the Other Half Lives: Studies Among the Tenements of New York. Kessenger Publishing, LLC. 2010.*

Rodrik, Dani. *One Economics, Many Recipes: Globalization, Institutions, and Economic Growth. Princeton University Press. 2008.*

Rolston III, Holmes. *Three Big Bangs: Matter-Energy, Life, and Mind. Columbia University Press. 2010.*

Rolston III, Holmes. *A New Environmental Ethics: the Next Millennium for Life on Earth. Routledge. 2011.*

Rothkopf, David. *Superclass: The Global Power Elite and the World They Are Making. Farrar, Straus, and Giroux. 2009.*

Rousseau, Jean-Jacques. *Discourses on Political Economy and the Social Contract. Oxford University Press. 2009.*

Rumi, Jalal al-Din. *The Essential Rumi. Harper One. 2004.*

Russett, Bruce M. *Grasping the Democratic Peace. Princeton University Press. 1994.*

Sachs, Jeffrey. *The End of Poverty: Economic Possibilities for Our Time. Penguin Books. 2006.*

Sachs, Jeffrey D. *Common Wealth: Economics for a Crowded Planet. Penguin Books. 2009.*

Sahlins, Marshall. *Stone Age Economics. Aldine Transaction. 1974.*

Sandel, Michael. *Liberalism and the Limits of Justice. Cambridge University Press. 1982.*

Sandel, Michael. *Democracy's Discontent: America in Search of Public Philosophy. Belknap Press of Harvard University Press. 1998.*

Sandel, Michael J. *Justice: What's the Right Thing to Do? Farrar, Straus, and Giroux. 2010.*

Schlesinger Jr., Arthur M. *The Disuniting of America: Reflections on a Multicultural Society.* W.W. Norton and Company. 1998.

Schumacher, E.F. *Small if Beautiful: Economics as if People Mattered.* Harper Perennial. 2010.

Schweitzer, Albert. *The Philosophy of Civilization.* The Macmillan Company. 1949.

Sen, Amartya. *Development as Freedom.* Anchor. 2000.

Sen, Amartya. *Identity and Violence: The Illusion of Destiny.* W.W. Norton and Company. 2007.

Senge, Peter M. Smith, Bryan. Kruschwitz, Nina and Laur, Joe. *The Necessary Revolution: How Individuals and Organizations are Working Together to Create a Sustainable World.* Crown Business. 2010.

Sheldrake, Rupert. *The Rebirth of Nature: The Greening of Science and God.* Park Street Press. 1994.

Shellenberger, Michael and Nordhaus, Ted. *Breakthrough: Why We Can't Leave Saving the Planet to Environmentalists.* Houghton Mifflin Co. 2009.

Shipler, David K. *Arab and Jew: Wounded Spirits in a Promised Land.* Penguin Books. 1987.

Simmel, George. *Conflict and the Web of Group Affiliations.* The Free Press. 1955.

Singer, Peter. *Famine, Affluence, and Morality.* Philosophy and Public Affairs. 1971.

Singer, Peter. *The Expanding Circle: Ethics and Sociobiology.* Farrar, Straus, and Giroux. 1981.

Singer, Peter. *One World: The Ethics of Globalization.* Yale University Press. 2002.

Singer, Peter. *The Life You Can Save: How to Do Your Part to End World Poverty.* Random House Trade Paperbacks. 2010.

Skee, David l. *Icarus in the Boardroom: The Fundamental Flaws in Corporate America and Where They Came From.* Oxford University Press.

2006.

Slaughter, Anne-Marie. *A New World Order.* Princeton University Press. *2005.*

Smil, Vaclav. *Energy Myths and Realities: Bringing Science to the Energy Policy Debate.* American Enterprise Institute Press. *2010.*

Smith, Adam. *The Wealth of Nations.* Modern Library. *1776.*

Smith, Adam. *The Theory of Moral Sentiments.* Barnes and Noble Books. *2004.*

Smith, Bradley A. *Unfree Speech: the Fallacy of Campaign Finance Reform.* Princeton University Press. *2003.*

Smith, William and Stray, Chris. *Dictionary of Greek and Roman Biography and Mythology.* I.B. Taurus. *2007.*

Sobel, Dava. *Longitude: the True Story of a Lone Genius Who Solved the Greatest Scientific Problem of His Time.* Walker and Company. *2007.*

Steffen, Alex and McKibben, Bill, intro. *Worldchanging: A Users Guide to the 21st Century.* Abrams, Revised ed. *2011.*

Steinberg, Jonathon. *European History and European Lives: 1715 to 1914.* The Teaching Company.

Steinfeld, Henning. Gerber, Pierre. Wasenaar, T.D. and Castel, Vincent. *Livestock's Long Shadow: Environmental Issues and Options. Livestock, Environment, and Development.* Food and Agricultural Organization of the United Nations. *2006.*

Stern, Nicholas. *The Global Deal: Climate Change and the Creation of a New Era of Progress and Prosperity.* Public Affairs. *2009.*

Stone, Christopher D. *Should Trees Have Standing: Law, Morality, and the Environment.* Oxford University Press. *2010.*

Sullivan, Robert. *The Thoreau You Don't Know.* Harper Perennial. *2011.*

Sunstein, Cass R. and Nussbaum, Martha R., eds. *Animal Rights: Current Debates and New Directions.* Oxford University Press. *2005.*

Sunstein, Cass. *Infotopia: How Many Minds Produce Knowledge*. Oxford University Press. 2008.

Swimme, Brian. *The Universe Story: From the Primordial Flaring Forth to the Ecozoic Era – A Celebration of the Unfolding of the Cosmos*. Harper One. 1992.

Tainter, Joseph A. *The Collapse of Complex Societies*. Cambridge University Press. 1990.

Taylor, Bron. *Dark Green Religion: Nature, Spirituality, and the Planetary Future*. University of California Press. 2009.

Taylor, Charles. *Hegel and Modern Society*. Cambridge University Press. 1979.

Taylor, Charles. *A Secular Age*. The Belknap Press of Harvard University Press. 2007.

Teilard de Chardin, Pierre. *The Phenomenon of Man*. Wm. Collins Sons & Co. Ltd. 1959.

The Economist. *Brain Scan: Watching the Web Grow Up*. March, 8, 2007.

The Economist. *Global Warming: Some Like it Cool*. Dec. 19, 2007.

The Economist. *Mobile Phones: Sensors and Sensitivity*. June 4, 2009.

The Federation of American Scientists and Dexter Mathews and Katharine Way, eds. *One World or None: A Report to the Public of the Full Meaning of the Atomic Bomb*. New Press. 1946.

The Onion. *Twitter Creator on Iran*. June 24, 2009.

Thoreau, Henry David. *Walden and Other Writings*. Modern Library. 1992.

Thurow, Roger and Kilman, Scott. *Enough: Why the World's Poorest Starve in an Age of Plenty*. Public Affairs. 2010.

Tickle, Phyllis. *Emergence Christianity: What It Is, Where It Is Going, and Why It Matters*. Baker Books. 2012.

Tillich, Paul. *The Courage to Be*. Yale University Press. 1952.

Toffler, Alvin. *Future Shock*. Random House. 1970.

Toffler, Alvin. The Third Wave. Bantam. 1984.

Toffler, Alvin. Revolutionary Wealth. How it will be created and how it will change our lives. Crown Business. 2007.

Tolstoy, Leo. Anna Karenina. Penguin Classics. 2004.

Traboulsi, Fawwaz. A History of Modern Lebanon. Pluto Press. 2007.

Tribe, Laurence H. The Invisible Constitution. Oxford University Press. 2008.

Trout, J.D. Why Empathy Matters: the Science and Psychology of Better Judgment. Penguin Books. 2010.

Unger, Peter. Living High and Letting Die: Our Illusion of Innocence. Oxford University Press. 1996.

United Nations Framework Convention on Climate Change. Investment and Financial Flows to Address Climate Change. United Nations Framework Convention on Climate Change. 2007

United Nations, Department of Economic and Social Affairs. World Population Prospects: the 2006 Revision. The United Nations. 2007.

US Department of Agriculture. Agricultural Statistics. US Department of Agriculture. 2001.

Varela, Francisco J. Thompson. Evan T. and Rosch, Eleanor. The Embodied Mind: Cognitive Science and Human Experience. MIT Press. 1992.

Virgil and Fagles, Robert, trans. The Aeneid. Penguin Classics. 2010.

Waldron, Jeremy. In Seyla Benhabib. Another Cosmopolitanism. Oxford University Press. 2008.

Wallerstein, Immanuel. World-Systems Analysis: An Introduction. Duke University Press. 2004.

Walzer, Michael. Spheres of Justice. Basic Books. 1984.

Wapner, Paul. Living Through the End of Nature: the Future of American Environmentalism. Massachusetts Institute of Technology Press. 2010.

Weber, Christopher. L. and Mathews, H. Scott. Food Miles and Relative Climate Impacts of Food Produced in the United States. Environment, Science, and Technology, 42 3508-3513. 2008.

Weber, Max. The Sociology of Religion. J.C.B. Mohr. 1922.

Weinberger, David. Everything is Miscellaneous: The Power of the New Digital Disorder. Holt Paperbacks. 2008.

Wilber, Ken. The Marriage of Sense and Soul: Integrating Science and Religion. Random House. 1998.

Wilber, Ken. Integral Psychology: Consciousness, Spirit, Psychology, Therapy. Shambhala Books. 2000.

Wilber, Ken. A Theory of Everything: An Integral Vision for Business, Politics, Science and Spirituality. Shambhala. 2001.

Wilber, Ken. Sex, Ecology, and Spirituality: the Spirit of Evolution. Shambhala Books. 2001.

Wilber, Ken. Integral Spirituality: A Startling New Role for Religion in the Modern and Postmodern

World. Shambhala. 2007.

Williams, Richard C. The Cooperative Movement: Globalization From Below. Ashgate Pub Co. 2007.

Wilson, E.O. Human Nature. The President and Fellows of Harvard College. 1978.

Wilson, Edward O. Consilience; the Unity of Knowledge. Vintage Books. 1999.

Wilson, Edward O. The Social Conquest of Earth. Liveright. 2012.

Wilson, James Q. The Moral Sense. The Free Press. 1997.

Wolf, Martin. Why Globalization Works. Yale University Press 2nd ed. 2005.

Wolfe, Alan. The Transformation of American Religion: How We Actually Live Our Faith. University of Chicago Press. 2005.

Woodard, Colin. American Nations: A History of the Eleven Regional Cultures of North America. Penguin Books. 2012.

Wordsworth, William. The Major Works. Oxford University Press. 2008.

Wright, Robert. Non-Zero: the Logic of Human Destiny. Vintage. 2001.

Wright, Robert. The Evolution of God. Back Bay Books. 2010.

Wrong, Michela. In the Footsteps of Mr. Kurtz: Living On the Brink of Disaster in Mobutu's Congo. Harper Perennial. 2002.

Wu, Tim. The Master Switch: The Rise and Fall of Information Empires. Knopf. 2010.

Yunus, Muhammad. Banker to the Poor: Micro-lending and the Battle Against World Poverty. Public Affairs. 2003.

Yunus, Muhammad. Creating a World Without Poverty: Social Business and the Future of Capitalism. Public Affairs. 2009.

Zakaria, Fareed. The Post-American World. W.W. Norton and Company. 2008.

Zalsiewicz, Jan, & Williams, Mark. The Goldilocks Planet: The 4 Billion Year Story of Earth's Climate. Oxford University Press. 2012.

Zimmerman, Michael E. Contesting Earth's Future: Radical Ecology and Postmodernity. University of California Press. 1997.

Zubok, Vladislov M. A Failed Empire: The Soviet Union in the Cold War from Stalin to Gorbachev. The University of North Carolina Press. 2008.

REFERENCES

INTRODUCTION

[1] Ken Wilber. A Theory of Everything: An Integral Vision for Business, Politics, Science and Spirituality. Shambhala. 2001.

[2] Kwame Anthony Appiah. Cosmopolitanism: Ethics in a World of Strangers. W.W. Norton and Co. 2007.

[3] Seyla Benhabib. Another Cosmopolitanism. Oxford University Press. 2008.

[4] David Held. Cosmopolitanism: Ideals and Realities. Polity. 2010.

[5] Ronald Inglehart and Christian Welzel. Modernization, Cultural Change, and Democracy: The Human Development Sequence. Cambridge University Press. 2005.

[6] William J. Bernstein. A Splendid Exchange: How Trade Shaped the World. Grove Press. 2009.

[7] Marshall Sahlins. Stone Age Economics. Aldine Transaction. 1974.

[8] Yokai Benkler. The Wealth of Networks: How Social Production Transforms Markets and Freedoms. Yale University Press. 2007.

[9] Alvin Toffler. Revolutionary Wealth: How it will be created and how it will change our lives. Crown Business. 2007.

[10] Ray Kurzweil. The Singularity is Near: When Humans Transcend Biology. Penguin. 2006.

[11] Lawrence Lessig. Free Culture: The Nature and Future of Creativity. Penguin. 2005.

[12] Alvin Toffler. The Third Wave. Bantam. 1984.

[13] Anne-Marie Slaughter. A New World Order. Princeton University Press. 2005.

[14] Pierre Teilard de Chardin. The Phenomenon of Man. Wm. Collins Sons & Co. Ltd. 1959.

[15] Amartya Sen. Identity and Violence: The Illusion of Destiny. W.W. Norton and Company. 2007.

[16] Peter Singer. One World: The Ethics of Globalization. Yale University Press. 2002.

[17] David Held. Cosmopolitanism: Ideals and Realities.

[18] David Held. Democracy and Global Order: From the Modern State to Cosmopolitan Governance. Stanford University Press. 1995.

[19] Paul Collier The Bottom Billion: Why the Poorest Countries are Failing and What Can Be Done About It. Oxford University Press. 2008.

[20] Ken Wilber. Integral Spirituality:

A Startling New Role for Religion in the Modern and Postmodern World. Shambhala. 2007.

[21] Warwick Fox. *Toward a Transpersonal Ecology: Developing New Foundation for Environmentalism.* State University of New York Press. 1995.

[22] Bill Devall. *Deep Ecology: Living as if Nature Mattered.* Gibbs Smith. 2001.

[23] Arne Naess. *Ecology, Community, and Lifestyle: Outline of an Ecosophy.* Cambridge University Press. 1993.

[24] Jeremy Rifkin. *The Empathic Civilization: The Race to Global Consciousness in a World in Crisis.* Tarcher. 2009

[25] Pankaj Ghemawat. *World 3.0: Global Prosperity and How to Achieve It.* Harvard Business Review Press. 2011.

[26] Jean Piaget. *The Psychology of Development.* Routledge and Kegan Paul. 1950.

[27] Daniel Kahneman. *Thinking, Fast and Slow.* Farrar, Straus, and Giroux. 2011.

[28] Ken Wilber. *Sex, Ecology, and Spirituality: The Spirit of Evolution.* Shambhala. 2001.

[29] Ibid.

[30] Ibid.

SECTION 1. GLOBALIZATION OF MIND

MAJESTIC & SUBLIME

[1] Annie Dillard. *Pilgrim at Tinker Creek.* Harper Perennial Modern Classics. 2007.

[2] Stephen Mitchell. *The Bhagavad-Gita: A New Translation.* Three Rivers Press. 2002.

[3] Immanuel Kant. *Critique of Judgment.* Cambridge University Press. 2001.

[4] Karl Polanyi. *The Great Transformation: The Political and Economic Origins of Our Time.* Beacon Press. 2001.

[5] Jacob Riis. *How the Other Half Lives: Studies Among the Tenements of New York.* Kessenger Publishing, LLC. 2010.

[6] Don Beck and Christopher Cowan. *Spiral Dynamics: Mastering Values, Leadership, and Change.* Wiley-Blackwell. 2005.

[7] Ken Wilber. *A Theory of Everything: An Integral Vision for Business, Politics, Science, and Spirituality.* Shambhala. 2001.

[8] The Economist. *Global Warming: Some Like it Cool.* Dec. 19, 2007.

[9] Anne-Marie Slaughter. *A New World Order.* Princeton University Press. 2005.

[10] Jeremy Rifkin. The Empathic Civilization: The Race to Global Consciousness in a World in Crisis. Tarcher. 2009.

[11] Amartya Sen. Identity and Violence: The Illusion of Destiny. W.W. Norton and Company. 2007.

[12] Will Kymlicka. Multicultural Citizenship: A Liberal Theory of Minority Rights. Oxford University Press. 1998.

[13] Karl Marx and Friedrich Engels. The German Ideology, including Theses on Feuerbach. Prometheus Books. 1998.

[14] Peter M. Senge, Bryan Smith, Nina Kruschwitz, and Joe Laur. The Necessary Revolution: How Individuals and Organizations are Working Together to Create a Sustainable World. Crown Business. 2010.

[15] Paul R. Ehrlich and Robert E. Ornstein. Humanity on a Tightrope: Thoughts on Empathy, Family, and Big Changes for a Viable Future. Rowan and Littlefield Publishers. 2010.

[16] Frances Moore Lappe. Eco-Mind: Changing the Way We Think, to Create the World We Want. Nation Books. 2011.

[17] Peter Singer. One World: The Ethics of Globalization. Yale University Press. 2002.

[18] Ibid.

[19] Ibid.

[20] Ramana Maharshi. The Spiritual Teachings of Ramana Maharshi. Shambala. 2004

[21] Jonathon Steinberg. European History and European Lives: 1715 to 1914. The Teaching Company.

[22] Eric Hobsbawm. Nations and Nationalism Since 1780: Programme, Myth, Reality. Cambridge University Press. 1992.

[23] Benedict Anderson. Imagined Communities: Reflections on the Origin and Spread of Nationalism. Verso. 1983.

[24] Ernst Gellner. Nations and Nationalism. Cornell University Press. 1983.

[25] Amartya Sen. Identity and Violence: The Illusion of Destiny. W.W. Norton and Company. 2007.

[26] Peter Singer. The Expanding Circle: Ethics, Evolution, and Moral Progress. Princeton University Press. 1981.

[27] Kwame Anthony Appiah. Cosmopolitanism: Ethics in a World of Strangers. W.W. Norton & Company. 2007.

[28] Michael J. Sandel. Justice: What's the Right Thing to Do? Farrar, Straus and Giroux. 2010.

[29] Peter Singer. *The Expanding Circle: Ethics, Evolution, and Moral Progress.* Princeton University Press. 1981.

[30] Martha C. Nussbaum. *Frontiers of Justice: Disability, Nationality, Species Membership.* Belknap Press of Harvard University Press. 2007.

[31] Tom Regan. *The Case for Animal Rights.* University of California Press. 2004.

HISTORIES OF CONSCIOUSNESS

[1] Guy Murchie. *The Seven Mysteries of Life.* Mariner Books. 1999.

[2] Homer. *The Odyssey.* Penguin Classics. 1997.

[3] Michael Coogan, Mark Z. Brettler, Carol A. Newsom, Pheme Perkins. *The New Oxford Annotated Bible with Apocrypha: New Revised Standard Version.* Oxford University Press. 2010.

[4] Hesiod. *Theogeny and Works and Days.* Oxford University Press. 2009.

[5] George Wilhelm Hegel. *Introduction to the Philosophy of History.* CreateSpace 2011.

[6] Herodotus. *The Histories, Revised.* Penguin Classics. 2007.

[7] Immanuel Kant. *Perpetual Peace and Other Essays on Politics, History, and Morals.* Hackett Pub

Co. 1983.

[8] Plato. *The Republic.* Simon and Brown. 2011.

[9] Jean-Jacques Rousseau. *Discourses on Political Economy and the Social Contract.* Oxford University Press. 2009.

[10] George Wilhelm Hegel. *Introduction to the Philosophy of History.* CreateSpace. 2011.

[11] Anne-Marie Slaughter. *A New World Order.* Princeton University Press. 2005.

[12] Francis Fukuyama. *The End of History and the Last Man.* Free Press. 2006.

[13] Fareed Zakaria. *The Post-American World.* W.W. Norton and Company. 2008.

[14] Leo Tolstoy. *Anna Karenina.* Penguin Classics. 2004.

[15] Fareed Zakaria. *The Post-American World.* W.W. Norton and Company. 2008.

[16] Dani Rodrik. *One Economics, Many Recipes: Globalization, Institutions, and Economic Growth.* Princeton University Press. 2008.

[17] E.F. Schumacher. *Small if Beautiful: Economics as if People Mattered.* Harper Perennial. 2010.

[18] Charles Kenny. *Getting Better: Why Global Development is Succeeding and How We Can Help

the World Even More. Basic Books. 2012.

[19] Freedom House. Freedom in the World 2010: The Annual Survey of Political Rights and Civil Liberties. Rowman and Littlefield. 2010.

[20] George C. Herring. From Colony to Superpower: US Foreign Relations Since 1776. Oxford University Press. 2011.

[21] Stephen Kinzer. Overthrow: America's Century of Regime Change from Hawaii to Iraq. Times Books. 2007.

[22] Bruce M. Russett. Grasping the Democratic Peace. Princeton University Press. 1994. Michael Doyle. Liberal Peace: Selected Essays. Routledge. 2011.

[23] Michael E. Brown, Sean M. Lynn-Jones, and Steven Miller. Debating the Democratic Peace. The MIT Press. 1996.

EVOLUTION OF ATLAS

[1] William Smith and Chris Stray. Dictionary of Greek and Roman Biography and Mythology. I.B. Taurus. 2007.

[2] Herodotus. The Histories, Revised. Penguin Classics. 2007.

[3] John G. Morris. Martin Behaim: The German Astronomer of the Times of Columbus. Kessinger Publishing LLC. 2007.

[4] Dava Sobel. Longitude: the True Story of a Lone Genius Who Solved the Greatest Scientific Problem of His Time. Walker and Company. 2007.

[5] Daniel J. Boorstin. The Discoverers. Vintage. 1985.

[6] Alan Moorehead. The Blue Nile. Harper and Row. 1962.

[7] Alan Moorehead. The White Nile. Harper and Row. 1960.

[8] Frederick Jackson Turner. The Frontier in American History. CreateSpace. 2011.

[9] Jared Diamond. Guns, Germs, and Steel: The Fates of Human Societies. W.W. Norton and Company. 2005.

[10] Joseph Conrad. Heart of Darkness. Tribeca Books. 2011.

[11] Al Gore. An Inconvenient Truth: The Planetary Emergency of Global Warming and What We Can Do About It. Rodale Books. 2006.

[12] Ted Nordhaus and Michael Shellenberger. Breakthrough: From the Death of Environmentalism to the Politics of Possibility. Houghton Mifflin Co. First Edition. 2007.

[13] Rupert Sheldrake. The Rebirth of Nature: The Greening of Science and God. Park Street Press. 1994.

[14] The Federation of American Scientists and Dexter Mathews and Katharine Way, eds. One World or

None: A Report to the Public of the Full Meaning of the Atomic Bomb. New Press. 1946.

[15] *Vladislov M. Zubok. A Failed Empire: The Soviet Union in the Cold War from Stalin to Gorbachev.* The University of North Carolina Press. 2008.

[16] *David Halberstam. The Fifties.* Ballantine Books. 1994.

[17] *Vladislov M. Zubok. A Failed Empire: The Soviet Union in the Cold War from Stalin to Gorbachev.*

[18] *John Lewis Gaddis. Cold War.* Penguin. 2006.

[19] *Tony Judt. Postwar: A History of Europe Since 1945.* Penguin. 2009.

[20] *Noam Chomsky and Edward Herman. The Washington Connection and Third World Fascism. South End Press. 1999.*

[21] *Pierre Teilard de Chardin. The Phenomenon of Man. Wm. Collins Sons & Co. Ltd. 1959.*

[22] *Brian Fagan. The Long Summer: How Climate Changed Civilization. Basic Books. 2004.*

[23] *Brian Fagan. The Little Ice Age: How Climate Made History 1300-1850. Basic Books. 2001.*

[24] *David Hackett Fischer. The Great Wave: Price Revolutions and the Rhythm of History. Oxford University Press. 1999.*

[25] *Ray Kurzweil. The Singularity is Near: When Humans Transcend Biology. Penguin. 2006.*

[26] *The Economist. Mobile Phones: Sensors and Sensitivity. June 4, 2009.*

[27] *Benedict Anderson. Imagined Communities: Reflections on the Origin and Spread of Nationalism. Verso. 1983.*

[28] *Ernst Gellner. Nations and Nationalism. Cornell University Press. 1983.*

THE DIALECTIC OF DEVELOPMENT

[1] *Henry David Thoreau. Walden and Other Writings. Modern Library. 1992.*

[2] *Robert Sullivan. The Thoreau You Don't Know. Harper Perennial. 2011.*

[3] *Immanuel Wallerstein. World-Systems Analysis: An Introduction. Duke University Press. 2004.*

[4] *William Wordsworth. The Major Works. Oxford University Press. 2008.*

[5] *Aldo Leopold. A Sand County Almanac. Ballantine Books. 1986.*

[6] *Christopher. L. Weber and H. Scott Mathews. Food Miles and Relative Climate Impacts of Food Produced in the United States. Environment,*

Science, and Technology, 42 3508-3513. 2008.

[7] *Stewart Brand. Whole Earth Discipline: Why Dense Cities, Nuclear Power, Transgenic Crops, Restored Wildlands, and Geoengineering are Necessary. Penguin Books. 2010.*

[8] *Michael Shellenberger and Ted Nordhaus. Breakthrough: Why We Can't Leave Saving the Planet to Environmentalists. Houghton Mifflin Co. 2009.*

[9] *Bron Taylor. Dark Green Religion: Nature, Spirituality, and the Planetary Future. University of California Press. 2009.*

[10] *Aldo Leopold. A Sand County Almanac. Ballantine Books. 1986.*

[11] *John Muir. My First Summer in the Sierra. Dover Publication. 2004.*

[12] *Arne Naess. The Ecology of Wisdom. Counterpoint. 2010.*

[13] *Albert Schweitzer. The Philosophy of Civilization. The Macmillan Company. 1949.*

[14] *William Cronon. Uncommon Ground: Rethinking the Human Place in Nature. W.W. Norton and Co. 1996.*

[15] *Ken Wilber. Sex, Ecology, and Spirituality: the Spirit of Evolution. Shambhala Books. 2001.*

[16] *James Lovelock. The Vanishing Face of Gaia: a Final Warning. Basic Books. 2009.*

[17] *Paul R. Ehrlich and Anne H. Ehrlich. The Dominant Animal: Human Evolution and the Environment. Island Press. 2008.*

[18] *Michael E. Zimmerman. Contesting Earth's Future: Radical Ecology and Postmodernity. University of California Press. 1997.*

[19] *Bron Taylor. Dark Green Religion: Nature, Spirituality, and the Planetary Future.*

[20] *Michael Shellenberger and Ted Nordhaus. Breakthrough: Why We Can't Leave Saving the Planet to Environmentalists. Houghton Mifflin co. 2009.*

[21] *Robert Paarlberg. Starved for Science: How Biotechnology is Being Kept Out of Africa. Harvard University Press. 2009.*

[22] *Robert Paarlberg. Food Politics: What Everybody Needs to Know. Oxford University Press. 2010.*

[23] *Stewart Brand. Whole Earth Discipline: Why Dense Cities, Nuclear Power, Transgenic Crops, Restored Wildlands, and Geoengineering are Necessary. Penguin Books. 2010.*

[24] *Robert Paarlberg. Food Politics: What Everybody Needs to Know. Oxford University Press. 2010.*

[25] Robert Paarlberg. Starved for Science: How Biotechnology is Being Kept Out of Africa. Harvard University Press. 2009.

[26] Stewart Brand. Whole Earth Discipline: Why Dense Cities, Nuclear Power, Transgenic Crops, Restored Wildlands, and Geoengineering are Necessary.

[27] Ibid.

[28] Ibid.

[29] James Lovelock. The Vanishing Face of Gaia: a Final Warning. Basic Books. 2009.

[30] David J.C. Mackay. Sustainable Energy – Without the Hot Air. UIT Cambridge. 2009.

[31] Richard A. Muller. Energy for Future Presidents: The Science Behind the Headlines. W.W. Norton and Company. 2012.

[32] Vaclav Smil. Energy Myths and Realities: Bringing Science to the Energy Policy Debate. American Enterprise Institute Press. 2010.

[33] Al Gore. Our Choice: A Plan to Solve the Climate Crisis. Rodale Books. 2009.

[34] Stewart Brand. Whole Earth Discipline: Why Dense Cities, Nuclear Power, Transgenic Crops, Restored Wildlands, and Geoengineering are Necessary. Penguin Books. 2010.

[35] Michael Shellenberger and Ted Nordhaus. Breakthrough: Why We Can't Leave Saving the Planet to Environmentalists. Houghton Mifflin. 2009

[36] Ibid.

[37] Benjamin M. Friedman. The Moral Consequences of Economic Growth. Knopf. 2005.

[38] Herbert Marcuse. One-Dimensional Man: Studies in the Ideology of Advanced Industrial Society. Beacon Press. 1991.

[39] Murray Bookchin. The Ecology of Freedom: the Emergence and Dissolution of Hierarchy. AK Press. 2005.

[40] Adam Smith. The Theory of Moral Sentiments. Barnes and Noble Books. 2004.

[41] Emile Durkheim. The Division of Labor in Society. Macmillan. 1933.

[42] Amartya Sen. Development as Freedom. Anchor. 2000.

[43] Michael Shellenberger and Ted Nordhaus. Breakthrough: Why We Can't Leave Saving the Planet to Environmentalists. Houghton Mifflin. 2009.

[44] Ronald Inglehart and Christian Weltzel. Modernization, Cultural Change, and Democracy: the Human Development Sequence. Cambridge University Press. 2005.

[45] Michael Shellenberger and Ted Nordhaus. Breakthrough: Why

We Can't Leave Saving the Planet to Environmentalists. Houghton Mifflin. 2009.

[46] *The Onion. Twitter Creator on Iran. June 24, 2009.*

[47] *Peter Drucker. The Discipline of Innovation. Harvard Business Review. 2009.*

[48] *Paul Hawken. Blessed Unrest: How the Largest Social Movement in History is Restoring Grace, Justice, and Beauty to the World. Penguin Books. 2008.*

[49] *John Maynard Keynes. The General Theory of Employment, Interest, and Money. Kessinger Publishing LLC. 1936.*

SECTION 2.
GLOBALIZATION OF COMMUNICATION

CONJURING DREAMS

[1] *Francisco J. Varela, Evan T. Thompson, and Eleanor Rosch. The Embodied Mind: Cognitive Science and Human Experience. MIT Press. 1992.*

[2] *Peter L. Berger and Thomas Luckman. The Social Construction of Reality: A Treatise in the Sociology of Knowledge. Anchor Books. 1966.*

[3] *Karl Marx. Capital: Volume 1: A Critique of Political Economy. Penguin Classics. 1992.*

[4] *G.A. Cohen. Marx's Theory of History. Princeton University Press. 2000.*

[5] *Joseph A. Tainter. The Collapse of Complex Societies. Cambridge University Press. 1990.*

[6] *Ken Wilber. Sex, Ecology, and Spirituality: The Spirit of Evolution. Shambhala. 2001.*

[7] *Adam Smith. The Wealth of Nations. Modern Library. 1776.*

[8] *Karl Marx and Martin Nicolaus trans. The Grundrisse: Foundations of the Critique of Political Economy. Penguin Classics. 1993.*

[9] *Karl Marx. The Poverty of Philosophy. Intl. Pub. 1982.*

[10] *Ivan Illich. Deschooling Society. Marion Boyars Publishers Ltd. 2000.*

WEAVING THE WEB

[1] *Tim Berners-Lee. Weaving the Web: The Original Design and Ultimate Destiny of the World Wide Web. Harper Collins. 1999.*

[2] *The Economist. Brain Scan: Watching the Web Grow Up. March, 8, 2007.*

[3] *Tim Berners-Lee. Weaving the Web: The Original Design and Ultimate Destiny of the World Wide Web.*

[4] Richard Florida. The Rise of the Creative Class: And How It's Transforming Work, Leisure, Community, and Everyday Life. Basic Books. 2003.

[5] Tim Wu. The Master Switch: The Rise and Fall of Information Empires. Knopf. 2010.

[6] Lawrence Lessig. Code: And Other Laws of Cyberspace, Version 2.0. Basic Books. 2006.

[7] Karl Marx and Friedriche Engels. The German Ideology, including Theses on Feuerbach. Prometheus Books. 1998.

[8] Hernando de Soto. The Mystery of Capital: Why Capitalism Triumphs in the West and Fails Everywhere Else. Basic Books. 2003.

[9] Karl Polanyi. The Great Transformation. Beacon Press. 2001.

[10] John Micklethwait. The Company. A Short History of Revolutionary Idea. Modern Library. 2005.

[11] David Skeel. Icarus in the Boardroom: The Fundamental Flaws in Corporate America and Where They Came From. Oxford University Press. 2006.

[12] Peter Drucker. Managing the Non-Profit Organization. Harper Paperbacks. 2006.

[13] Robert William Fogel. The Fourth Great Awakening and the Future of Egalitarianism. University of Chicago Press. 2002.

[14] Peter Drucker. Post-Capitalist Society. Harper Business. 1994.

[15] Daniel Bell. The Coming of Post-Industrial Society: A Venture in Social Forecasting. Basic Books. 1976.

[16] Manuel Castells. The Rise of the Network Society: The Information Age: Economy, Society, and Culture Volume I. Wiley-Blackwell. 2009.

[17] Alvin Toffler. The Third Wave. Bantam. 1984.

[18] Yokai Benkler. The Wealth of Networks: How Social Production Transforms Markets and Freedoms. Yale University Press. 2007.

[19] Stephen Kinzer. A Thousand Hills: Rwanda's Rebirth and the Man Who Dreamed It. Wiley. 2008.

Gerard Prunier. The Rwanda Crisis: History of a Genocide. Columbia University Press. 1997.

[20] Alison Des Forges. Leave None to Tell the Story. Genocide in Rwanda. Human Rights Watch. 1997.

THE NEW CLASS

[1] Peter F. Drucker. Management Challenges for the Twenty-First Century. Harper Business. 2001.

[2] Peter F. Drucker. Post-Capitalist Society. Harper Business. 1994.

[3] Peter F. Drucker. The Age of Discontinuity: Guidelines to Our Changing Society. Harper and Row. 1969.

[4] Daniel Bell. The Coming of Post-Industrial Society: A Venture in Social Forecasting. Basic Books. 1976.

[5] Richard Florida. The Rise of the Creative Class: And How It's Transforming Work, Leisure, Community, and Everyday Life. Basic Books. 2003.

[6] Robert William Fogel. The Fourth Great Awakening and the Future of Egalitarianism. University of Chicago Press. 2002.

[7] Ron Pernick. The Clean Tech Revolution: The Next Big Growth and Investment Opportunity. Collins Business. 2007.

[8] Nicholas Stern. The Global Deal: Climate Change and the Creation of a New Era of Progress and Prosperity. Public Affairs. 2009.

[9] Ken Wilber. Sex, Ecology, and Spirituality: The Spirit of Evolution. Shambhala. 2001

[10] Jeremy Rifkin. The Empathic Civilization: The Race to Global Consciousness in a World in Crisis. Tarcher. 2009.

[11] John B. Judis and Ruy Teixeira. The Emerging Democratic Majority. Scrubber. 2004.

[12] Michael Lind. Up from Conservatism. Free Press. 1997.

[13] Alvin Toffler. Revolutionary Wealth: How it will be created and how it will change our lives. Crown Business. 2007.

[14] Nicholas Carr. The Shallows: What the Internet is Doing to Our Brains. W.W. Norton and Company. 2011.

[15] Thomas Frank. What's the Matter With Kansas? How Conservatives Won the Heart of America. Holt Paperbacks. 2005.

[16] Robert Jay Lifton. The Protean Self: Human Resilience in an Age of Fragmentation. University of Chicago Press. 1999.

[17] Jedediah Purdy. For Common Things: Irony, Trust, and Commitment in America Today. Vintage. 2000.

[18] Michael Sandel. Democracy's Discontent: America in Search of Public Philosophy. Belknap Press of Harvard University Press. 1998.

[19] Amartya Sen. Identity and Violence: The Illusion of Destiny. W.W. Norton and Company. 2007.

SECTION 3.
GLOBALIZATION OF INFORMATION

OCEANS OF EXPERIENCE

[1] William James. The Principles of Psychology Vols. 1-2. Harvard University Press. 1981.

[2] David Hume and Eric Steinberg, ed. An Inquiry Concerning Human Understanding. Hackett Pub. Co. 1993.

[3] Immanuel Kant, Marcus Eaglet trans., and Max Muller trans. Critique of Pure Reason. Penguin Classics. 2008.

[4] Alasdair MacIntyre. After Virtue: A Study in Moral Theory. University of Notre Dame Press, 3rd ed. 2007.

[5] James G. March. A Primer on Decision Making: How Decisions Happen. Free Press. 2009.

[6] Peter L. Berger and Thomas Luckman. The Social Construction of Reality: A Treatise in the Sociology of Knowledge. Anchor Books. 1966.

[7] Jared Diamond. Collapse: How Societies Choose to Fail or Succeed. Penguin Books, Revised edition. 2011.

[8] Emile Durkheim. The Division of Labor in Society. Macmillan. 1933.

[9] Arthur M. Schlesinger Jr. The Disuniting of America: Reflections on a Multicultural Society. W.W. Norton and Company. 1998.

[10] Jared Diamond. Guns. Germs, and Steel: The Fates of Human Societies. W.W. Norton and Company. 2005.

[11] Donald E. Brown. Human Universals. Temple University Press. 1991.

[12] Steven Pinker. The Blank Slate: The Modern Denial of Human Nature. Penguin Books. 2003.

[13] Immanuel Kant, Marcus Weigelt trans., and Max Muller, trans. Critique of Pure Reason. Penguin Classics. 2008.

[14] Karl Marx and Martin Nicolaus trans. The Grundrisse: Foundations of the Critique of Political Economy. Penguin Classics. 1993.

[15] John Rawls. Political Liberalism. Columbia University Press 2nd edition. 2005.

[16] Noam Chomsky. Aspects of the Theory of Syntax. MIT Press. 1965.

[17] George Lakoff and Mark Johnson. Metaphors We Live By. University of Chicago Press, 2nd edition. 2003.

MAPPING THE WORLD OUTSIDE

[1] Gregory Bateson. Steps to an Ecology of Mind: Collected Essays in Anthropology, Psychiatry,

Evolution, and Epistemology.
University of Chicago Press. 2000.

[2] *James Hansen. Storms of My Grandchildren: The Truth About the Climate Change Catastrophe and Our Last Chance to Save Humanity. Bloomsbury. 2010.*

[3] *Michael E. Mann and Lee R. Kump. Dire Predictions: Understanding Global Warming. DK Publishing. 2008.*

[4] *Paul N. Edwards. A Vast Machine: Computer Models, Climate Data, and the Politics of Global Warming. MIT Press. 2013.*

[5] *Alvin Toffler. Future Shock. Random House. 1970.*

[6] *David Weinberger. Everything is Miscellaneous: The Power of the New Digital Disorder. Holt Paperbacks. 2008.*

[7] *Ibid.*

[8] *Ibid.*

MAPPING THE WORLD INSIDE

[1] *Herbert Marcuse. One Dimensional Man: Studies in the Ideology of Advanced Industrial Society. Beacon Press, 5th edition. 1991.*

[2] *Erich Fromm. To Have or To Be? Bloomsbury Academic, Revised edition. 2005.*

[3] *Emile Durkheim. The Division of Labor in Society. Macmillan. 1933.*

[4] *Karl Marx and Friedrich Engels. The Communist Manifesto. A Modern Edition. Verso. 2012.*

[5] *Cass Sunstein. Infotopia: How Many Minds Produce Knowledge. Oxford University Press. 2008.*

[6] *Ibid.*

[7] *John Stuart Mill. On Liberty and the Subjection of Women. Penguin Classics. 2007.*

[8] *Robert D. Putnam. Bowling Alone: The Collapse and Revival of American Community. Touchstone Books. 2001.*

[9] *George Simmel. Conflict and the Web of Group Affiliations. The Free Press. 1955.*

[10] *Steven Pinker. The Better Angels of Our Nature: Why Violence Has Declined. Penguin Books. 2011.*

[11] *Erich Fromm. The Sane Society. Fawcett Book, Reprint edition. 1965.*

[12] *Ken Wilber. Integral Psychology: Consciousness, Spirit, Psychology, Therapy. Shambhala. 2000.*

SECTION 4.
GLOBALIZATION OF EMPATHY

BINDING MINDS

[1] Adam Smith. *The Theory of Moral Sentiments.* Barnes and Noble Books. 2004.

[2] Frans de Waal. *The Age of Empathy: Nature's Lessons for a Kinder Society.* Broadway. 2010.

[3] Marco Iacoboni. *Mirroring People: The Science of Empathy and How We Connect With Others.* Picador. 2009.

[4] Paul R. Ehrlich. *Human Nature: Genes, Cultures, and the Human Prospect.* Penguin Books. 2001.

[5] E.O. Wilson. *Human Nature.* The President and Fellows of Harvard College. 1978.

[6] Patricia S. Churchland. *Braintrust: What Neuroscience Tells Us About Morality.* Princeton University Press. 2011.

[7] J.D. Trout. *Why Empathy Matters: the Science and Psychology of Better Judgment.* Penguin Books. 2010.

[8] James Q. Wilson. *The Moral Sense.* The Free Press. 1997.

[9] Yokai Benkler. *The Penguin and the Leviathan: How Cooperation Triumphs Over Self-Interest.* Crown Business. 2011.

[10] David Brooks. *The Social Animal: the Hidden Sources of Love, Character, and Achievement.* Random House. 2012.

[11] Jeremy Rifkin. *The Empathic Civilization: the Race to Global Consciousness in a World in Crisis.* Tarcher. 2009.

[12] Marco Iacoboni. *Mirroring People: The Science of Empathy and How We Connect With Others.* Picador. 2009.

[13] Adam Smith. *The Theory of Moral Sentiments.* Barnes and Noble Books. 2004.

[14] Aristotle. *Aristotle's Poetics.* Hill and Wang. 1961.

[15] Frans de Waal. *The Age of Empathy: Nature's Lessons for a Kinder Society.*

[12] John Dewey. *Human Nature and Conduct.* Henry Holt and Co. 1922.

[13] J. Krishnamurti. *The Awakening of Intelligence.* Harper and Row. 1987

[14] Simon Baron-Cohen. *The Science of Evil: On Empathy and the Origins of Cruelty.* Basic Books. 2012.

[15] Martin Luther King Jr. and Clayborne Carson ed. *Autobiography of Martin Luther King Jr.* Warner Books. 2001.

[16] Yokai Benkler. *The Penguin and the Leviathan: How Cooperation Triumphs Over Self-Interest.*

[17] Robert Axelrod. *The Evolution of*

Cooperation. Basic Books. 1984.

[18] Benjamin Franklin. Autobiography and Other Writings. Oxford University Press. 2009.

[19] Daniel Boorstin. The Americans: the National Experience. Vintage. 1967.

[20] Alexis de Tocqueville and Stuart Gilbert, ed. The Old Regime and the French Revolution. Anchor Books. 1955.

[21] Alexis de Tocqueville. Democracy in America. Penguin Classics. 2003.

[22] Fernand Braudel and Sian Reynolds trans. Identity of France: People and Production. Perennial. 1992.

[23] Akhil Reed Amar. America's Constitution: A Biography. Random House. 2006.

[24] Daniel Boorstin. The Americans: the Colonial Experience. Vintage. 1964.

[25] David Hackett Fischer. Albion's Seed: Four British Folkways in America. Oxford University Press. 1989.

[26] Reinhold Niebuhr and Andrew J. Bacevich intro. The Irony of American History. University of Chicago. 2008.

[27] Jack N. Rakove. Original Meanings: Politics and Ideas in the Making of the Constitution. Vintage.

1997.

[28] Colin Woodard. American Nations: A History of the Eleven Regional Cultures of North America. Penguin Books. 2012.

[29] Karl Marx and Friedriche Engels. The German Ideology, including Theses on Feuerbach. Prometheus Books. 1998.

[29] John Rawls. The Law of Peoples, with "The Idea of Public Reason Revisited." Harvard University Press. 2001.

[30] George Wilhelm Hegel and Hugh Barr Nisbet trans. Lectures on the Philosophy of World History. Cambridge University Press. 1981.

[31] Immanuel Kant. Perpetual Peace and Other Essays. Hackett Pub Co. 1983.

[32] Marcus Aurelius. The Meditations. Penguin Classics. 2006.

COOPERATIVE APES

[1] Richard C. Williams. The Cooperative Movement: Globalization From Below. Ashgate Pub Co. 2007.

[2] David C. Korten. The Post-Corporate World: Life After Capitalism. Berrett-Koehler Publishers. 2010.

[3] Richard C. Williams. The Cooperative Movement:

Globalization From Below. Ashgate Pub. Co. 2007.

[4] *Richard Dawkins. The Selfish Gene. Oxford University Press. 1976.*

[5] *W.D. Hamilton. Narrow Roads of Geneland: Evolution and Social Behavior. Oxford University Press. 1998.*

[6] *Frans de Waal. The Age of Empathy: Nature's Lessons for a Kinder Society. Broadway. 2010.*

[7] *Edward O. Wilson. Consilience: The Unity of Knowledge. Vintage. 1999.*

[8] *Robin Dunbar. Grooming, Gossip, and the Evolution of Language. Harvard University Press. 1998.*

[9] *Ibid.*

[10] *Robin Dunbar. How Many Friends Does One Person Need? Dunbar's Number and Other Evolutionary Quirks. Harvard University Press. 2010.*

[11] *Robin Dunbar. Grooming, Gossip, and the Evolution of Language. Harvard University Press. 2010.*

[12] *Ibid.*

[13] *Jimmy Carter. Palestine, Peace Not Apartheid. Simon and Schuster. 2006.*

[14] *Henry Kissinger. Diplomacy. Simon and Schuster. 1995.*

[15] *Henry Kissinger. On China. Penguin Books. 2012.*

[16] *Laurence H. Tribe. The Invisible Constitution. Oxford University Press. 2008.*

[17] *Jeffrey D. Clements. Corporations Are Not People: Why They Have More Right Than You Do and What You Can Do About It. Berrett Koehler Publishers. 2012.*

[18] *Lawrence Lessig. Republic Lost: How Money Corrupts Politics - and a Plan to Stop It. Twelve. 2012.*

[19] *Bradley A. Smith. Unfree Speech: the Fallacy of Campaign Finance Reform. Princeton University Press. 2003.*

[20] *Lawrence Lessig. Code: And Other Laws of Cyberspace, Version 2.0. Basic Books. 2006.*

[21] *Elinor Ostrum. Governing the Commons: the Evolution of Institutions for Collective Action. Cambridge University Press. 1990.*

[22] *Cass R. Sunstein and Martha R. Nussbaum, eds. Animal Rights: Current Debates and New Directions. Oxford University Press. 2005.*

[23] *Christopher D. Stone. Should Trees Have Standing: Law, Morality, and the Environment. Oxford University Press. 2010.*

[24] *Hernando De Soto. The Mystery of Capital: Why Capitalism*

Triumphs in the West and Fails Everywhere Else. Basic Books. 2003.

[25] Jeremy Rifkin. The Empathic Civilization: the Race to Global Consciousness in a World in Crisis. Tarcher. 2009.

[26] Ken Wilber. Sex, Ecology, and Spirituality: The Spirit of Evolution. Shambala. 2001.

[27] Robert Henson. The Rough Guide to Climate Change, 3rd ed. Rough Guides. 2011.

[28] Eric A. Posner and David Weisbach. Climate Change Justice. Princeton University Press. 2010.

PUZZLING POVERTY

[1] Ted C. Fischman. China, Inc: How the Rise of the Next Superpower Challenges America and the World. Scribner. 2006.

[2] Leslie T. Chang. Factory Girls: From Village to City In a Changing China. Spiegel and Grau. 2009.

[3] Population Reference Bureau. World Population Data Sheet. Population Bulletin. 2007.

[4] Robert Chambers, Deepa Narayan, Meera Shah, and Patt Petesch. Voices of the Poor: Crying Out for Change. World Bank Publications. 2001.

[5] James Martin. The Meaning of the 21st Century: A Vital Blueprint for Ensuring Our Future. Riverhead Trade. 2007.

[6] Branko Milanovic. Worlds Apart: Measuring International and Global Inequality. Princeton University Press. 2007.

[7] Paul Polak. Out of Poverty: What Works When Traditional Approaches Fail. Berrett Koehler Publishers. 2009.

[8] C.K. Prahalad. The Fortune at the Bottom of the Pyramid: Eradicating Poverty Through Profits. Wharton School Publishing. 2009.

[9] Muhammad Yunus. Creating a World Without Poverty: Social Business and the Future of Capitalism. Public Affairs. 2009.

[10] Jean Drezé and Amartya Sen. An Uncertain Glory: India and Its Contradictions. Princeton University Press. 2013.

[11] Edmund S. Phelps. Mass Flourishing: How Grassroots Innovation Created Jobs, Challenge, and Change. Princeton University Press. 2013.

[12] Deepa Narayan and Patti Petesch Ed. Voices of the Poor: From Many Lands. Oxford University Press. 2002.

[13] Simon Baron-Cohen. The Science of Evil: On Empathy and the Origins

of Cruelty. Basic Books. 2012.

[14] Patricia S. Churchland. Braintrust: What Neuroscience Tells Us About Morality. Princeton University Press. 2011.

[15] Deepa Narayan. Voices of the Poor: Crying Out for a Change. Oxford University Press. 2000.

[16] Robert Chambers, Deepa Narayan, Meera Shah, and Patt Petesch, eds. Voices of the Poor: Crying Out for Change. Oxford University Press. 2001.

[17] Deepa Narayan and Patti Petesch Ed. Voices of the Poor: From Many Lands. Oxford University Press. 2002.

[18] Thomas Nagel. The View From Nowhere. Oxford University Press. 1986.

[19] Jagdish Bhagwati and Arvind Panagariya. Why Growth Matters: How Economic Growth in India Reduced Poverty and the Lessons for Other Developing Countries. Public Affairs. 2013.

[20] Abhijit Banerjee and Esther Duflo. Poor Economics: A Radical Rethinking of the Way to Fight Global Poverty. Public Affairs. 2012.

[21] Ibid.

[22] Daryl Collins, Jonathan Morduch, Stuart Rutherford, and Orlanda Ruthven. Portfolios of the Poor: How the World's Poor Live on $2 a Day. Princeton University Press. 2010.

[23] Muhammad Yunus. Banker to the Poor: Micro-lending and the Battle Against World Poverty. Public Affairs. 2003.

[24] Daryl Collins, Jonathan Morduch, Stuart Rutherford, and Orlanda Ruthven. Portfolios of the Poor: How the World's Poor Live on $2 a Day. Princeton University Press. 2010.

[25] Abhijit Banerjee and Esther Duflo. Poor Economics: A Radical Rethinking of the Way to Fight Global Poverty. Public Affairs. 2012.

[26] Jeffrey Sachs. The End of Poverty: Economic Possibilities of Our Time. Penguin Books. 2006.

[27] Amartya Sen. Development as Freedom. Anchor. 2000.

SECTION 5.
GLOBALIZATION OF ETHICS
SHALLOW PONDS

[1] Peter Singer. Famine, Affluence, and Morality. Philosophy and Public Affairs. 1971.

[2] Peter Unger. Living High and Letting Die: Our Illusion of Innocence. Oxford University Press.

1996.

[3] Peter Singer. The Life You Can Save: How to Do Your Part to End World Poverty. Random House Trade Paperbacks. 2010.

[4] Jeffrey Sachs. The End of Poverty: Economic Possibilities for Our Time. Penguin Books. 2006.

[5] Peter Singer. Famine, Affluence, and Morality. Public Affairs. 1971.

[6] Kwame Anthony Appiah. Cosmopolitanism: Ethics in a World of Strangers. W.W. Norton and Company. 2007.

[7] Immanuel Kant. Grounding for the Metaphysic of Morals. Hackett Publishing Company. 1981.

[8] George Kateb. Human Dignity. Belknap Press of Harvard University Press. 2011.

[9] Adam Smith. The Theory of Moral Sentiments. Barnes and Noble Books. 2004.

[10] Peter Singer. The Life You Can Save: How to Do Your Part to End World Poverty. Random House Trade Paperbacks. 2010.

[11] Ibid.

[12] Kwame Anthony Appiah. Cosmopolitanism: Ethics in a World of Strangers. W.W. Norton and Company. 2007.

[13] Michael Sandel. Justice: What's the Right Thing to Do? Farrar, Straus, and Giroux. 2010.

[14] Mohamed Choukri and Paul Bowles trans. For Bread Alone. Telegram Books. 2007.

[15] Taha Hussein. The Days: His Autobiography in Three Parts. The American University of Cairo University Press, 2nd ed. 2010.

[16] Thomas W. Pogge. World Poverty and Human Rights. Polity. 2008.

[17] Peter Singer. The Life You Can Save: How to Do Your Part to End World Poverty. Random House Trade Paperbacks. 2010.

[18] Paul Collier. The Bottom Billion: Why the Poorest Countries Are Failing and What Can Be Done About It. Oxford University Press. 2008.

[19] Thomas W. Pogge. World Poverty and Human Rights. Polity. 2008.

[20] Paul Collier. The Bottom Billion: Why the Poorest Countries Are Failing and What Can Be Done About It. Oxford University Press. 2008.

[21] Daren Acemoglu and James Robinson. Why Nations Fail: The Origins of Power, Prosperity, and Poverty. Crown Business. 2012.

[22] William Easterly. The White Man's Burden: Why the West's Efforts to Aid the Rest Have Done

So Much Ill and So Little Good. Penguin Books. 2007.

[23] Roger Thurow and Scott Kilman. Enough: Why the World's Poorest Starve in an Age of Plenty. Public Affairs. 2010.

[24] William Easterly. The White Man's Burden: Why the West's Efforts to Aid the Rest Have Done So Much Ill and So Little Good. Penguin Books. 2007.

[25] Dambisa Moyo. Dead Aid: Why Aid Is Not Working and How There Is a Better Way for Africa. Farrar, Straus, and Giroux. 2010.

[26] Jeffrey D. Sachs. Common Wealth: Economics for a Crowded Planet. Penguin Books. 2009.

[27] Michela Wrong. In the Footsteps of Mr. Kurtz: Living On the Brink of Disaster in Mobutu's Congo. Harper Perennial. 2002.

[28] Paul Collier. The Bottom Billion: Why the Poorest Countries Are Failing and What Can Be Done About It. Oxford University Press. 2008.

[29] Fareed Zakaria. The Future of Freedom: Illiberal Democracy at Home and Abroad. W.W. Norton and Company. 2008.

[30] Peter Singer. The Life You Can Save: How to Do Your Part to End World Poverty. Random House Trade Paperbacks. 2010.

[31] Charles Kenny. Getting Better: Why Global Development Is Succeeding - and How We Can Improve the World Even More. Basic Books. 2012.

[32] Jean Dreze and Amartya Sen. Hunger and Public Action. Oxford University Press. 1990.

[33] Thomas Malthus. An Essay on the Principle of Population. Oxford University Press. 1991.

[34] Paul Ehrlich. The Population Bomb. Sierra Books. 1969.

[35] Donella H. Meadows, Dennis L. Meadows, Jorgen Randers, and William W. Behrens III. The Limits to Growth: A Report for the Club of Rome's Project on the Predicament of Mankind. Universe Books. 1974.

[36] United Nations, Department of Economic and Social Affairs. World Population Prospects: the 2006 Revision. The United Nations. 2007.

[37] Abhijit Banerjee and Esther Duflo. Poor Economics: A Radical Rethinking of the Way to Fight Global Poverty. Public Affairs. 2012.

[38] Amartya Sen. Development as Freedom. Anchor. 2000.

[39] Charles Kenny. Getting Better: Why Global Development Is Succeeding - and How We Can Improve the World Even More. Basic Books. 2012.

[40] *Muhammad Yunus. Banker to the Poor: Micro-Lending and the Battle Against World Poverty. Public Affairs. 2003.*

[41] *Paul Polak. Out of Poverty: What Works When Traditional Approaches Fail. Berrett-Koehler Publishers. 2009.*

[42] *Alex Steffen and Bill McKibben intro. Worldchanging: A Users Guide to the 21st Century. Abrams, Revised ed. 2011.*

[43] *Jeffrey Sachs. The End of Poverty: Economic Possibilities for Our Time. Penguin Books. 2006.*

[44] *William Easterly. The White Man's Burden: Why the West's Efforts to Aid the Rest Have Done So Much Ill and So Little Good. Penguin Books. 2007.*

[45] *Jeffrey Sachs. The End of Poverty: Economic Possibilities for Our Time. Penguin Books. 2006.*

[46] *Ibid.*

[47] *Charles Kenny. Getting Better: Why Global Development Is Succeeding - and How We Can Improve the World Even More. Basic Books. 2012.*

[48] *Martha C. Nussbaum. Creating Capabilities: The Human Development Approach. Belknap Press of Harvard University Press. 2011.*

[49] *Amartya Sen. Development as Freedom. Anchor. 2000.*

[50] *Martha C. Nussbaum. Creating Capabilities: The Human Development Approach. Belknap Press of Harvard University Press. 2011.*

[51] *Amartya Sen. Development as Freedom. Anchor. 2000.*

[52] *Ibid.*

[53] *Peter Singer. The Expanding Circle: Ethics, Evolution, and Moral Progress. Princeton University Press. 1981.*

SEAS OF SUFFERING

[1] *Dante Alighieri and Mark Musa trans. The Divine Comedy: Volume 1: The Inferno. Penguin Classics. 2002.*

[2] *Michael J. Sandel. Justice: What's the Right Thing to Do? Farrar, Straus, and Giroux. 2010.*

[3] *Amartya Sen. Development as Freedom. Anchor. 2000.*

[4] *Bjorn Lumborg ed. How to Spend $50 Billion to Make the World a Better Place. Cambridge University Press. 2006.*

[5] *Peter Singer. Famine, Affluence, and Morality. Philosophy and Public Affairs. 1971.*

[6] *Stephen Mitchell. The Bhagavad-*

Gita: A New Translation. Three Rivers Press. 2002.

THE OCEAN OF LOVE

[1] Edward O. Wilson. The Social Conquest of Earth. Liveright. 2012.

[2] Karl Marx and Friedriche Engels. The German Ideology, including Theses on Feuerbach. Prometheus Books. 1998.

[3] Bill McKibben. The End of Nature. Random House Trade Paperback. 1989.

[4] Paul Wapner. Living Through the End of Nature: the Future of American Environmentalism. Massachusetts Institute of Technology Press. 2010.

[5] Food and Agriculture Organization. FAOSTAT. Food and Agriculture Organization of the United Nations. 2011.

[6] Robert Costanza et al. The Value of World's Ecosystem Services and Natural Capital. Nature 387. 1997.

[7] National Research Council. Nutritional Requirements of Beef Cattle. National Academy Press. 2000.

[8] US Department of Agriculture. Agricultural Statistics. US Department of Agriculture. 2001.

[9] David Pimentel. Sustainability of Meat-Based and Plant-Based Diets and Sustainability. The American Journal of Clinical Nutrition. 2003.

[10] Robert Paarlberg. Food Politics: What Everyone Needs to Know. Oxford University Press. 2010.

[11] Henning Steinfeld, Pierre Gerber, T.D. Wasenaar, and Vincent Castel. Livestock's Long Shadow: Environmental Issues and Options. Livestock, Environment, and Development. Food and Agricultural Organization of the United Nations. 2006.

[12] United Nations Framework Convention on Climate Change. Investment and Financial Flows to Address Climate Change. United Nations Framework Convention on Climate Change. 2007.

[13] Sergio Margulis. Causes of Deforestation of the Brazilian Rainforest. World Bank. 2004.

[14] Henning Steinfeld, Pierre Gerber, T.D. Wasenaar, and Vincent Castel. Livestock's Long Shadow: Environmental Issues and Options. Livestock, Environment, and Development. United Nations. 2006.

[15] Albert Schweitzer. The Philosophy of Civilization. The Macmillan Company. 1949.

[16] Holmes Rolston III. A New Environmental Ethics: the Next Millennium for Life on Earth. Routledge. 2011.

SECTION 6.
GLOBALIZATION OF SPIRITUALITY

EVOLUTION OF GOD

[1] *Karen Armstrong. The Great Transformation: the Beginning of Our Religious Traditions. Anchor 2007.*

[2] *Robert Bellah. Religion in Human Evolution: From the Paleolithic to the Axial Age. Belknap Press of Harvard University Press. 2011.*

[3] *Karl Jaspers. The Origin and Goal of History. Routledge and Kegan Paul Ltd. 1953.*

[4] *Luke Timothy Johnson. Among the Gentiles: Greco-Roman Religion and Christianity. Yale University Press. 2009.*

[5] *Karen Armstrong. The Great Transformation: the Beginning of Our Religious Traditions. Anchor Books. 2007.*

[6] *Ibid.*

[7] *Robert Wright. The Evolution of God. Back Bay Books. 2010.*

[8] *Ibid.*

[9] *Ibid.*

[10] *William H. McNeill. Keeping Together in Time: Dance and Drill in Human History. ACLS Humanities. 1995.*

[11] *Robert Wright. The Evolution of God. Back Bay Books. 2010.*

[12] *Karen Armstrong. History of God: the 4,000-Year Quest of Judaism, Christianity, and Islam. Ballantine Books. 1994.*

[13] *Karen Armstrong. The Case for God. Anchor. 2010.*

[14] *Benedict de Spinoza and Edwin Curley trans. Ethics. Penguin Classics. 2005.*

[15] *G.W.F. Hegel and A.V. Miller trans. The Phenomenology of Spirit. Oxford University Press. 1976.*

[16] *Charles Taylor. Hegel and Modern Society. Cambridge University Press. 1979.*

[17] *Thomas Berry. The Dream of the Earth. Sierra Club Books. 2006.*

[18] *Pierre Teilard de Chardin. The Phenomenon of Man. Wm. Collins Sons & Co. Ltd. 1959.*

[19] *Karen Armstrong. The Case for God. Anchor Books. 2010.*

[20] *Karen Armstrong. The Great Transformation: the Beginning of Our Religious Traditions. Anchor Books. 2007.*

[21] *Robert Wright. The Evolution of God. Back Bay Books. 2010.*

[22] *Catholic Church. Catechism of the Catholic Church. Image. 2005.*

[23] Seyyed Hossein Nasr. Islam: Religion, History, and Civilization. Harper One. 2002.

[24] Vali Nasr. The Shia Revival. How Conflicts Within Islam Will Shape the Future. W.W. Norton and Co. 2007.

[25] Max Dimont. Jews, God, and History. Mentor. 1964.[26] Ken Wilber. Sex, Ecology, Spirituality: the Spirit of Evolution. Shambhala. 2001.

[27] Joseph A. Tainter. The Collapse of Complex Societies. Cambridge University Press. 1990.

[28] Robert Wright. Non-Zero: the Logic of Human Destiny. Vintage. 2001.

THE GREAT RECONFIGURATION

[1] Samuel P. Huntington. The Clash of Civilizations and the Remaking of World Order. Simon and Schuster Inc. 1996.

[2] John King Fairbank and Merle Goldman. China: A New History. Belknap Press of Harvard University Press. 2006.

[3] Valerie Hanson. The Open Empire: A History of China to 1600. W.W. Norton and Company. 2000.

[4] William James. Varieties of Religious Experience. Penguin Books. 2007.

[5] Peter Berger. The Sacred Canopy: Elements of a Sociological Theory of Religion. Anchor Books. 1967.

[6] Karen Armstrong. The Great Transformation: the Beginning of Our Religious Traditions. Anchor Books. 2007.

[7] Peter Berger. The Sacred Canopy: Elements of a Sociological Theory of Religion. Anchor Books. 1967.

[8] Robert D. Putnam and David E. Campbell. American Grace: How Religion Divides and Unites Us. Simon and Schuster. 2012.

[9] Robert Wright. The Evolution of God. Back Bay Books. 2010.

[10] Karen Armstrong. The Case for God. Anchor Books. 2010.

[11] Samuel P. Huntington. The Clash of Civilizations and the Remaking of World Order. Simon and Schuster. 1996.

[12] Christopher Hitchens. God Is Not Great: How Religion Poisons Everything. Hachette Book Group Inc. 2007.

[13] Karen Armstrong. The Great Transformation: the Beginning of Our Religious Traditions. Anchor Books. 2007.

[14] Robert Wright. The Evolution of God. Back Bay Books. 2010.

[15] Charles Taylor. A Secular Age. The Belknap Press of Harvard

University Press. 2007.

[16] Charles Kenny. Getting Better: Why Global Development is Succeeding – And How We Can Improve the World Even More. Basic Books. 2012.

[17] Marcus J. Borg. Meeting Jesus Again for the First Time: the Historical Jesus and the Heart of Contemporary Faith. Harper Collins Publishers. 1994

[18] Harvey Cox. The Future of Faith. Harper Collins Publishers. 2009.

[19] Phyllis Tickle. Emergence Christianity: What It Is, Where It Is Going, and Why It Matters. Baker Books. 2012.

[20] Reza Aslan. Beyond Fundamentalism: Confronting Religious Extremism in the Age of Globalization. Random House Trade Paperbacks. 2009.

[21] Charles Taylor. A Secular Age. The Belknap Press of Harvard University Press. 2007.

[22] Morris Berman. The Reenchantment of the World. Cornell University Press. 1981.

[23] Max Weber. The Sociology of Religion. J.C.B. Mohr. 1922.

[24] Edward O. Wilson. Consilience; the Unity of Knowledge. Vintage Books. 1999.

[25] Ken Wilber. The Marriage of Sense and Soul: Integrating Science and Religion. Random House. 1998.

[26] Peter Singer. The Expanding Circle: Ethics and Sociobiology. Farrar, Straus, and Giroux. 1981.

[27] Karen Armstrong. The Case for God. Anchor Books. 2010.

[28] Ken Wilber. Sex, Ecology, Spirituality: the Spirit of Evolution. Shambhala. 2001.

[29] Karen Armstrong. The Case for God. Anchor Books 2010.

[30] Ibid.

[31] Robert N. Bellah. Religion in Human Evolution: From the Paleolithic to the Axial Age. Belknap Press of Harvard University Press. 2011.

[32] Charles Taylor. A Secular Age. The Belknap Press of Harvard University Press. 2007.

[33] Karen Armstrong. The Case for God. Anchor Books. 2010.

[34] Robert Novak. No One Sees God: the Dark Night of Atheists and Believers. Doubleday. 2008.

[35] Paul Tillich. The Courage to Be. Yale University Press. 1952.

[36] Robert Wright. Non-Zero: the Logic of Human Destiny. Vintage. 2001.

THE SPIRITUAL RENAISSANCE

[1] Robert N. Bellah. *Religion in Human Evolution: From the Paleolithic to the Axial Age.* Belknap Press of Harvard University Press. 2011.

[2] Charles Taylor. *A Secular Age.* The Belknap Press of Harvard University Press. 2007.

[3] Robert D. Putnam and David E. Campbell. *American Grace: How Religion Divides and Unites Us.* Simon and Schuster. 2012.

[4] Karen Armstrong. *The Case for God.* Anchor Books. 2010.

[5] Karen Armstrong. *The Battle for God.* Ballantine Books. 2001.

[6] Bill Devall and George Sessions. *Deep Ecology: Living as if Nature Mattered.* Gibbs Smith. 2001

[7] Bron Taylor. *Dark Green Religion: Nature, Spirituality, and the Planetary Future.* University of California Press. 2009.

[8] Moojan Momen. *The Baha'i Faith.* One World Publications. 2007.

[9] Alan Wolfe. *The Transformation of American Religion: How We Actually Live Our Faith.* University of Chicago Press. 2005.

[10] Ken Wilber. *Integral Psychology: Consciousness, Spirit, Psychology, Therapy.* Shambhala Books. 2000.

[11] Robert M. Hazen. *The Story of Earth: The First 4.5 Billion Years, From Stardust to Living Planet.* Penguin Books. 2013

[12] Jan Zalsiewicz and Mark Williams. *The Goldilocks Planet: The 4 Billion Year Story of Earth's Climate.* Oxford University Press. 2012.

[13] Charles H. Langmuir and Wally Broecker. *How to Build a Habitable Planet: The Story of Earth from Big Bang to Humankind.* Princeton University Press. 2012.

[14] Tim Flannery. *Here On Earth: A Natural History of the Planet.* Atlantic Monthly Press. 2011.

[15] Terrence W. Deacon. *Incomplete Nature: How Mind Emerged From Matter.* W.W. Norton of Company. 2012

[16] Edward O. Wilson. *The Social Conquest of Earth.* Liveright. 2012.

[17] David Christian. *Maps of Time: An Introduction to Big History.* University of California Press. 2004.

[18] Michael Cook. *A Brief History of the Human Race.* W.W. Norton and Company. 2005.

[19] Holmes Rolston III. *Three Big Bangs: Matter-Energy, Life, and Mind.* Columbia University Press. 2010.

[20] Brian Swimme. The Universe Story: From the Primordial Flaring Forth to the Ecozoic Era – A Celebration of te Unfolding of te Cosmos. Harper One. 1992.

SECTION 7.
GLOBALIZATION OF CIVILIZATION
NEW WORLD LEADERS

[1] Immanuel Kant. Grounding for the Metaphysic of Morals. Hackett Publishing Company. 1981.

[2] H.H. Dalai Lama. Beyond Religion: Ethics for a Whole World. Mariner Books. 2012.

[3] H.H. Dalai Lama. Ethics for a New Millennium. Riverhead Trade. 1999.

[4] Isaac Deutscher. The Non-Jewish Jew. The Merlin Press Ltd. 1981.

[5] Thomas Friedman. From Beirut to Jerusalem. Harper Collins Ltd. 1989.

[6] Gershon Gorenberg. The Unmaking of Israel. Harper Perennial. 2012.

[7] David K. Shipler. Arab and Jew: Wounded Spirits in a Promised Land. Penguin Books. 1987.

[8] Karen Armstrong. Jerusalem: One City, Three Faiths. Alfred A. Knopf. 1996.

[9] Fawwaz Traboulsi. A History of Modern Lebanon. Pluto Press. 2007.

[10] Jimmy Carter. Palestine, Peace Not Apartheid. Simon and Schuster. 2006.

[11] Plato and Allen Bloom trans. The Republic of Plato. Basic Books. 1968.

[12] Ken Wilber. Sex, Ecology, Spirituality: the Spirit of Evolution. Shambhala. 2001.

[13] Charles Taylor. A Secular Age. The Belknap Press of Harvard University Press. 2007.

[14] Michael Lerner. Embracing Israel/Palestine: A Strategy to Heal and Transform the Middle East. North Atlantic Books. 2011.

[15] John Broome. Climate Matter: Ethics in a Warming World. W.W. Norton and Company. 2012.

[16] Stephen M. Gardiner. A Perfect Moral Storm: the Ethical Tragedy of Climate Change. Oxford University Press. 2011.

[17] Eric A. Posner and David Weisbach. Climate Change Justice. Princeton University Press. 2010.

[18] Holmes Rolston III. A New Environmental Ethics: the Next Millennium for Life on Earth. Routledge. 2011.

[19] John Broome. Climate Matters: Ethics in a Warming World. W.W. Norton and Company. 2012.

[20] Mike Hulme. Why We

Disagree About Climate Change: Understanding Controversy, Inaction, and Opportunity. Cambridge University Press. 2009.

[21] George Lakoff. *The Political Mind: A Cognitive Scientist's Guide to Your Brain and Its Politics.* Penguin Books. 2009.

THE GLOBAL CONTRACT

[1] John Rawls. *A Theory of Justice.* Belknap Press of Harvard University Press. 1999.

[2] *Ibid.*

[3] Ronald Dworkin. *Taking Rights Seriously.* Harvard University Press. 1978.

[4] Robert Nozick. *Anarchy, State, and Utopia.* Basic Books. 1977.

[5] Allen E. Buchanan. *Marx and Justice: The Radical Critique of Liberalism.* Rowman and Littlefield Publishing Inc. 1984.

[6] G.A. Cohen. *Rescuing Justice and Equality.* Harvard University Press. 2008.

[7] Susan Moller Okin. *Justice, Gender, and the Family.* Basic Books. 1991.

[8] Michael Sandel. *Liberalism and the Limits of Justice.* Cambridge University Press. 1982.

[9] Michael Walzer. *Spheres of Justice.* Basic Books. 1984.

[10] Peter Singer. *One World: The Ethics of Globalization.* Yale University Press. 2002.

[11] Friederich List. *National System of Political Economy.* J.B. Lippincott and Co. 1856.

[12] Ha-Joon Chang. *Bad Samaritans: The Myth of Free Trade and the Secret History of Capitalism.* Bloomsbury Press. 2008.

[13] Ha-Joon Chang. *Kicking Away the Ladder: Development Strategy in Historical Perspective.* Anthem Press. 2002.

[14] Martin Wolf. *Why Globalization Works.* Yale University Press 2nd ed. 2005.

[15] Anne-Marie Slaughter. *A New World Order.* Princeton University Press. 2005.

[16] Jeremy Waldron in Seyla Benhabib. *Another Cosmopolitanism.* Oxford University Press. 2008.

THE NEXT GREAT CIVILIZATION

[1] Virgil and Robert Fagles Trans. *The Aeneid.* Penguin Classics. 2010.

[2] Kevin Phillips. *American Theocracy: the Peril and Politics of Radical Religion, Oil, and Borrowed Money, in the 21st Century.* Viking

Penguin. 2006.

3 Chalmers Johnson. *The Sorrows of Empire: Militarism, Secrecy, and the End of the Republic.* Metropolitan Books. 2004.

4 Christopher Lasch. *The Culture of Narcissism: American Life in an Age of Diminishing Expectations.* W.W. Norton and Co. 1979.

5 Lawrence E. Harrison and Samuel P. Huntington. *Culture Matters: How Values Shape Human Progress.* Basic Books. 2001.

6 Brian Arthur. *The Nature of Technology: What It Is and How It Evolves.* Free Press. 2009.

7 Mark Elvin. *The Retreat of the Elephants: An Environmental History of China.* Yale University Press. 2006.

8 Tamim Ansary. *Destiny Disrupted: A History of the World Through Islamic Eyes.* Public Affairs. 2010.

9 Albert Hourani. *A History of the Arab Peoples.* Warner Books. 1991.

10 Jacques Barzun. *From Dawn to Decadence: 500 Years of Western Cultural Life, 1500 to the Present.* Harper Perennial. 2001.

11 Fareed Zakaria. *The Post-American World.* W.W. Norton and Company. 2008.

12 Walter Russell Mead. *Power, Terror, Peace, and War: America's Grand Strategy in a World at Risk.* Vintage Books. 2005.

13 Benedict Anderson. *Imagined Communities: Reflections on the Origin and Spread of Nationalism.* Verso. 1983.

14 Immanuel Wallerstein. *World-Systems Analysis: An Introduction.* Duke University Press. 2004.

15 David Rothkopf. *Superclass: The Global Power Elite and the World They Are Making.* Farrar, Straus, and Giroux. 2009.

16 Amartya Sen. *Identity and Violence: The Illusion of Destiny.* W.W. Norton and Company. 2007.

17 Eric Hobsbawm. *Nations and Nationalism Since 1780: Programme, Myth, Reality.* Cambridge University Press. 1992.

18 Benedict Anderson. *Imagined Communities: Reflections on the Origin and Spread of Nationalism.* Verso. 1983.

19 Ernst Gellner. *Nations and Nationalism.* Cornell University Press. 1983.

PERSONAL POSTSCRIPT

1 Douglas Adams. *Life, the Universe, and Everything.* Del Ray. 2005.

2 Jalal al-Din Rumi. *The Essential Rumi.* Harper One. 2004

CPSIA information can be obtained
at www.ICGtesting.com
Printed in the USA
FSOW02n2253050215
5037FS